A book of Storms

A book of
Storms
The story of my turbulant life

Ann Young

PEN&FORGE
PRODUCTIONS

Pen&Forge Productions

This book is based on the best recollection of my memories, events and experiences throughout my life. Names and places were left out, except with explicit permission or in the case of public figures, so as to protect peoples' privacy (and keep me from being sued). All scriptural passages are from the King James Version of the Bible.

I am grateful to my loving husband, for his patience and understanding, and that together our joint creation became this book.

Edited and designed by Chris Young
Proofread by Edna Tunke
Portrait by Judy Woods (2009)

ISBN-13: 978-0-9880979-4-0
Trade Paperback

I dedicate this book to anyone who finds themselves at a place in their life when the question of 'Why' seems unanswerable.
You are not alone.
I hope you find comfort within these pages.

Contents

Chapter One

Running Away from Home

Just about anybody you talk to knows a story about running away from home as a kid, either their own or from someone they know. It usually involves a dispute of some kind where children don't get their own way and decide that they'll be better off somewhere else, although where this 'someplace else' is isn't always clear. Some stories will have the child that never makes it out the door, while others can tell you about the disgruntled toddler getting all the way down the street, packed suitcase in tow. My husband, Chris, has just such a story about his older sister, but my story about running away from home is a little different. It wasn't a sudden decision to just head out the door, but a carefully planned mission that was years in the making.

Let me first say that in no way did I have bad parents. They are both European immigrants, two of the many who made their way to Canada after surviving the Second World War. To be honest, to use the word 'survive' is an understatement. My father, Czech born, lied about his age to get accepted into the Polish army, but I honestly don't know anything else about that experience. Despite what he went through he would never talk about that time. All I do know is that he was in Italy when it was all over and took the opportunity to start a new life in Canada. My mother's story is not so simple.

Born into an affluent family of Russian-Jewish heritage, my mother was only a young girl when her family home was taken by Hitler's army. Her mother was carrying her third child and was too far along in the pregnancy to flee the country. One of the invading soldiers had compassion on her and she, along with my mother and her younger brother, were sent to a concentration camp where they were pretty much treated as slaves. The hardship took her mother's life as well as the child that she had given birth to, so my mother's new sister never made it to her first birthday. At the end of the war mom was ten years old, and like many of the children of that time she and her brother were now orphans.

They ended up in a Belgian convent which was a common solution for war orphans, but instead of finding peace after such a harrowing experience they were treated as servants and faced with hardship once again. That went on for a few years and my mother had pretty much resigned herself to the fact that she too would become a nun, but then a married couple heading for Canada had asked to adopt her. She was elated to have a chance to leave but insisted that her brother be part of the adoption. She refused to lose her last family member. Making the demand risked her one chance for freedom should the couple decide against it, but they agreed and soon traveled to Canada as a family, settling in a small mining town in northern Ontario. Once there it was decided that, for whatever reason, education was not an option for both children. Only one could attend school and the other would have to stay home. My mother decided to let her brother be the one to go to school while she stayed at home to be a servant yet again, this time to her foster parents. It was here that she met and married my father and was finally able to start a new life that would be her own.

You could probably say that my mother reinvented herself in Canada. Though not ashamed of her Jewish heritage it was now instinctive to keep that aspect of her life tucked away. This was also the era of the Cold War when the U.S.S.R. was viewed as the next official threat to world peace. It definitely wasn't a good time to proclaim that you were Russian. Since my mother is a natural linguist she adopted French as her native tongue and was able to pass for being Belgian. Blending in with Canadian culture was paramount for her, but she still kept a spark of her true heritage alive in the home through cooking, baking, and the stories that went along with those traditions.

It wasn't long before I was born, but I don't remember much about my early years. Dad worked in the gold mines but soon realized the dangers of the job and headed south to find more civilized work. Once he secured a position at the General Motors plant in Oshawa he brought us to our new home which he was building himself. For the first year or so we lived in a boarding house while our home was being built, and we moved in when there was only tar paper on the walls, but in the end we lived in our own brick house with a full basement on a double lot with no mortgage. My parents still live there to this day. With all of the licences and permits needed to start such a task, building a house like that nowadays is unheard of. Back then there was plenty of opportunity for any who were hard working and willing to carve their own niche in the growing Canadian mosaic, long before the generous government handouts that are doled out to today's new Canadians.

Dad quickly gained a reputation at work for being both hard working and conscientious. It also turned out that GM had a policy to reward good work ethics; the employee to suggest the best money-saving idea of the year would be given a new car. I can't remember which year it was that dad got his first car, but it seemed to me that every year after that he was having it upgraded to the latest model as a thank-you from his bosses at General Motors. In fact, I'm sure that he would have been placed in upper-management if not for the common language-barrier that handicapped many war immigrants arriving in Canada. Speaking English came gradually for both of my parents, but reading and writing was a hardship. That's when I got my first official family job title of Translator.

Now, since we initially spoke Polish in the family home I was in the same boat as my parents. I started kindergarten without knowing a stitch of English and my teacher would have nothing to do with me. I was promptly put in the corner of the classroom and told that I would stay there until I could speak English. Can you believe that? What an injustice to place upon a child! I mean, I must have known a bit of English to understand why I was segregated from the class, but those memories are a bit hazy. I'm pretty sure that my mother advocated for me when I told her how my first day of school went, but I honestly can't recall how I eventually came to learn the language aside from interacting with the other kids when I was permitted to go outside with them for recess. All I can figure is that God must have had his hand in the matter.

My two brothers never really knew Polish to any degree because my parents resolved to speak more English in the house so that they wouldn't have the go through same difficulties when growing up. I, on the other hand, continued to grow with both languages because every letter that came to the house was brought to my attention. "Ann, what does it say?" They would ask, and only by switching between both languages could I explain, and teach, what was written. I felt as if I had suddenly become indispensable, and for some reason that worried me.

These days, being the oldest child and also being the only girl in the family can grant you a special status above your other siblings. For me, however, it was only a double whammy. Being the oldest meant that I was responsible for both of my brothers, and since my mother became quite sick after giving birth to my second brother I was responsible for them more often than I would have liked. Being the only girl meant that I was the one to help my mother with the cleaning, even accompanying her on her part time job of cleaning nearby houses for the affluent. While it was never demanded of me I could feel the expectation to help, and I did so willingly, but to this day I feel that I was robbed of my childhood or at least the same type of childhood that my two brothers had.

Perhaps it was the 'old European' way of thinking, but my parents never held me to the same esteem as my brothers so my feminism was more of a burden than anything. When it was time for a haircut my father would walk all three of us down to the barber shop, and all three of us were given the same, generic haircut as if I were just one of the boys. It wasn't until I went off to university that I was able to grow out my hair and start to gain the appearance of a young woman. Clothing me was treated in the same manner on most occasions, but the skirt and stockings were brought out now and then and I suspect that was my mother's doing. To be honest, those who remember women's fashion in the sixties will understand that I didn't complain all that much about the simplicity of dressing as a boy. This ruse, however, only lasted for as long as it was convenient.

Every time there was a domestic problem, usually involving cooking or cleaning, the boy was gone and suddenly it was remembered that Ann was in fact a girl. Heaven forbid that the two boys should take care of themselves! Being able to carry on the family name was asking enough of them apparently, and this became more and more evident as the years wore on. When I wanted to take piano or violin lessons I was told that there was no money for that, but there was money for both of my brothers to get into any sport that they wanted. When I asked for money to go to university it was the same story.

"Why do you need to go to university?" My father would ask. "You're just going to get married and have a family." Again, the old European way of thinking. If I wanted to further my education then I'd have to find the money on my own. I thank God that my mother and I did house cleaning for a GM executive who could help me with this dilemma.

Normally only department managers could get their kids in for summer work at GM, and only after their first year of university, but I was determined to be the exception. The executive and his wife were a kind couple who didn't have children of their own, and they had watched me grow up over the past five years as I helped my mother. They both knew the strong work ethics of my parents, but I'm sure my pleading played an important role as well. I earnestly explained that I needed the GM job before my first year of school or I wouldn't be able to pay for the tuition or residence. Perhaps he saw me as a surrogate for the child they never had, but he told me that I would have this summer to prove myself and that I was only given the chance because of my parents' reputation. So without doing so intentionally my parents did help me get to university, but it was up to me to carry on the hard-working reputation of our family name which is exactly what I did for that summer and the next four after that.

Some might think that a few years away from home would satisfy the craving of independence, and perhaps under different circumstances for different people it would have, but nothing could change my father's way of thinking. Doing well at school didn't bring pride to his heart, only confusion as to why I was working so hard at what he thought was a waste of time. After all, why would a house wife need to be so highly educated? The confusion continued when it came time for me to buy my first car.

In the summer of 1973 I had the opportunity to buy a new Firebird at factory cost. It was a chocolate brown special order that the original buyer backed out of for some reason, so it was offered up to the workers. We're talking about the nice hood emblem and everything! It was a dream come true for any student and I begged my father to loan me the money which I promised to pay back. His response had nothing to do with a concern for getting paid back, only that he didn't understand why I needed the car at all. "Why do you need a car? Your boyfriend can just drive you around." To this day I'm not sure what boyfriend he was thinking of since I would rarely let a boy near me until I got into university. You see, all through high school my mother had me convinced that if a boy so much a kissed me then I would become pregnant. You're laughing as you read this, but it's true!

Discouraged and heart-broken about the car I resorted to bumming rides from anyone I could during my university years and biking down the highway, in my work boots, to my summer factory job when I wasn't on the same shift as my dad. It was hard not to feel resentful towards my brothers when the money pot seemed endless for their post-secondary education, and each being given a car to boot. So it really isn't a mystery that after completing my final glorious year of university (with Honors) I felt that my destiny was finally my own. You could say that I hit the ground running and never looked back, and can anyone really blame me?

STARTING A RELATIONSHIP WITH GOD

As I reflect upon these years and the ones that follow, it has occurred to me that running from my parents resembles the way that most of us run from God as well. Early in a relationship with our heavenly Father it's easy to be disgruntled, not with what He does in our lives but with what we feel He *isn't* doing. The beginning of this relationship is hard because His ways are new to us. Living up to His expectations is not only difficult but also confusing at times. Why does it need to be difficult? Why do I have to do that now? Why can't He give me what I want? Why can't I do what I want to? Sticking it out with this new commitment can be taxing for most and usually results in little, if any, obvious reward in the beginning.

My parents had always provided for me, were never cruel to me, and I know to this day that they always loved me. Unfortunately they just didn't understand me. To be more accurate, we didn't understand each other. They couldn't fathom why a girl would need, or even want, to look after herself or have a career when she could just get married and have a man to do all that for her. They couldn't, or maybe wouldn't, see the drive that I was born with, and I couldn't understand how they could be so blind to what I was. However, I have come to attribute all things to God's wisdom, and my parents' constant denial to my wishes only ensured that I would leave home to go on the journey that He needed me to. And when God needs you to do something, no matter how hard, it's always for our benefit no matter how obscure the task may seem. The lifelong lesson is to figure out when a difficult task is His bidding or just the enemy trying to waste your time.

Chapter Two

Beating Up the Boys

For most of my life I have been at odds with the opposite sex whether it was my brothers, co-workers, or just about any guy that was interested in me. I don't know if it was the feeling of inadequacy that I would inadvertently bestow upon them by either not needing their help or simply by being better at something than they were, or if it was that male feeling of conquest that would inevitably get quashed when their advances were flatly dismissed. Even before I left home there was one thing that was certain to me; I would always be needed but never needy.

Mid-way through elementary school I acquired my second title: Protector. You see, though neither my brothers nor I were ever small children, my first brother was growing at an alarming rate even for our family. Luckily the diagnosis of a growth on his pituitary gland was found early, halting his growth at six-feet and six inches tall by the age of fifteen. Now you would think that being as tall as he was would give him a free pass for life from bullies, but for some reason it had the opposite effect. It seemed that every schoolyard tough guy needed to take him on to prove themselves to everyone else. You have to realize that, as big a he was on the outside, he was still a little kid on the inside who was terrified of these others who were years older than him. Plus he wasn't a mean spirit to start with. He didn't know how to fight and he didn't want to fight so it was up to me to solve the problem every time it came up. For years I came home with skinned knees, a black eye or a bloody nose from defending him, and I don't regret doing it, but unfortunately I was a little too good at doing it. Soon my youngest brother was having a similar problem and I was fighting on his behalf as well, but a medical condition wasn't the root of the problem this time. Instead, I soon found out that he was instigating the fights on purpose! His condition was that he was born a little jerk, and there's no medical procedure to fix that. Once I figured this out I left him to his own devices the next time someone wanted to beat him up, and I'm pretty sure that he got what he deserved.

My most memorable fight happened when I was in grade eleven and teaching Sunday school to the younger kids during church. One of the boys was picking on my brother and I told him to stop it.

"Why? Who's gonna make me?" He answered.

"I'll make you," I shot back, "so quit it!"

Perhaps he didn't take me seriously because of my Sunday dress, or maybe he felt that nothing would happen with all of the little kids around, but the teasing continued so the fists started flying. Some adults heard the ruckus and came down to the basement to investigate, so imagine their surprise to see me and him slugging it out! Even their arrival wasn't enough to get us to stop and we had to be physically pulled apart for that fight to end. After taking a few weeks off I went back to teaching Sunday school, but I never saw that boy at church again. Incidentally, all that fighting was what got me introduced to make-up. These days girls are mastering the art of cosmetic image enhancement as early as grade school, but I never had that interest until a few years later. I did, however, become quite good at learning to cover up a black eye.

Once that phase ended another soon began: dating. It was a brief chapter of my high school life, but not because I had an aversion to the opposite sex. I was around boys all the time during my younger years; climbing trees, running around and hanging out as school kids did back then. I was one of those tomboys that you've read about in old novels, and with my haircut and lanky build I'm sure lots of onlookers thought I actually *was* a boy. But eventually I was asked out on a date, and everything went as fine as could be expected until he got up the nerve to lean in close for a kiss. POW! I'm sure a punch in the mouth wasn't what he was expecting, but that's what he got for trying to get me pregnant! I don't know what exactly he told everyone at school the next day, but I wasn't asked out on too many dates after that.

Turning the Other Cheek

These days, standing up for something that you think is right can be a difficult decision. Today's society is adopting the 'ethics' that everybody is entitled to their opinion, no matter how perverse or distorted it may be, and anyone who openly opposes such opinions is labeled as being a troublemaker. To make matters worse, Christians have been led to think that they must always turn the other cheek whenever somebody does anything against them, and I know that's just wrong. Should my brother have just stood there and let the bullies hit him or else he wasn't being a good Christian? I don't think so. This whole problem starts with a misinterpretation of the famous passage in the book of Matthew:

[38] Ye have heard that it hath been said, An eye for an eye, and a tooth for a tooth:
[39] But I say unto you, That ye resist not evil: but whosoever shall smite thee on thy right cheek, turn to him the other also.
[40] And if any man will sue thee at the law, and take away thy coat, let him have thy cloak also.
[41] And whosoever shall compel thee to go a mile, go with him twain.
[42] Give to him that asketh thee, and from him that would borrow of thee turn not thou away. ~ Matthew 5:38-42

In "That ye resist not evil", the word "resist" is more accurately translated as "retaliate" in the form of revenge. Jesus wasn't against justified, lawful defense, but spiteful revenge which apparently was common among the Jews back then. Support for this is found in the book of John:

[19] The high priest then asked Jesus of his disciples, and of his doctrine.
[20] Jesus answered him, I spake openly to the world; I ever taught in the synagogue, and in the temple, whither the Jews always resort; and in secret have I said nothing.
[21] Why askest thou me? ask them which heard me, what I have said unto them: behold, they know what I said.
[22] And when he had thus spoken, one of the officers which stood by struck Jesus with the palm of his hand, saying, Answerest thou the high priest so?
[23] Jesus answered him, If I have spoken evil, bear witness of the evil: but if well, why smitest thou me?

24 Now Annas had sent him bound unto Caiaphas the high priest. ~ John 18:19-24

In verse 23 Jesus didn't turn the other cheek for another slap from the officer, nor did He retaliate in spite, but our Lord instead challenged the man to justify his actions. That is the example that I feel we as Christians are obligated to do as well. If someone does us wrong then call them on it and make them justify their actions. If there is some sort of misunderstanding then it can be solved right away, otherwise you run the risk of becoming resentful towards the other person and also letting them think that they are justified in their behaviour.

Back at Matthew 5:39-40 where we're getting slapped and then sued for our tunic, a different perspective needs to be taken. In biblical times, if you got slapped or sued it was usually because you had wronged someone. Remember, Jesus was preaching to spiteful, vengeful Jews at this time, not a bunch of do-gooders. He was telling them that after they had wronged someone, don't just repay in kind (an eye for an eye) but go a little further to show that you are truly sorry for what you had done. Proof on this is found at verse 42, "Give to him that asketh thee, and from him that would borrow of thee turn not thou away." This phrase would be redundant if verses 39-40 did indeed want us to lie down and give everything up to the other guy. How could we give and let others borrow from us in verse 42 if we've already let them take all our stuff back in verse 40? That would be a redundant statement and a contradiction, and Jesus did neither of those things, so a better interpretation is to pay back more than you owe for any trouble you cause and to help another person more than they ask. Go the extra mile!

And about that extra mile back at Matthew 5:41, apparently the Roman army had the authority to demand any citizen to carry a load for up to a mile in distance. It's a strange old law, and they probably didn't just pick one guy out of a crowd and tell them to carry something for a mile up the road, but more likely they enlisted a large group at once. The Roman army were no wimps, but it's possible that on the march home after a hard battle they might want to give the troops a bit of a break without actually stopping for a rest, so they would enlist all able bodies of a village to help carry stuff for a mile. It's not so far that it would harm the villagers, nor would it take them so far from home that they couldn't get back after. This may have been Jesus' way of encouraging people to do more than what they were obligated to do.

So was it wrong for me to fight those boys? I don't think so. They weren't just shoving my brother or calling him names and running away, they were looking for a fight and they weren't leaving without one. I stood up for what I thought was right, and when words wouldn't settle things I used my fists. And each time it was over, it was over. There was no revenge being plotted, but there were spiteful feelings for a while which is normal for kids and people in general. It isn't just the action that's important but the actions that follow as well.

Many years after this phase in my life was over, during one of the times I was visiting my parents, my brother dropped by with a surprise.

"You'll never guess who I just ran into at the barber shop," he said. When he told me who it was I couldn't believe it so I drove on over to the shop myself. Sure enough, standing behind the chair was the same boy I was fighting with in the church basement, only now he was all grown up! I just smiled when he looked up to see who had walked in.

"Remember me?" I said.

"I sure do!" He replied with an equally big smile on his face.

"You wouldn't stop bothering my brother all those years ago and now you're cutting his hair!"

We recounted the show-stopping event and traded stories on how we each dealt with our black eyes and wounded pride after committing such an atrocity in the church basement, and in some ways I wish I had a chance to do more of that with everything that happened in my past. Everyone makes mistakes as a kid, especially during those awkward years of puberty where the child's mind is trying to be re-wired into a responsible adult. Reconnecting with the boy from the church gave some unplanned closure on an event from my past. Being able to laugh about it with him did more for me than if I'd just turned the other cheek or had simply forgiven him on my own terms without him even knowing about it. I think closure is the best remedy for any altercation, even if it's years after the event, and certainly better than simply paying back for doing something wrong. As for my younger brother, I think he ended up paying back more than he owed for the trouble he caused, and I'm okay with that.

Chapter Three

Flirting with the Boys

University in the 70s was very different from what we see today. Everybody had manners, most of the people who were there were serious about their education, being in residence meant having access to cooked meals three times a day, seven days a week, and you could hang out with a group of people in your spare time and not have to worry about being obligated to sleep with them. In fact, I'm pretty sure that university today is pretty much the opposite of what it was like in the 70s, but be that as it may it was all new to me.

My first year in residence was very exciting for me, and also a little scary. Ever since we moved into our house in Oshawa I had enjoyed the privilege of having my own room with a double bed. The down side to this meant that when company came over I was sleeping on the couch. It was a common inconvenience in those days, a time before the lavish middle-class houses that now come standard with dens, guest rooms and finished basements, but it was a worthy sacrifice to ensure my privacy for most of the time. Now, however, I had to adjust to my new surroundings that consisted of only a single bed and a roommate. I shared the room with a girl from Toronto who was pleasant enough, but unfortunately she wasn't the sort of person whom I made that special, roommate bond with. I had finally taken the first step in running away from home, only to be stuck sharing my room with a complete stranger. Baby steps, I suppose.

I think part of the reason that I had trouble connecting with most girls during my first year of university could be traced back to my complete lack of sex education. I hadn't even kissed a boy yet, and knew nothing about dating or, well, anything else really. More importantly I didn't want anyone to know this about me, and hanging out with guys was a good way to avoid the topic. The type of young men who went to university back then were not the sort to openly speak of crude, sexual conquest like you see in everyday society now. In fact, these days it's almost impossible to go a single day without hearing somebody speaking about who they've slept with and how proud they are about it, either on television, the internet, or the coffee shop, but back then it just didn't happen. That's probably why it took me this long to start figuring everything out, and who knows how much longer it would have taken if I hadn't left home to go to school.

Even in the good ol' days of completely separate buildings for boys' and girls' dorms it wasn't unheard of for a girl to have her boyfriend come for a weekend visit, although the proper protocol was to arrange for him to stay with a friend in the boys' dorm during the nights. Of course my roommate had to be the exception. You know the girl in the movies who can't watch a couple kissing without turning away in uncomfortable embarrassment? You guessed it. That was me! It was bad enough when I had to witness their first smooch session, but when she casually let me know that he'd be spending the night on the floor, *our* floor, in the same room as us, I didn't know what to do.

"Oh, it's alright. Nothing's going to happen," she assured me, but I'd barely gotten used to having her in my room and I sure as hell wasn't going to spend the night in a room with a boy sleeping on the floor. My real dilemma, however, was handling the situation without letting her know just how ignorant I was about the whole 'sleeping arrangement' of life. Thankfully by this time I had managed to make a friend in the girls' dorm and made some sleeping arrangements of my own. To me a weekend on somebody else's floor was better than an uncomfortable weekend in my own bed. I suppose I could have just complained to the don about the arrangement, but I was still getting the hang of dorm life and didn't want to rock the boat at this time. The last thing I needed was a spiteful roommate from hell for the rest of the year.

The one good thing that did come about from this encounter was that I was starting to figure things out for myself, and I was pretty sure that kissing did not lead to pregnancy as my mother had forewarned me. This new realization, along with my regular Sunday attendance at the local church, finally led to a new milestone in my life: my first official boyfriend. He was studying Ministry nearby and had the ethics which I could relate to. He wouldn't dare even hold my hand in public, but he was good company on Sundays and the other outings that we managed to attend together like going to youth groups or a night out skating. I even mustered up the courage to engage in some kissing, though I'm sure that I must have been horrible at it since I can't exactly recall those 'magical moments' as I think back. There were definitely no fireworks going off at this momentous occasion. These weren't the make-out sessions that kids perform nowadays, just quick pecks of affection to test the waters. Alas, it was not to be. By the end of the school year I had come to the realization that in no way was I prepared to be a Minister's wife anytime soon.

I returned home for the summer a little wiser and a little more confident. Boys were no longer taboo, but they were still icky in general. Of all the summers I spent at the GM plant, this was the most memorable for a few reasons. Returning to a summer job and no longer being one of the new kids is always a good feeling, and this was also the year that dad rejected my decision to own my own car. This isn't to say that I never got to drive a nice car—I just didn't get my own. Being an assembly line worker meant that you got rotated down the entire assembly line throughout the summer, including the job of driving the finished cars off of the line and out to the loading area. If you were really lucky then your turn came when some of the performance vehicles were getting finished, allowing you to zip down the quarter mile lane in brand new sports cars all day long.

It was never officially encouraged to 'bury the needle' on those little jaunts to the shipping lot, but then the regular workers could hardly expect less from students with lead feet. A blind eye was turned to the occasional squeal of rubber since these were essentially test drives as well. Prompt acceleration was an important part of quality control with those larger engines, but there's always someone to spoil it for everybody else in the end. While you would think that the trouble came with the top-end sports cars, it instead came from a less obvious, but understandable source. This was the year that we were building a new fleet of police cars for the Quebec Police Department, and boy could those things move! It was only a matter of time before a couple of lads decided to push the supped-up engines to the limit by drag racing down the lane side-by-side thinking that a reprimand would have been the least of their worries. I didn't get to witness this particular lapse of judgement, but a lot of people heard the crash that signaled the end of the race as one of the drivers lost control. I'm not sure if the Quebec Police Department got two less cars than expected that year, but after the foreman was done with them we definitely has two less line workers by the end of the day. Surprisingly enough, this is not my most vivid memory of working summers at GM. That memory comes from a far less obvious, everyday pantry item.

Being the era before microwave ovens were a common, kitchen appliance, factory workers would get creative, if not innovative, with what they had on hand. At the end of the paint line was the drying booth where freshly painted cars were slowly passed through the room on a conveyor belt. Electricity-sucking heat lamps turned the room into a large oven that cured the paint in under an hour, and it was in here that workers realized you could get a warm lunch. A favourite trick was to punch some holes in a soup can and put it just inside the door of the paint booth an hour or so before lunch, enabling them to retrieve a pre-heated meal mid-shift.

One day a new student asked one of the regulars how to heat up his can of beans before lunch. "Just put it in the paint booth," was the common answer, although not the entirely correct one. The student did as he was told, without puncturing the lid, and you probably know where this is going. An hour later there was a tremendous "BANG!" as the sealed can could no longer contain the pressure of being heated, sending beans and sauce flying to coat everything within the can's blast radius. You may be smiling now, but here's the punch line. How many of you readers know the Mary Kay makeup company? Those who do will know that they reward select sales members with a custom-painted, powder pink Cadillac, and of all the cars to be in the paint booth at that exact time, that would be the absolute worst one.

Stopping the assembly line was not an option, so by the time that pink Caddy made it out the door those beans were baked right into the fresh paint. Some workers tried to make light of the small disaster for the kid's sake. "Mary Kay was always full of beans anyways," they said, trying to cheer him up, but the entire car had to be stripped and painted again, which is an expensive mistake with custom paint. Had it been a regular car with a common paint job it might have been overlooked, but not this time. We seemed to go through more students than usual that summer.

It would also seem that my confidence wasn't the only thing I had grown in the past year, and I wasn't the only person to notice either. No more regular trips to the barber shop with my dad and brothers meant that I was finally able to grow out my hair, and while I was never an overly well-endowed girl I seemed to be getting more mature in other areas as well. Factory coveralls aren't flattering by any means, but they can only hide so much from factory workers. Being a girl who could handle herself on an assembly line was just another way of getting unwanted attention, and I gradually learned to develop a tolerance towards the snips and innuendos that would float past me on a regular basis.

Mind you, crudeness back then would be considered tame by today's standards, but the tomboy in me had no problem telling those guys off. "Get lost!" Was my usual comeback, and in the end I think that's all those guys really wanted. I'd keep walking and they'd get a chuckle and then it was over. Another saving grace was my father's reputation at the plant. He wasn't upper management, but he was the type of man that upper management listened to, so while the line workers would insist on having their fun it never got to the point where I actually worried about my safety. Still, the constant interaction with those guys may have helped me to overcome my fear of the opposite sex and start to see them in a new light. By my second year in university men had moved from 'ick' to 'potential companion'.

Not having my own car, specifically my own '73 chocolate brown Trans Am Firebird with the gold hood emblem, meant that I constantly needed rides from other people. Not that this was uncommon back then since the frivolous "want it now but pay for it later" mentality hadn't really started yet. If you had something then you either earned it or had it given to you, and there were plenty of young men also attending Trent University who were being put through school by their parents, and that usually included the use of a car. It would seem that the old European way of thinking was not isolated to my parents as I had first thought.

My second year of dorm life was a considerable improvement since I managed to get a room all to myself that year, but it was still dorm life. The room was small, we all had to share the common bathrooms on our floor and wash our laundry in a utility room, and there was just the one phone per floor for everybody to use. If you wanted to make a private call then you did it someplace else. There was plenty of room for improvement in my mind, but that would have to wait until next year.

By reconnecting with returning acquaintances from last year I had become part of a small network of friends who would hang out together when time permitted. This year was different, though, since I was no longer rushing off to spend time with the student Minister, leaving me open to consider my options that were closer at hand. I would have been spoiled for choice if I'd been a regular girl with a regular dream of the white wedding and the picket fence house, but of course I was not a regular girl.

My group of friends consisted of five guys and five girls who would get together for communal recreation when we needed a break from our studies. There was no facebook back then, so socializing was done face to face with people you actually knew and had similar interests with. One thing we had in common was that we weren't in university to waste time, so when we did find time to take a break we did so as a group and with responsibility. You also have to realize that Trent University was on the outskirts of Peterborough, on the edge of the Otonabee River, pretty much in the middle of nowhere. Its nick-name was "Little Oxford", in reference to the prestigious Oxford University in England, and many of our profs came over from England just to teach there. It was a beautiful place, but if you wanted to do anything off campus it was either a planned car ride or bus trip to get into town.

There wasn't always time to take the journey into Peterborough so we would find ways to amuse ourselves on site. This would include activities like cross-country skiing across the picturesque university grounds, a quick game of floor hockey in the hallway of the boy's dorm, or if we were really in the mood for a beer we'd get our own case and just hang out together in somebody's room. I guess we were the poster kids for naivety and innocence without even knowing it. There were also trips into town for a movie or if a very special show was playing at the theater, and we would attend the odd party which would look more like a social gathering by today's outrageous standards of what a party is supposed to be like. It was very special to get an entire weekend off from our studies and we would sometimes congregate to one of our houses (not mine) for few days of snowmobiling. Before you knew it, April was just around the corner and the task of year-end finals was at hand.

Of the five guys I hung out with, three had potential to become a steady companion for me. All of them were very nice, of course, but it took a while to weigh the pros and cons of embarking on such an arrangement. Spontaneity was never one of my dominant qualities. One of the boys was the son of a wealthy family that owned a very successful wallpaper company in Toronto. Pairing this with all of his personal qualities would make him a no-brainer for most girls, but the prospect of never leaving the Toronto area, and thus never really leaving home, was a major con in my mind. Bachelor number two was the son of a predominant parliament member who worked in the Canadian embassy. He came with money and prestige, but I got the impression that he was only attending school to make his parents happy. He would have rather been pursuing his hobby as an artist and I saw his half-hearted attempt at university as a type of laziness, so that put him out of the picture. My third friend was studying to be a geologist and was quite serious with his education, so by the end of the year I had settled on him to be my steady companion, not that he knew it at the time. My seemingly clinical process of elimination took the entire school year and the only thing on my mind by the end of April was getting back to work at the GM plant and surviving another summer at home.

By my third year at Trent I had decided that I'd had enough of dorm life and went hunting for my own apartment in town, as did most of my friends. I finally settled for renting out the servant's quarters in an elderly lady's downtown estate home. It was a short walk from the bus stop, I had my own entrance off of the back lane and the room came furnished with a couch, which also served as my bed, plus a few odds and ends to make the space livable. Through my door was the downstairs bathroom, a full bathroom which I pretty much had to myself (cha-ching!) plus the kitchen was just a bit further down the hall. There was no direct heating into my room but it was instead kept warm(ish) from whatever heat crept into the space from the main house, and with the aid of an electric blanket to keep me warm at night I had my very own Den of Solitude for a nominal price of $200 a month. It was more expensive than residency but I considered the privacy to be well worth the lack of amenities. Compared to today's living prices you would consider that a bargain, but a recent on-line check with the Bank of Canada inflation calculator shows that a $200 value from back then converts to just over one thousand dollars today, and I don't think it was even close to being a $1000 per month apartment by today's standards.

Despite its majestic character, the most interesting part about my new home wasn't the house itself but the neighbour outside my door. Across the lane was the back of another century-home and I had a splendid view of the large, two-door garage with an apartment above it. That in itself isn't so unusual, nor was the renter who was a pleasant enough young man, but his practicing occupation is what intrigued me the most. You see, he was interning to become an embalmer and the house across the lane was the local funeral home. I'm not sure if my new landlady had left out that tidbit of information on purpose, worried that I wouldn't want the room, or if she genuinely gave it no second thought after all her years of living there.

He and I would have short conversations now and then if he happened to be outside having a smoke break as I was coming home from school. The smell of stale cigarette smoke and formaldehyde was a potent mix, so our talks weren't long, but I'm sure he got a laugh from my reaction to his chosen occupation. I had never had any exposure to funeral experiences and was both horrified and intrigued at what I was learning from him. I don't know what my face looked like as he described the process of flushing the body with formaldehyde, especially the part about the body 'farting' as air bubbles passed through, but I'm sure my expression was more memorable than the actual procedure. Then one autumn day, as he butted out his cigarette, our usual chat went for a different turn.

"You want to take a look inside?" He asked. It certainly wasn't how I expected our conversation to start out, and I didn't know what to say right away, but he did his best to reassure me. A cosmetics student was on her way over to fix up the "customer's" hair and make-up, and I was welcome to tag along when she arrived. I can't remember my exact response, but I'm sure the look on my face was along the lines of, "Hair and make-up? Are you kidding me?" But soon enough there she was, and not the least bit freaked out about her assignment.

Seeing my first dead body was an unforgettable experience, and watching the girl give the old woman a make-over was a little on the surreal side. He explained that the cosmetics students get good practice this way since the customer is more forgiving of any mistakes. The girls were actually more relaxed about working on cadavers than with a live customer, which kind of made sense to me. As grossed out as I was, I still watched the procedure in fascination. It was almost hypnotic in a strange sort of way, but I still thought the corpse looked more natural before she started than with the make-up plastered all over the face in an attempt to make her look less dead. But that's what the mourning family wants, and who's going to argue with them? My only comment was that it certainly wasn't a job that I could do.

The embalmer said that he liked it because it was peaceful with very little stress. The person was already dead so it was kind of hard to mess anything up. Getting a body back after an autopsy was a little more work because it usually had to be re-done. After the coroner had finished his procedure the organs were usually just plopped back into the chest cavity like a pile of meat, with just enough stitches to hold everything in. My neighbour would then have to open the corpse, put everything back where it belonged so that the body didn't look like an over-stuffed apple pie and carefully sew the chest closed so nothing was noticeable underneath the clothing. I'm sure he could tell that I was completely engrossed in the story, and who know how many times he'd told it before, but my reaction to his next line must have been priceless.

"The worst part, really, is when they sit up on me," he said, almost casually. I don't know what opened wider, my eyes or my mouth! I thought I was ready to leave, but I knew I had to hear one last story. It had happened unexpectedly enough as he was going about his work, his customer lying on the table with hands folded neatly on its lap. He had dropped something on the ground accidentally and bent down to pick it up from under the table. Unbeknownst to him the corpse had sat up suddenly as they sometimes do, and one of the hands had slipped off to the side and smacked him on the back! He said he almost jumped out of his skin that time, but I'm sure that such an experience would traumatize most regular people. Having heard enough stories for one day, if not for the rest of my life, I thanked them both for the opportunity and headed back to the land of the living.

My remaining two years of school are a bit of a blur to me now, only memories of studies and social breaks with my friends. Some of that time was spent solely with the geologist, and many of those 'dates' were road trips to geological sites in the area. He needed to do field research at designated locations, so I would accompany him on these little day trips. Of course nothing happened on these excursions. He was a perfect gentleman and I was not a promiscuous girl, and though there wasn't any intimacy in our relationship there was some sort of unspoken agreement that we were a steady item, and I was okay with that.

A clearer acknowledgement of our relationship was made during the summer after my third year of school. After getting home I ran into one of the few boys I had become actual friends with during high school. He never really left home and was content to work at the local grocery store for now, but I never thought less of him for it and I guess he knew that. As it turned out he had won an all-expense paid trip but had nobody to go with at the time. There were no strings attached, no 'funny business' of the sort would be expected from him in return of the favour. He just needed somebody to bring along since going alone would be no fun.

"So?" He asked. "Would you like to go to Hawaii?"

Now who in their right mind would turn that down? The timing was perfect because I had a few weeks to kill before starting at GM, and I called my geologist to let him know that it was a completely plutonic affair which he was okay with. The fact that I called him at all is enough to tell me that I acknowledged some sort of relationship, and followed proper protocol, but the idea of being in a relationship was still a foreign concept to me. All that aside, the trip to Hawaii was a lot of fun and just as beautiful as what you would see in one of those travel brochures. Something like that could still be considered a big deal today, so imagine how big of a deal it was back then when global travel was generally only experienced by the affluent and privileged.

During the last year of university I spent several weekends at my geologist's house with his parents, so I guess you could say we had taken our relationship to the next level. We had met before, but as an entire group of friends during one of the weekend visits from earlier years. Now it was just the four of us. His parents were a delightful British couple, older than most parents, with the geologist being their only child. His mother was an incredible cook and the visits were always enjoyable, making the general atmosphere a distinct contrast to my own home life. A normal girl would have probably considered this to be a match made in Heaven.

At the end of that year, my final year of university, I got the chance to spend six months in Florida with my mother's foster parents. They had property there and spent a lot of time in the pan handle state, and half a year away from home, from everything, certainly couldn't hurt. I let my geologist know that I would be gone for a while and we parted ways amicably, knowing that I would be returning in a few months. Time to myself was something that I rarely had so I felt that this opportunity could not be passed up. The world seems more open when you're finally done with school and I wanted to see what was out there. Not being one to waste all of my time with idle sight-seeing I kept myself busy by taking some courses towards a Mediation law diploma, which was a much simpler process back then even though I was not an American citizen.

I duly returned home at the appointed time, albeit a little reluctantly, bitten by the Florida bug that claims so many northerners. A few days later I was paid a visit from my geologist whom I have to admit was the furthest thing from my mind at that point. I can't even describe my surprise when what I thought was a friendly visit turned out to be a marriage proposal! I was momentarily speechless, and anyone who knows me can attest to how rarely that happens. Every girl's dream was happening to me; the gallant man with the promise of a white wedding and perfect in-laws. A moment like this deserved the proper response, and I could see in his face that he was fully anticipating it. Unfortunately he had to hear the truth instead, that I had only returned home to apply for a green card. I had met someone in Florida and was going to marry him and live there permanently.

Love, Hate & Being Sorry

As I look back to that event in my life, to say that I broke his heart would be a severe understatement. You break eggs to make breakfast. I'm sure to him it felt like I had ripped out his heart, crushed it in front of him, thrown the pieces to the ground, stomped on them and then kicked them about the floor for good measure, thought that was never my intention nor do I wish for that description to be taken in a comical way. He was devastated and I was to blame for it. It is said that some people are blind in love, so I must be blind, deaf and dumb where matters of the heart are concerned. What he must have perceived as a two-year courtship (and how could he not?), I only saw as a relationship of mutual convenience. I honestly couldn't understand how he, or anyone, could get that attached to me, but regardless of my ignorance somebody ended up getting hurt. It certainly isn't something I am proud of, nor was it intentional, but it happened all the same and I am truly sorry for the pain I had cause him and his parents who also thought that the proposal was a sure thing.

1 John 4:8 states "He that loveth not knoweth not God; for God is love." These days the word "love" is used almost entirely out of context and can properly be replaced by the words "like" or "enjoy". Those who are overly emphatic about a particular food or activity could add the word "really" in front of

either of those words, perhaps even multiple times to get the point across. To actually feel love is to have an uncompromising dedication towards someone that cannot possibly be replaced by any other individual, and certainly not by some food or activity. Loving somebody fills a void inside of us, maybe one that we didn't realize was there, but when that someone is suddenly removed from your life you definitely notice it. Poets through the ages have written of love, about the joys it brings to life and the pain it leaves behind.

Some would argue that if God is love, then why do so many bad things happen? Why does the Bible depict Him getting angry? To understand this we must first understand that, above all, God is also balance. Everything He makes is perfectly balanced and harmonious no matter how complex it is. All of his creation starts out pure and equal and fair, with nothing going against the natural laws that the entire universe adheres to. God is love, but not *only* love. He is balanced as well, and we all know what happens when love is not reciprocated by both sides of a relationship, which is the proper way to view your life with Him; it's a relationship above anything else.

Many of you reading this book are parents, so imagine how you would feel if your child had grown up and decided that they suddenly wanted nothing to do with you for no apparent reason. You loved and cared for your child for all those years, giving them everything that you possibly could without spoiling them, but then one day they decide that the good things you are teaching them don't make sense. Other kids they know get to do fun stuff, like take drugs and have lots of sex, so off your child goes to join them. Despite everything you say or do to show them how bad of a decision that is there is nothing you can do to stop them. It would probably be very hard to describe how you would feel at that moment, but take those feelings and multiply them by God-like proportions, then multiply it again by the number of people on this world that have turned away from Him. It is impossible to conceive that amount of rejection. Because God is love I think that He must also be able to feel the pain that is associated with the feeling of love being ripped away, only it would be so much greater than we can possibly imagine.

The usual response to this kind of situation is to be defensive, and that's understandable. "I didn't know" or "I didn't meant too" is the normal way to react, and often genuine, but that doesn't take the pain away for the other person. "I'm sorry" is the kinder approach to hurting someone, but where love is concerned it won't heal the pain unless the apology is sincere and a true relationship is desired. It simply was not meant to be for the geologist and myself, and all of the apologies in the world, no matter how sincere, were not going to mend that relationship, but with God it is possible.

Now some people might say "Why bother? I was taught that God is all-forgiving. I don't have to be sorry for anything because I'm already forgiven, right?" Well, that would depend on your interpretation of apology and forgiveness I suppose. Does it make sense to you that somebody can be the most horrible person on the planet yet still expect forgiveness from God because we are taught that he is all-forgiving? It might help to think of it this way; before anyone can be forgiven for something, that person must first be truly and genuinely sorry for whatever it is that they have done.

Sorry is both a word and an action, and it's important to distinguish between the two. The word "sorry" can be said many times without actually being meant, and it's probably another word that is improperly used, and over-used, in our society these days. Quite often when somebody has done something wrong and they are confronted about it, they will offer the apology because they know it's expected of them. Truth be told, many of those people are not sorry for what they have done but only sorry that they got caught, and will soon be committing the same act as before only this time being a bit more careful. That is not being sorry. On the other hand, the *act* of being sorry can often speak volumes without any words being uttered, and it is only through those actions that true forgiveness can be earned. This is done by truly recognizing and acknowledging whatever it is you did, whether it was intentional or not, and making sure that it never happens again.

So what are these things that we need to be sorry for concerning our relationship with God? While the Bible is full of scripture telling us what not to do, most of these can be considered as advice to be taken under strong advisement for our own good and not necessarily forbidden. There are, however, several distinct passages that should not be viewed as optional and by turning to the book of Proverbs we can find one such passage:

16 *These six things doth the Lord hate: yea, seven are an abomination unto him:*
17 *A proud look, a lying tongue, and hands that shed innocent blood,*
18 *An heart that deviseth wicked imaginations, feet that be swift in running to mischief,*
19 *A false witness that speaketh lies, and he that soweth discord among brethren.* ~ Proverbs 6:16-19

There are many detailed studies on these few lines, but in short God hates it when we're arrogant, when we lie or are dishonest, when we kill and when we intentionally cause trouble of all sorts. When lists like these appear in the Bible the order in which the items are written can be from most important to least important, but it can also be the other way around with the list ending at the most important item. Modern scholars don't completely agree as to whether this list starts with the most hated action, being arrogant and vain, or if the last item of causing trouble among fellow men is the greatest abomination to Him, but the fact that lying is covered twice speaks volumes. Lying is also second on the list no matter which way you look at it, being hated even more than shedding innocent blood, and it's also one of the easiest to do. It may seem strange that lying is hated more than something as awful as killing, but I think that's because of what lying can become.

Those who live a life of dishonesty will eventually justify it with the excuse that it's easier than being good. A life of lies is the beginning of a downward slide that will lead to all of those other horrible actions that God abhors. The opposite, always being truthful, is a courageous way to live believe it or not, especially in these times when immorality is becoming a way of life for many. Not being afraid to be honest in a situation, especially one that many of your peers see nothing wrong with because 'everybody else is doing it', can be a difficult way of life, even lonely at times, but the narrow path of truth is the only one that leads to God as long as we don't become arrogant in our beliefs along the way.

But the Bible says that God is love, and now it says that he hates us if we even do so much as tell a lie? No. Those verses from Proverbs tells us what God hates most. It doesn't say that He hates us when we do it; it is telling us that He hates *when* we do those things. The difference is that He still loves us despite the fact that he hates what we're doing, and that's where true forgiveness comes into the picture. Despite the terrible things that we've done we can still be forgiven IF we are truly sorry for doing them in the first place, and we show this by never doing it again. For some people this is easier to do than for others, and for some this can be a very long road to forgiveness, but starting the journey is the most important step we can take.

So was I truly sorry for what happened to my friend and his parents? Absolutely, and I showed that to God by learning from my mistake and never getting into that situation again. Even though I had never meant to hurt them in the first place

I still took responsibility for that action and adjusted my life accordingly. I would also hope that my rejection wasn't too hard on the geologist and that he managed to find the woman who was right for him, who properly appreciated and deserved all that he had to offer. In fact, to hear from him again and know that he found Miss Right would be a greater reward than any gold or treasure.

Chapter Four

Husband Number One

Yes, I'm starting to number my husbands. Definitely an indication as to how my married life went, but don't worry it isn't a spoiler. There's still lots to keep you turning these pages. I would also like to add, probably unnecessarily, that even though he was husband number one in no way should he be confused with, or even qualified for, the position of #1 husband. That is a completely different status for a completely different man who is a long way off in my life at this point.

We met in a hair products store, of all places, and he came over to ask my opinion on what he should buy for himself. He did landscaping in the summer and his long, golden locks dried out like straw in the Florida heat so he asked me what I thought would work best for him. What a pick-up line! But it worked. Instead of telling him to ask one of the store clerks I helped the tall, tanned hunk with piercing blue-eyes to find a product that would work for him and then indulged him a little more when I was invited to dinner a few days later.

Being a newcomer to the area, and still suspicious of anyone who would be interested in me, I agreed to meet him at the restaurant and drove myself there in my foster grandparents' car. If things went sour then it would be nothing to excuse myself and simply head back home, but that is the exact opposite of how the date went. Over the course of the meal I learned that my soon-to-be suitor was actually a full-time teacher who did landscaping over the summer to make extra money. Definitely not a lazy man. His family of German descent is originally from Pittsburgh, which is still a decent distance from my home town, and I could tell from his mannerism that he was not a womanizer of any sort. On top of all that I simply loved Florida and couldn't imagine going back to live and work in, or anywhere near, Ontario. While I'm not a girl to make hasty decisions my clinical approach to match-making was already doing the calculations: tall, fit, hard-working, reasonably attractive, nice personality and lived quite far from the home town that I desperately wanted to escape from. How could I NOT consider marrying this guy?

Over the next few months I tried to give myself a reason to end the relationship but found none. Not only did he meet all of my standards but I met his as well. I could tell that I was more than just a pretty face to him. One blip on the radar was when he told me about his recently failed marriage to his high school sweetheart. She thought she could make a go of it in Florida but ended up missing her family too much back in Pittsburgh. He was determined to stay in Florida and that was that. His openness about this part of his life is probably what sealed the deal, or perhaps it was the idea of being able to live in Florida permanently, but I returned home after those six decisive months to tell my parents of my planned nuptials.

Despite my somewhat distant relationship with my parents I did not blind-side them with this decision. Not completely. During our chats over the phone I did mention to them that I had met someone in Florida and that we were seeing each other on a regular basis. How they did or did not interpret this information was simply something that I felt was beyond my control. Either way I think it was an affair filled with mixed emotions. My parents were happy for me of course, but the sudden realization that I would be leaving for good was a sad moment as well. Be that as it may, my mother still managed to organize our betrothal at the local Greek Orthodox Church for that Friday while my husband-to-be was driving up from Pittsburgh with his parents so that we could all meet for the first time.

His mother was a tiny woman with the heart of a giant, the kind of person whom you liked from the moment you met her. His father was a giant of a man with a heart of gold and a smile that could put anyone at ease, and despite their obvious physical differences it was clear that his parents were made for each other. The joy of meeting them for the first time, and the way they welcomed me into their family, is a very special feeling that I will never lose and a memory that I could never forget. I could see their son beaming with pride while the introductions were being made and if I'd had any doubts about the decision I had made then they disappeared right then and there. I had never felt so special in all my life, and it didn't matter to me one bit that we weren't having a lavish, picture book wedding with all the trimmings.

I had bought myself a burgundy summer dress for the occasion and he managed to rustle up a suit. A quick trip to the Sears jewelry department solved the problem of the rings, and making sure that my brothers had properly fitting dress clothes finished off the to-do list. In a matter of days the eight of us walked into that church as the sole witnesses to my beginning of marital bliss that we later celebrated with a splendid dinner at the Holiday Inn, which incidentally also consisted of my honeymoon. Then without wasting any time we were packed up and rolling out, heading across the American border as an officially married couple. So how many people do you know who can sum up their wedding in one paragraph?

Once back in Florida everything seemed to fall into place for us. I found work at a Wendy's restaurant and performed some mediation on the side which is how we found our house. While mediating a divorce neither member of the couple wanted to keep the house or any of the furnishings. Each just wanted to take a few personal belongings and leave everything behind to start a fresh, new life somewhere else. While I don't generally like profiting from other people's misfortune, this was a win-win situation for everyone. It didn't take long for me and my husband to assume the payments on the house, thus saving the divorcing couple from having to go through the hassle of selling it, and there we were moving into a fully furnished home long before we would have thought it possible.

During that first year one of my husband's best friends from Pittsburgh came to live with us for a bit until he could get himself set up on his own. Our new house had plenty of rooms so space was not an issue, and to top it off he was a very devout Christian. Having him around helped me get back to my beliefs which I had been slightly negligent in for the past few years. He got a job as a personal trainer at a nearby gym and that encouraged me to work out in my spare time, which I had quite a lot of when the landscaping season started. There were some days when I would see more of my husband's friend than my husband himself, but that gave us time for long talks about religion and faith and everything in between. It wasn't long before I was promoted to be the first woman manager of a Wendy's restaurant in the Tampa Bay area. I was definitely living the American dream. Then we got the phone call from Canada.

In mid-May I got a phone call about a teaching job in Canada. My first brother, the gentle giant, had gone directly into teaching when he finished school and got a job at a fly-in native community in northern Saskatchewan. Somehow he got talking with his Superintendent, who needed more teachers in that area, and mentioned that my husband and I were both teachers. That's a grand-slam for northern school divisions when they can get a couple of teachers in one shot, so he wasted no time getting our number and giving us a call. I told him that while my husband was indeed a teacher, I was a few credits short from getting my teaching degree and that I was sorry he had made the call for nothing. I wasn't trying to be rude but I was really getting used to Florida weather.

Hardly dissuaded, the man on the other end of the phone assured me that I'd be given a temporary teaching certificate if I committed to finishing my degree over the next summer. He wasn't making this easy so I asked a little more about the assignment. Apparently some people had 'gone across the river' and broken away from their band, and it didn't look like they were going back. We were needed to go in and make an assessment, then provide any teaching that was required. It was good money, but I still wanted to know more about what I was getting into so I questioned him about the facilities where he was. "Oh, the usual," he casually replied, then named off some places like the hospital, bank and bowling alley. I told him that I would discuss it with my husband and get back to him as soon as possible. I didn't give it much thought at the time since the demand of leaving Florida ended his first marriage, so why would he want to go all the way to Canada?

When I mentioned the whole thing to husband number one his eyes lit up at the opportunity. You see, teachers are not paid well in the United States, and even less so in Florida. A large portion of Floridian residents were retirees who didn't want their tax dollars being spent on an education system that they didn't use. Being faced with the notion of getting paid double to be a teacher, and both of us making that kind of money, was too much for him to resist. We called back to accept the job, which started in August, and just as fast as it came my Florida dream was now sold as we liquidated everything to start another new life. Our roommate moved back to Pittsburgh and we bought a pick-up truck to make the journey north. In a couple of months we were packed and rolling once again, onwards to an exciting new chapter in our life, or at least that's what I kept telling myself. Little did I know that this was the beginning of the end of my marriage.

The trek to central Saskatchewan was going to be long enough as it was, but we decided to make it even longer by visiting my parents along the way. It was more of an obligatory visit than a social occasion since my relationship with my mom had become strained since university. A rift started to grow once she realized that I wasn't going to be the dutiful daughter that married a local boy. My desire to live more than a few minutes away was hard on her, and I'm sure she viewed it as a form of abandonment, but the real problem was that we could never connect. I could never relate to the life-changing horror she had lived through as a child and she couldn't understand my need to be more than a kept housewife. I can't say that I completely understood myself either, but I also knew that I couldn't ignore how I felt about my quest for accomplishment. I grew up in a time when a girl's ultimate goal was to marry a local star athlete, and the truly aspiring ones got a full time secretarial job before settling down with a family. So not only did my mother not understand me, I don't think anybody really did.

While I'm sure they were probably happy to see me the visit with my parents was strained and short. Just a few months ago I was settled down with a home in Florida and a career in the newly expanding food services industry, yet now I was heading to the near opposite end of the continent to be a teacher, all of my worldly possessions in the back of a pickup truck. As I look back to that time it's no wonder we couldn't relate to each other because even I had no clue what was happening. All we could do was pretend that everything was fine and make the most out of our awkward situation. A few days later we were in Prince Albert, Saskatchewan, meeting with our new boss at the Northern Lights School Division.

I never really had a first impression of Prince Albert, and I think that's because I kept expecting to see the rest of it before coming to a conclusion. Part of me couldn't believe that this bare-bones community was the central hub of a school division. What it lacked in substance was made up for in northern charm, but it was no St. Petersburg. Thankfully my first impression of our Superintendent was a good one. He was welcoming, easy to talk to, seemed very genuine, and I could tell that he would be a nice man to work for. My apprehension was eased a bit, but I could never shake the feeling that we weren't being told the whole story about this job we had signed up for. It took a few days to get the paperwork sorted out, and once all of our p's and q's in order we checked into the hotel for the last time and got what rest we could. It was a long drive up to our next stop, La Loche, and by the end of the day we would be in our new home.

We awoke with the sun which wasn't hard since I could hardly sleep the entire night. Our journey went as well as could be expected for the first half, passing though several small communities before making it to Green Lake for some gas and a quick stretch. The second half of the trip was about the same time and distance, but the complete lack of civilization along this piece of highway made the drive seem that much longer. Even to call it a highway was being a bit generous when it was really just a paved logging road winding its way ever northward, completely void of any distinct landmarks. I half expected to see a lonely hitchhiker appear around the next bend, and then hear the movie audience all scream, "No! Don't pick him up! He's the murderer!" Instead, after a very long couple of hours we finally reached the end of the road: Buffalo Narrows. And when I say the end of the road, I mean it literally.

The highway ended at Kiezie Channel, which we had to cross to get to Buffalo Narrows, but the bridge across the channel was not completed yet. Our momentary confusion was cleared up by talking to one of the bridge crew who told us we just had to wait for the ferry to return. Looking across the two-hundred meter wide channel I could make out a vessel of some sort at the other side, so wait we did. I watched the bobbing spec as it approached from the far bank, but it didn't seem to be getting a whole lot bigger as it closed the gap. It soon became apparent that the ferry was actually a wooden barge which looked like it was built with turn of the century know-how. Criticism aside, that old barge got us to where we needed to be as I'm sure it had been doing for years on end, and after a choppy ride across the water we were in civilization once again. Sort of.

At this time, the end of the '70s, Buffalo Narrows had just gone through the transition from being a fishing and trapping resource settlement to a government-run town. The introduction of a local government brought a huge amount of infrastructure improvements, including the nearly completed bridge to replace the ferry, and we were witnessing the end result. New construction was everywhere making it easy to forget that you were a few hundred miles out in the middle of nowhere. We gassed up the truck one more time and got directions to our final destination of La Loche, only a hundred kilometers away. Unfortunately the infrastructure boom had not gone beyond Buffalo Narrows yet, so we were now facing one hundred kilometers of gravel road. Yay.

After what was probably the longest and bumpiest ninety minutes of my life, which topped off one of the longest days of my life, we had finally reached our goal. The village of La Loche was yet another remote settlement turned town in the last decade, sporting telephone poles galore that carried hydro and phone lines throughout the community. Despite this evidence of modern progress I still felt as if I had gone back in time to one of those places you see in the old western flicks.

We drove around the dirt road town, every head turning to check out the obvious newcomers, until finding the float plane service at the edge of the lake. Introductions were not needed as we stepped out of the truck since they were expecting us. It would appear that my husband and I were the talk of the town before we'd even arrived.

The couple running the float plane service were very nice, helping us unload our truck and bringing it to the '54 Beaver at the side of the dock. For those of you who have never been in a float plane before, imagine being inside of a narrow, elongated delivery van with wings. Unlike a van, you can't pack a plane to the ceiling and go merrily on your way. Cargo weight is an important issue and we had enough stuff to warrant two trips, so my husband sent me out first with half of our belongings and he'd follow up with the rest. This was my first time in a single-engine aircraft and the best word to describe the experience is 'loud'. Not only is the engine right in front of you, ten times louder than any car you've driven in, but the body of the plane rattles and vibrates as the sky rushes past, pounding on the sides like an angry mob desperate to get in. After a deafening twenty minutes of flying over water and forest the pilot suddenly pointed to the lake below, banked the plane, and started his descent towards the long dock that jutted out into the pristine waters of Garson Lake.

A crowd was waiting for us when we glided into place, and they all eagerly helped to unload my stuff and carry it towards shore. The green banks of the lake climbed steeply to the town up top, or at least I could only assume that it was up there since I couldn't even see rooftops from my vantage point. Before we had even reached the end of the dock I looked back to see the plane taking off again to get the other half of his fare. The row of people ahead of me just kept on walking, off of the dock and up the hill, climbing the well-worn path to my new home. Even for a young woman in good shape I was a bit winded at the end of the hike, so I stopped to get a quick look around. Ahead of me were only wooden shacks and simple log houses.

That sense of panic I had been fighting for most of the journey was getting stronger, but I managed to get moving again and walked to the group of people that had stopped outside one of the log houses, its windows boarded up as if it were condemned. Another man was approaching the group as well and he gave me a welcoming smile. My head was swimming with confusion now, and I desperately tried to communicate with the people around me. I can't remember the words I used, but never before had I felt like such an outsider. The man who had smiled continued to do so and pointed to the boarded-up house. "Teacherage," he said, as if to confirm a question that I don't even remember asking. He then produced a claw hammer and started ripping the plywood from the windows as casually as if he were opening a brown paper parcel. When the door was accessible all of my stuff was brought into the building, placed in the main room and I was left alone to unpack.

My new home was a dirty, empty shell of a house with one wall dividing it into two rooms, three if you count the small mudroom that consisted of the front foyer. Garbage and debris were strewn about the floor and collected in the corners, leftovers from the previous occupants who may or may not have been human. A large, black wood stove sat in the middle of the floor like a monolith, while a crude counter top with a sink occupied some space on the back wall to complete the kitchen ensemble. The adjoining room was completely barren except for some marks on the floor to indicate where a bed must have been at one point in time. Mere weeks ago I had been the proud owner of a bungalow home in the Florida Keys, complete with palm trees on the front lawn, and for the first time I had been happy. I quietly walked back and sat down on one of my suitcases, put my face into my hands and cried, and cried, and cried.

Leaving Your Comfort Zone

In the Bible, God sent His people all over the place; different cities, different lands, usually places that they knew nothing about. Actually, He didn't really send them so much as He requested them to make those journeys, but it's difficult to deny a request from the ominous voice of God. These weren't vacations either. Most of the time there was some degree of danger involved, but God was always there to help His servants through the hardships they ran into. You'll notice I didn't say that God kept them from trouble, which some people view with mixed feelings. Why can't He just be nice and keep everything nasty from ever happening to His chosen children? I'll answer that question with a dramatized depiction of a part of life that we're all familiar with.

A young couple with their first toddler is proudly watching him stagger around the shopping mall, the baby's stern expression shows his focused concentration as he successfully places one tiny foot in front of the other. While quietly mastering this new found skill it becomes apparent to the mother that he's wandering further away than probably intended. She instinctively moves to bring him back but dad gently grabs her arm.

"Hang on," he says without taking his eyes off of his son, "Let's see if he figures it out." Sure enough, when the child is only fifty feet away he turns to look at his parents but can't see them past the other patrons shopping at the mall. The toddler is easily confused when facing a forest of grown-ups walking to and fro, and the look of puzzlement on the baby's face is soon followed by tears. Both parents rush to his side to comfort the child who was never out of their sight, but hopefully he has learned not to wander off again.

Now you can be sure that if the same father saw that his child was about to fall down a flight of stairs or walk out into traffic he would run to stop the accident from happening, and our walk with God is the same idea. He will help us through anything that we can't handle on our own, and by allowing us to take a few steps in a new direction outside of our comfort zone He is encouraging us to grow as individuals. This isn't an invitation to take unnecessary risks because you think God will always be there to bail you out. Learning to live within our Father's boundaries is a lifetime achievement and testing the waters along the way is a must. Gradually getting accustomed to what you can and can't do will strengthen you in such a way that eventually you'll ignore the emotional bumps and bruises as if they were nothing at all, even though earlier in your life you would have been terrified of the same dangers.

Chapter Five

Hauling Water Uphill

I was still sitting on my suitcase, crying, when my husband finally entered the house almost an hour later. He could be thick in the head at times, but one look around the teacherage was enough for even him to understand the situation. He spoke to the smiling man with the hammer, who it turned out was our janitor and also the person in the village who spoke the best English, and asked him to get some water to clean the house. With a nod he was off, and once we were alone my husband tried to be reassuring about our seemingly hopeless situation.

"It's going to be alright," he said. "We'll find a way to make this work."

Our janitor soon returned with brooms, a mop, and some buckets of water fresh from the lake. Thankfully I had calmed down by then, or maybe I just ran out of tears, and did what I could to compose myself. It had been a long, long day, and this was definitely not the way I wanted it to end, but it was what it was and there was no going back. While the men started to clean up I poured some water into the sink and washed my face.

The cold water actually helped to calm me down and I slowly regained my composure. I could hear the men talking about using a radio to contact our boss, meaning that we weren't utterly cut off from the rest of the world, and that little piece of information was enough to bring me back to the task at hand. With a deep breath of resolve I stood up straight, cleared my head of all the negative feelings that had been crushing down on me, and pulled the stopper out of the sink to let it drain. It took a second for my brain to register the sound of splashing water coming from under the counter, and I bent down to open the cupboard doors just in time for the draining water to spill out onto the floor at my feet. It was no surprise to see that the sink was not connected to any plumbing whatsoever, with the drain ending in mid-air above the cupboard floor where a bucket should be. I was starting to make a shopping list in my head, and that bucket was the first thing on it.

After having had enough of cleaning for one day we headed over to our janitor's house. Since he was the most fluent at speaking English it was decided that the community two-way radio would be kept there. We managed to get in touch with our Superintendent over in Prince Albert, informed him of the living conditions that we found at Garson Lake and told him that we'd need some living essentials if we were expected to stay here. He understood completely and told us to order anything and everything we wanted from the Sears catalogue and he would get it shipped to us as fast as possible. It turned out that he was half expecting us to quit on the spot, contract or no contract, so he never bothered to look into the living situation. Once it was understood that my husband and I fully intended to live up to our end of the bargain he was overjoyed and gave us an open budget, within reason of course. With that out of the way I was feeling better about the situation and went right to work making my shopping list. Our janitor would put us up in his place until the living arrangement could be made more suitable in the teacherage, and we were made to feel more welcome in this small community than I had ever felt out there in the modern world. I was starting to realize that the term 'civilized' could apply to more than just the twentieth-century amenities that people had to offer you.

I slept surprisingly well that night and awoke to a native breakfast of fresh bannock and tea. It's strange how such a simple meal could revitalize me in both body and spirit, and I looked around the village with a new sense of vision. Wooden racks were seen everywhere. Some were those long, triangular racks on which fish were hanging to be smoked and dried while others were stretching racks of various sizes displaying every manner of hide and pelt that the land had to offer. It was clear to me now that this place was not the desolate point of no return that my fears had lead me to believe upon my arrival, but it was in fact a small but vibrant community that was very much full of life. I could even look at our new home in a different light as I mentally placed all of the Sears catalogue items around the rooms. There weren't as many items in comparison to furnishing a modern day house, but the basic comforts that each item would bring was enough to help me carry on.

As the day unfolded my husband and I started to grasp the complete picture that had only been revealed in parts since we first talked to our Superintendent back in May. We were led to believe that this group had broken away from La Loche not too long ago and stubbornly refused to return, but it was easy to see that this was not the case. The community had actually been here for decades, living quite happily in their traditional ways, but their separated presence threw the proverbial monkey wrench into the ideas of the new local government. A large sum of money was already being allocated to build new structures in La Loche, including a new athletics arena and a high school. It would certainly be easier for the government if everybody here would simply abandon their home and move to the town, but it was clear to us that this wasn't going to happen. This tiny settlement of three hundred people had history here, they were happy living here, and if that was an inconvenience to the local government and the school division then so be it.

A few days later the sound of the float plane broke the natural silence of the lake and I hurried to the dock with the rest of the crowd in anticipation of our expected Sears order. My worries were immediately put to rest because even from a distance it was clear that the plane was fully loaded with our catalogue items, complete with the bed strapped securely to the plane floats. Many hands make light work, and in no time at all the entire shipment was up the hill and in front of the teacherage leaving my husband and I to the task of unpacking our new essentials. Comparing me to a child on Christmas morning didn't even come close to how I felt about the pile of parcels outside our door. When it came time to set up the bed we noticed that there was no frame to keep it off of the floor, just the mattress and box spring. My husband asked our janitor if anything got left on the dock but he just shook his head and said that it must have fallen off the plane. We took him seriously for a bit, but it turns out that that's what they say about anything that goes missing from a delivery and is likely never to be seen. To solve our problem the janitor soon returned with four wide stumps to set our bed on. I was starting to think that there wasn't anything they couldn't solve by taking a short trip into the surrounding bush.

I think that aside from our bed, the item I was most happy to see was the galvanized bathtub just like the ones you see in those old western movies. While not large enough to stretch out in it still held enough water to give you a good soak, which is the first thing I did once all of the unpacking was done. Hauling water from the lake was a necessity, and carrying it up that hill two buckets at a time was the best fitness regime that anyone could go through. At first I needed to take several breaks along the way, stopping on the hillside and looking around at the scenery while pretending that I wasn't dying from exhaustion. Heating the water on the wood stove and filling that tub for the first time was a huge ordeal, but the end result was worth it. Unfortunately that magic moment couldn't last forever and I was now faced with the task of getting rid of this tub-full of water. My husband just laughed and said, "Now what? It's too heavy to carry to the door." He was right of course, so I ended up tossing it all out the front door one bucket at a time, no help from him. I felt like I needed another bath after that workout! I can't remember what he was so busy doing that he couldn't help me but I was getting used to the fact that, while he was a hard worker, it was only when that work benefitted him directly. I quickly learned to make do with less while living at Garson Lake, and by the time the leaves were falling from the trees I could haul water uphill with the best of them. I had been transformed from Annie – girl from Florida to Natasha – strong like bull!

Now with everything as it should be, or at least as well as it could be, we were finally able to address the situation that we had been hired for: educational assessment. Another nearby log structure was designated as the school and was furnished with wooden desks and chairs, but with almost thirty prospective students, all of different ages, it wasn't going to be big enough. The only teaching aids available were flip chart easels, but these were next to useless at this point when we would be starting all of the students at the same rudimentary level of first grade. Mind you, this isn't to say that these children weren't educated. By simple definition, education is the teaching of skills that allow a child to grow and function productively and independently in society, and these children were already well on their way to doing that. The youngest of them had already developed Native skills that were beyond anything that I would learn in my lifetime, and I can remember one particular instance when a group of them demonstrated this point very well.

"Teacher! Teacher!" One of the smiling children beckoned, waving his hand and indicating for me to follow him and his buddies. He was carrying a long pole that had a wire loop at the end, something I don't remember learning about in university, so I followed out of curiosity. Before we had gone very far into the bush the junior hunting party all crouched down simultaneously, alerted by something that I was oblivious to, but I followed suit anyways. We all hung back while our leader slowly advanced upon an unseen target, pole at the ready, until one of his steps triggered his quarry. A bunch of partridge suddenly flew up from the tall grass when our leader deftly swung his pole at one of the birds, striking it with the wire hoop and neatly lopping off its head. He then retrieved his trophy and held it up proudly for me to see. While a city child of his age would be learning their ABCs and basic math skills so that they could become the household bread winner may years down the road, these children were already capable of bringing the main course to the dinner table. In the back of my head it was occurring to me that the definition of education was not as cut and dry as the government would like it to be.

During the next couple of months my husband and I set up a school agenda and established a regular school-day routine with our new students. We did what we could to work from the Saskatchewan curriculum, but this wasn't exactly a textbook scenario that we were dealing with. Our first goal was to introduce the idea of school time even though we didn't always stick to the classroom. Excursions into the bush were a regular part of their life so we did what we could to incorporate that into our lessons whenever possible. We needed the community to embrace the idea of regular education without making them feel that there was something wrong with the way that they were living. It soon became clear that we could expect some dedication on the community's part to support our ideas of schooling so we let our Superintendent know that he would have to take the next step to make it all possible.

To fully develop a proper schooling system out here we would need a proper school. Constructing a new building in such a remote location wasn't feasibly possible, but dragging in a retrofitted ATCO trailer was. In fact, that's how they solved many of these types of issues up in the north. We were told that it was in the works and would be brought on site once the winter road was ready. Winter roads are wide trails that connect to lakes. Not very useful during warm weather, but once the snow comes and the lakes freeze over they are a main road for heavy equipment, snowmobiles and trucks with four wheel drive. One such road existed between Garson Lake and La Loche which was used by the locals to haul lumber and other large items to the lake along with bulk quantities of non-perishable food items like flour and condensed milk. As far as I know, this was the first time it had been used to drag a full-sized building to the community.

It was quite an eye-opener for the kids of Garson Lake when the bulldozer came chugging through the bush while dragging a forty-foot trailer behind it. The new school had everything we would need to do a proper job of delivering an education such as blackboards and new furniture, but more importantly it was wired for electricity and ready to be hooked up to the generator that came with it. This wasn't the pull-start gizmo that men bring "camping" these days, but a full-sized diesel generator that was the size of a small building complete with extra-large capacity fuel tank. The twentieth century had finally made its way to the people of Garson Lake.

As you can imagine, introducing a constant source of electricity to this traditional community opened the doors to many opportunities, but the electrically heated school building was one of the most significant for us. Having never had to heat a house with wood before, maintaining a constant temperature in the teacherage was a challenge, if not an adventure. Our janitor did an excellent job of keeping us stocked with firewood and kindling, but it had never occurred to him that we wouldn't know the first thing about starting a proper fire. Mind you, we didn't think that it was the kind of thing that we needed to ask instructions for either, so on that first cold autumn day when an extra layer of clothing just wasn't going to cut it I went about to accomplish the simple task. Logs in the stove? Check. Matches? Check. Gasoline? Absolutely. Now, not being a science-minded person myself I was not well versed in the expansion properties of heated gasses within a confined space, so I crouched down right in front of the stove and tossed my match onto the freshly moistened logs. WUF! Luckily being young and stupid is often accompanied by quick reflexes so I avoided most of the flames that leapt out at me. I carefully felt my face for any permanent damage and was relieved to feel my eyebrows and lashes intact. My success was short-lived since the flames dwindled quickly once the gasoline burned away leaving me with sputtering, smouldering logs that barely gave off any heat. I poked and prodded the fire all night but never got the warm, roaring fire that I was hoping for.

It had cooled off quite a bit over night, and we awoke to one of those mornings when getting out of bed suddenly became optional. My husband made it quite clear that he wasn't about to do anything to remedy the situation, as was becoming a pattern with him, so I took it upon myself to get the job done. Being a smart girl and not wanting the same results as last night I realized where I had gone wrong and changed my technique. Logs? Check. Matches? Check. A healthier dose of gasoline? Bingo. Having learned from my previous mistake (I am a teacher after all) I stood off to the side and tossed the match onto the soaked logs with an air of confidence. KA-THOOM!

"You're gonna burn the frikin' cabin down!" My husband screamed. I'm not sure what was more impressive; the gout of flame that shot past me and almost scorched the opposite wall or how quickly he got out of bed. It was clear that I couldn't keep lighting fires in this manner all winter long (we only had a small can of gas) so we did the right thing and got proper instruction from our janitor who showed us how to build up a small fire with dried moss and kindling before piling on the larger pieces of wood. It wasn't as instantaneous as my method but it got the job done.

With the onset of winter we spent fewer school days out in the bush and more time in the new, heated school. Due to the language barrier between us and our students teaching by the book was literally not an option at this point, but with the introduction of electricity we were able to get past that obstacle with the age-old fascination of moving pictures. Back then an assortment of National Geographic films was our lifeline to the outside world just as the internet is today. The students were captivated by anything that showed them the animals of far off lands like Africa or South America. It was such a hit that we had weekly movie nights for the entire community and the kids had no problem sitting through the same films a second time with their parents and family members. Of all the films we showed that winter, I would have to say that the one with the largest impact was the ten year old movie of the American moon landing. What was regarded as old news to most of the world was a real eye-opener for our community who had no idea that such events were taking place beyond their borders.

Since the school and generator were located so close to out teacherage it was no big deal to run some extension cords to our house and finally make use of those electrical appliances that we had brought with us. Hello hairdryer! The rest of the community was located a fair distance from the school but that didn't keep them from following our example. Once they realized the full potential of the generator it wasn't long before strings of extension cords were being run to other houses, all propped up on forked sticks to keep them off the ground. The evening tradition of gathering around the two-way radio had come to an abrupt end as each household engaged in the modern tradition of sitting around their own black and white television watching CBC. Most people would probably feel proud to be the ones who made such a significant improvement to the community's lifestyle, but it made me sad in a way. There was no such thing as idle, wasted time before we had arrived, with every moment of these people's lives either put into productive traditions or communal gathering. Now with everyone getting their own television I could see a decline in both of those elements, especially during the rest of the long winter. It wasn't a catastrophic change by any means, and perhaps I was just being sentimental about something that was bound to happen eventually, but it has always been at the back of my mind that, by bringing something new to the people of Garson Lake we were also taking something away from them.

Understanding Fear

In the Bible there are generally two types of fear; the fear of God and the similar yet different act of being afraid. The fear of God is a concept that, until properly understood, can be the deciding factor that turns people off from Christianity in general. Godly fear is usually misinterpreted as the ever-present fear that we'll be struck down for the slightest scriptural infraction, when instead it should be related more to a feeling of reverence or respect. The closest concept that I can relate to this is the fear that we have towards our parents when growing up.

While I may not have agreed with my parents in every aspect of life I was still afraid to disappoint them. This wasn't a type of fear that kept me from going home. I was never afraid to be with my parents but I was definitely afraid to upset them. Eventually this type of relationship is developed with anyone whom you have a true bond with, and it is mutually shared by both sides of the relationship. This type of fear stems from feelings of love and respect, which makes sense when we remember that God is love, and the fear of doing something that would hurt your loved one is what keeps you from committing the act. Thus the fear of God should be thought of as the respect that you hold for your parents or a good spouse (emphasis on *good*). Sometimes, before you even do something, you know that it will upset that person whom you care so much about so you avoid the situation altogether. Other times you may have to figure out the hard way that something you have done is hurtful to a person whom you care about, even if it was unintentional.

It's always a learning process as you explore these boundaries, and it will lead you to making changes in your lifestyle which is of course another fine line between right and wrong. When these changes are for the better, which may be hard to admit at times, then they're probably the good changes that we all need in our lives from time to time which also help us to grow as individuals. But if these changes are purely one-sided in that somebody thinks you should change what you do, "or else", then it might be time to change the relationship instead. The bottom line is this: if you are afraid to upset somebody because you love them then you are probably headed in the right direction with that relationship, and this is also the type of relationship that God wants to have with you. However, if you are constantly afraid to upset somebody because it will make them angry, and there will be consequences for that person getting angry, then that is the type of fear which nobody should have in a relationship, nor is it the type of controlling relationship that God wants with us.

This second type of fear is the irrational fear that, while seemingly related to Godly fear, has an opposite effect on us, keeping us from growing as individuals. It is generally associated with the fear of the unknown, which stops us from going outside of our comfort zone, or the fear of consequences which is used by unscrupulous people to control other people. Sometimes they can both be present in a single situation, such as a bad relationship, and they are quite often ignored or not recognized for what they truly are. The fear of consequences will usually be associated with a threat: "Dinner had better be on the table when I get home, *or else*!", or "Don't go kissing boys, *or you'll get pregnant!*" Fear of the unknown can often be the fear which keeps someone from ending such a relationship because the person being controlled has no idea what will happen if they leave, and it can also be associated with a threat: "You'll never find another woman who'll love you like I do!" Being on our own is probably one of the biggest fears, and challenges, in the world these days, leading many people to believe that being in a bad relationship is better than being in no relationship at all.

Unfortunately, living with this fear causes us to be stunted inside, growing inward with weakness as those who are causing the fear remain stronger and in control. What few people realize is that these types of people, the bullies of the world, are struggling with their own fears at the same time. They are afraid that the people they are controlling will get strong enough to eventually leave, so they constantly apply their fear tactics to keep others in line and in doubt of themselves. Encouragement and strength are the last things they want us to receive and they will do anything they can to keep it from us. As long as we are afraid to face and conquer our fears then we can never grow to the potential that God has planned for each and every one of us. So while living in fear of disappointing God can be tedious, challenging, and even boring sometimes, not to mention lonely, you can only grow stronger for it in the end because that is His goal for all of us; to be as strong as we can be.

When I first set foot in that teacherage at Garson Lake I was overcome with the crippling fear of doubt. At that moment I had no idea how I was going to remedy the seemingly horrible situation that I had walked into; how would I sleep, eat or wash in this empty, filthy cabin? How could I possibly live here? I was definitely way out of my comfort zone and I stayed in that frame of mind until my husband arrived. In reality, it was what

I *didn't* know that triggered my fear. Had I known ahead of time that the cabin was unfurnished and a complete mess BUT we were more than welcome to stay with our janitor until new furniture arrived then I probably would have dealt with that moment in a completely different way.

I also had no idea just how well the community as a whole was going to look after me and my husband. The regular gifts of their traditional foods were more than enough, but on top of that were the gifts of beaded leather items. I still have them all in a box and occasionally go through the hand-made gloves, moccasins and boots, all trimmed with fur and meticulously decorated with bead work. Knowing all of that ahead of time would have definitely kept me from being afraid that day, but then I wouldn't have grown stronger for the experience. God hadn't abandoned me at that point in my life even though it sure felt that way. I was always in good hands but I just didn't know it, and every time I was shown a gesture of goodwill my spirit grew a little bit stronger. That definitely wouldn't have happened if I knew about them ahead of time. Instead of being gracious I'd be expecting all of those gifts, possibly even being judgemental because of pre-conceived ideas of how I felt the gift should be. In a way I could have ruined those moments before they'd even happened and robbed myself of the growth that they would bring. Living a life that's full of surprises can be challenging, but it also ends up being the most rewarding.

Chapter Six

Beating the Odds

It's amazing how a couple of years in Florida could make me forget all about the extremes of the Canadian seasons. Winter at Garson Lake came much sooner than we had expected, and as you can imagine our Florida wardrobe didn't quite cut it when the snow began to fly. Unfortunately the option of flying out for a quick shopping trip wasn't in the books with a five-hundred dollar price tag for a one way plane trip, and since it took weeks of sub-zero weather for the ice road to form we were pretty much stranded no matter how you said it: SOL, without a paddle, SNAFU, you get the idea. So we put a call in to our Superintendent to see what he could do for us, and as always he came through. We were told that a box of winter clothes would be sent on the next possible delivery plane, and sure enough there it was with our other school materials. Everything we could have wanted to protect our frail, Floridian hides was in that box: socks, long underwear, parkas, snow pants, hats, mitts, scarves and boots. However, in order to get us what we needed that quickly our boss made a one-stop shopping trip to the army surplus store, and thus everything he had sent was that wonderful army green colour, right down to the socks and underwear. Even when bundled up for winter we stuck out like a sore thumb, but at this point we weren't complaining.

Since flying in and out of isolated communities was such an expensive ordeal the school board always provided a few guaranteed flights for teachers like us. Flying us in and out at the beginning and the end of the school year was paid for, of course, but they also footed the bill to get us in and out for in-services with the other teachers of the division. We may have been an isolated oddity but we were still given the same opportunities for upgrading and local networking as any other teachers. Though they were far and few between, these Professional Development days always fell on a Friday which allowed us to make the most out of our weekend before flying back to north country on Monday morning. So what does a woman do for a whole weekend after being cooped up in a cramped, isolated cabin for weeks on end? That's right, laundry!

We were fortunate enough to have become friends with one of the local Vice-Principals and his wife, so we'd bunk with them whenever we made it into town. Since La Loche had no hotels at this time the administrative staff were given larger than average houses so that they could accommodate visitors such as ourselves, and the fact that they didn't have children made the arrangement all the easier. We'd show our appreciation for their hospitality by bringing moose steaks with us on every trip and the Vice would fire up his barbecue no matter what the weather. His wife and I got along well and she made sure that the washing machine was always free for my duffle bag of laundry that I brought on each visit. This was one of those extra-large military duffle bags that was big enough to fit an entire person, and it was packed to the seams with everything I wanted to wash.

This isn't to say that I was all work and no play on these outings. This was still considered no-man's land by most people, occupied mainly by hunters, trappers and loggers. The small population of the professional working class stuck together and were united by some sort of unwritten code. It's not like there was an "us vs. them" mentality, but we generally stuck to our own kind, for lack of a better term, since it was an accepted fact that single professionals mixing with local labourers usually turned out badly with the professional having to leave town. It could be tough living up here at the end of the highway, so on every PD day when the school division gathered in La Loche it was followed by an evening social event.

Holding a social event could be a tricky affair in La Loche since it was a "dry" town, meaning that no alcohol was sold or served there, but it wasn't forbidden to bring your own liquor into town as long as it didn't cause any trouble with the law. Another factor to keep in mind was that the professional population was purposely mixed in with the working population as far as housing was concerned, so if you wanted a private party it couldn't be held at anyone's house without the neighbours finding out about it. Once the neighbours found out then you were faced with two situations: they would get into the booze, and then a fight would break out, or you would have to keep them away from the booze, and then a fight would break out. The RCMP detachment was only a small force up there, and the jail was even smaller, so keeping the peace could only be attained by following the old saying, "An ounce of prevention is worth a pound of cure." Thankfully, one of our teachers just so happened to be dating that ounce of prevention.

She was a young teacher from the East coast who had come up here for a bit of adventure and the extra-large pay cheque that was awarded for enduring the northern isolation, and he was a young entrepreneur who started a fuel business and was kept busy by fueling pretty much every vehicle in the area. Like many people in those days his home was located with his business, which in this case was a large, lake side lot on the outskirts of town. The entire compound was fenced in and isolated, making it the perfect spot for our gatherings. This makes it sound like we were into some very controversial forms of entertainment, but you need to understand that just about every professional in town was earning a government pay cheque; nurses, RCMP, teachers and our support staff, and it simply wasn't publicly acceptable back then to be seen in a non-professional situation like drinking and partying. I like to think that we lived by the old adage of working hard and playing hard, but our version of "playing hard" back then was staying up until two in the morning and still being able to drive home. It's laughable by today's standards for debauchery but we thought we were cray-zee! But seriously, how was I going to get a weekend's worth of laundry done if I was nursing a hangover on Saturday? Laundry wasn't the end of the chore list either since a trip into town meant shopping for those essential items, and when you found them you bought them in bulk. Top that off with our janitor's regular request for tobacco and bullets (where do you think the moose steaks came from?) and we were ready to head back.

Despite my traumatic initiation upon first arriving here, returning to our northern outpost got easier with each trip. We were making excellent money and spending very little of it, the school division gave us all the support we needed, plus we were promised a new, less isolated assignment for next year. Every day became a step forward, which wasn't hard to do considering how we started, and by mid-December we had established the new school which was a considerable mile stone by anyone's standards. Mid-December also heralded the most anticipated fly-out of them all: Christmas Break. It had been a challenging four months, but the community was happy with the progress we had made, the school board was happy that the community was happy and our boss was happy because the school board was happy. We were just happy to get out of there for two weeks.

When the plane came to pick us up we were strapped in with our bags loaded before the prop could finish spinning. Despite the noisy conditions out pilot made an attempt at small talk.

"So, you're that couple from Florida, right?" He asked over the howl of his engine.

"That's us!" I hollered back.

"Heading out for the holidays?"

"Yes, we're going to check out Saskatoon!"

"Nice!" He responded, seemingly genuine. "So are you coming back?"

"Uh, yeah." I replied, a little confused. "Why?"

"Oh, no reason!" He shouted back with an awkward smile as if he'd been caught at something. I looked at my husband who just shrugged it off, and we enjoyed the rest of our short flight without any more dialogue.

The school division was putting on a big holiday bash so we stuck around town for the next couple of days before hitting the highway. The semi-formal event was a nice way to end the first half of the school year, and it was here that I found out what the pilot was getting at. When it was first noticed that there was a truck parked at the airport with a Florida licence plate most people thought it was a joke, or stolen, and I guess you couldn't really blame them. Once it was realized that an honest-to-goodness Florida couple had come all the way up here to teach, well, that was a little out of the norm for this northern town. Speculation had started as to just how long some people from Florida could actually last way up here, and the next thing you knew there was a betting pool started. Our 'survival' dates were all over the calendar, from running out screaming before the first day of school to sneaking away at Christmas break and never coming back. At first I wasn't sure how to react to this information, but reflecting back to my first day at Garson Lake I could see how such an idea could get started. We probably wouldn't have been the first people to high-tail it from such a demanding assignment, and who can say if those following us will fare as well as we did? All I know is that we were giving them a much better situation than what we started with.

Our week in Saskatoon would probably be considered a low-key vacation by today's standards, but a week in that hotel room was like being in a five-star resort compared to our cabin on the lake. Having the option to go out for dinner anywhere we wanted to was a treat in itself, and a variety of shopping locations besides the IGA or the hardware store was a real bonus. Unfortunately it had to end. You've heard the old saying: All work and no play makes Jack a dull boy. Well, my husband was as Jack as it gets. It turns out that my hand-picked, hard-working man couldn't relax until he got back to La Loche so he could spend the second week of our break doing school work. It's nice that he wanted to impress our Superintendent, but I was pretty sure we had already done that. Oh well, be careful what you wish for I guess.

The remainder of our year was relatively uneventful, and I was finally getting used to living out in the middle of nowhere. Not because I was growing accustomed to that type of living, but because we had a plan. My husband and I would put a few more years of hard work into this northern style of living until our financial nest egg was large enough to buy a home in a city where we could start a family. I had visions of the stereotypical married life that we were all told as kids; the house with the white picket fence, two kids and a dog, and the early retirement on full pension. It was a realistic goal with the start we had here, made possible by the guarantee of two healthy pay cheques for as long as we could bear it. Work hard while you're young and everything will fall into place, right? That was the natural order of things as far as I was concerned, so I threw myself into that dream whole-heartedly, making it my solace and my guiding light for the hard years ahead.

As we wrapped up our year at Garson Lake our Superintendent was true to his word and relocated us to a community that was accessible by road. My husband had also been successful with his goal of proving himself and was awarded the job of Principal of Turnor Lake, the next town over from La Loche. With a population in the hundreds, Turnor Lake warranted a full-sized and fully staffed school, from Kindergarten to grade eight, with me taking the position of the grade eight teacher. We were given a two-bedroom house, with electricity, plumbing and free satellite television, heated with a fully-automated oil furnace. It was a definite improvement from our previous teacherage, although Garson Lake will always hold a special place in my heart despite the rough beginnings.

While newcomers were a regular occurrence in these northern communities there was always the expectation that we should prove ourselves in some way before being fully accepted, and with schools this was usually done by holding extra-curricular activities. My husband turned to his love of basketball and coached an after-school boys' team that played in tournaments against nearby schools, but I didn't really have a hobby to fall back on. Holding after-school classes on how to work hard probably wouldn't have gone over well, but it just so happened that I stumbled upon a hidden gem in the industrial arts room that would give me a hobby for years to come. Tucked away in a corner, still wrapped in the shipping package, was a brand new, un-assembled, electric ceramics kiln, and it was calling my name.

At the time I knew absolutely nothing about ceramics, but I saw the potential and asked around if anyone knew how to put it together. Nobody in town did, and the person who ordered it was long gone, but I was told that a woman in Green Lake had a ceramics studio and might be able to help me. After giving her a call and telling her about my plans she was more than willing to drive the 300 kilometers and spend the weekend to help me out. We assembled the kiln and she told me all that I'd need to know about running a beginner's class. I took lots of notes and guaranteed her some steady business of buying green ware and other supplies if enough ladies showed an interest in my idea. It was a good turnout for my first class but we decided to take it slow and just make some coffee mugs for the first project, but once they held the finished products in their hands the ladies of Turnor Lake were hooked.

For those of you who don't know, the hobby of ceramics involves green ware, which are rough, unfinished clay forms such as cups, plates and vases, then taking the time to sand them down, glaze them, then fire the prepared pieces in the kiln to produce the hardened, glazed items that are as unique and personal as the artist's imagination. With the success of the coffee mugs my ladies were ready to take on all sorts of projects, and for the next two years we made everything from elegant water pitchers to complete eight-setting dish sets. I think we made just about everything that our supplier in Green Lake could bring in.

To add to the success of my brain child, when the art teacher saw what I was producing in my evening class she decided to teach pottery to the students. Pottery is the process of creating items from a lump of clay, letting it dry, and then going through the same steps that you would with green ware. While you don't get the professional look of pre-molded green ware, students were thrilled to see something that they had made with their own bare hands. And while you would think that the hardest part of pottery was forming a decent object, the real challenge for the kids was making sure that there wasn't a single air bubble in their hand-crafted items. If even the tiniest pocket of air got trapped during the molding and pounding of the clay then what went into the kiln as an ashtray or bowl would end up becoming a miniature time bomb when the hardened clay could no longer contain the expanding bubble of air. The kiln was built to withstand these miniature explosions, but unfortunately all of the other projects being fired at the same time were not so durable, getting shattered in the process. The kids were understandably disappointed when their projects got wrecked this way, but they also thought it was kind of cool to have accidentally blown something up.

As much as this sounds like our new assignment was a walk on easy street there was one detail that we didn't know about our new community; the population of Turnor Lake was roughly half Chipewyan and half Cree, which made for a potent mix at times. Under normal, every-day circumstances the people of Turnor Lake got along as well as any other community, but when there was a public disagreement of sorts then their differences would come out in flying colours. It was never anything serious that started the trouble, but it was always at a school meeting.

The first time it happened took us completely by surprise as we innocently asked for volunteers to help with an approaching function. The uncomfortable silence was obvious from the start, and then the accusations started. One side would "suggest" that it was the other side's turn to step up to the plate and volunteer, then the other side would remind the first side that they donated more money at the last function, so maybe they should be excused from this event until the first side had done enough to even things out. Before my husband and I knew what was going on there was shouting and yelling and wives holding their husbands back while accusations of all sorts were thrown around at the loudest possible volume. It usually ended with one side storming out of the gymnasium while the other side brooded in their seats, and nothing having been decided. After two successful years of running that school my husband applied for a Vice Principal position at the high school in La Loche and thankfully he got it.

As you will remember, after arriving in La Loche three years ago my first impression of the dirt-road town was not high. I never would have guessed that I would now look at the same town as a step up in my career. Mind you, a lot of progress had been made in those three years, and we were going to teach in a brand new high school that was as modern as any other school built in the early '80s. Along with the brand new school we were also assigned a brand new duplex to live in. In fact it was so new that it wasn't quite finished when we moved to La Loche so we took up temporary residence in another teacher's basement. We were used to such situations by now, and a few months of inconvenience was a fair compromise when our house was the payoff. Being the new Vice Principal, my husband was in charge of the orientation at the start of the school year and gave the standard "don't get involved with the locals" speech for all of the new teachers, but every once in a while you get somebody who just doesn't listen. Unfortunately for us this also happened to be one of the lady teachers whose basement we were temporarily living in.

She had been charmed by one of the locals and saw no harm in spending her free time with him, which usually involved attending some of the town parties. When it became obvious that our new roommate was ignoring my husband's advice we were as subtle as could be to advise her against getting involved with the man, but to no avail. It wasn't long before his ex-partner caught wind of the relationship. In fact, it wouldn't surprise me if he himself had told her out of spite. He'd had a couple of kids with his ex, and though she was the one who tossed him out of the house it still burned her britches that he was strutting around town with a new girlfriend. The fact that this new girlfriend was not a local just added fuel to the fire. What the new girl didn't understand was that, even though the relationship between her new boyfriend and his ex was indeed over, the ex would never really be out of his life. That's just the way small town life could be. Occasional socializing soon became regular weekend parties together, sometimes in the teacher's own house directly above our heads, and the ex made sure that she was a regular attendee at these gatherings as well.

Though he was her superior my husband had no authority to tell this woman how to spend her free time as long as it didn't carry over into her professional life, but when she started showing up to work with black eyes and scratches from scrapping with the ex we knew it was getting bad. Since this was not the big city with a large work pool to choose from these types of indiscretions could be over-looked for a brief amount of time. We had hoped that standing in front of her students with black eyes and scratches would be her wake-up call, but unfortunately the worst-case scenario was just around the corner. By the time winter had set in our house was pretty much complete and just waiting for furniture, but we happened to be around to witness the ex's Grand Finale. You see, it wasn't that the ex wanted the man back into her life, but she would be damned if any other woman was going to have him either. And to drive the point home during one weekend party, the ex decided to drive her car right though the teacher's front window. What a mess. We decided that we could manage just fine without furniture for a while and moved into our own home, but that teacher could no longer live with the choices she had made and had to move on to find a new beginning.

HOW TO ACT AS A CHRISTIAN

The Bible is full of passages about perseverance, from David fighting Goliath to Job facing his trials, but one that sticks in my mind is from the book of Hebrews:

Wherefore seeing we also are compassed about with so great a cloud of witnesses, let us lay aside every weight, and the sin which doth so easily beset us, and let us run with patience the race that is set before us. ~ Hebrews 12:1

In this particular passage the 'great cloud of witnesses' refers to a specific group mentioned in the previous chapter of the Bible, but the idea is still the same: somebody is always watching. This isn't meant to be treated as the creepy type of watching, where somebody won't take their eyes off of you, but instead it is a reminder that our actions are seen whether we realize it or not. In the Bible, getting through life is often compared to running a race, with references made to the man running it (Psalm 19:5), to those who win it (Ecclesiastes 9:11), to the prize at the end of it (1 Corinthians 9:24), but in this case the reference is to *how* we should run it, keeping in mind that we are being watched.

The concept of being watched isn't meant to make us paranoid, nor an encouragement to show off, but instead it's a reminder to set an example. To declare yourself as a follower of Christ is actually a big title with big responsibilities as seen in 2 Corinthians:

> [20] *Now then we are ambassadors for Christ, as though God did beseech you by us: we pray you in Christ's stead, be ye reconciled to God.* [21] *For he hath made him to be sin for us, who knew no sin; that we might be made the righteousness of God in him.* ~ 2 Corinthians 5:20-21

In short, Jesus took on our sins to give us the chance to prove ourselves, and we do this by setting a proper example. This doesn't mean that we are all expected to behave the same way. Everybody has their own strengths that they can use to set an example, usually by helping somebody else through a rough patch in life. Some people volunteer in soup kitchens for the homeless, or help to build houses for the less fortunate, or even the simple act of visiting the elderly, even when they aren't related to you in any way, are some of the many ways that people can use their gifts to help others. But what we do to set an example for others is only the half of it. What we *don't* do is the other half.

Looking back to Hebrews 12:1 it says, *let us lay aside every weight, and the sin which doth so easily beset us.* Our second instruction on how to run this race is to get rid of the weight, the sin, that is slowing us down. This refers to the swearing, smoking, drunkenness, promiscuous behaviour, laziness, idiotic acts, drug use, and any other bad habit that is quickly becoming fashionable in today's society. Not only are most of these bad traits displayed proudly under the guise that everybody "has the right" to be whomever they want, but anyone who shows intolerance towards these "life choices" is quickly branded as being judgemental, non-accepting, or my personal favourite: not a team player.

The term, *let us lay aside every weight,* is the indication that this is a voluntary act. We voluntarily choose to act poorly, and therefore we can also choose to stop acting this way. Most will simply brush it aside, stating that they'll quit when they're good and ready or that it's nobody's business but their own, which is entirely true, but their tone usually changes once the consequences start to set in. Despite being a bad example for others, acts of indiscretion are also bad for our bodies. The human body can only take so much, and while it's easy to argue with scripture, nobody can argue with bad health. Running a race can be hard enough, but doing it while in bad health makes it considerably harder.

Some will say that their life choices are somebody else's fault, usually their parents or a relative who treated them badly, and they use this as a reason to justify their actions claiming that they have no choice in the matter. The only way that this argument can be valid is if every single person who has gone through such hardships makes the same claim, yet I can personally say that I know many people who have gone through some type of abuse but you would never know it by meeting them. They made the choice to lay that part of their life aside and move on. I don't know where they found the strength to do it, but if some can do it then it would seem that every person can do it, but nobody can make that choice for them. Only one person can lay aside the weight that holds us back and that person is ourself.

My race at this point in my life was a little different from what I've been talking about. I was weighed down with doubt and fear at the beginning, and if I hadn't chosen to drop those burdens then I wouldn't have been able to carry on. I could have very easily refused to accept the original assignment at Garson Lake and even the Superintendent wouldn't have blamed me. In fact, he was expecting us to do just that. Instead I made the decision to do the opposite, and I did so by finding hope in the smallest things. From the radio at Garson Lake to the kiln at Turnor Lake, I chose to focus on something that would help me through the race of life that I had found myself running. My other means of dealing with this race was to have an end in sight. If somebody had told me that I would be stuck in the north for the rest of my life then I may have given up right there, but we had a plan to get out soon and that was where I found my endurance to run this race that had been set before me, to beat the odds that always seemed against us.

Chapter Seven

Big Fish in a Little Pond

As my husband took on his new administrative role I ventured forth to teach the fields of home economics, food studies and cosmetology (that's 'beauty classes' for those of you who don't know what cosmetology is). This involved coordinating the student-run cafeteria, complete with industrial kitchen, managing a small hair salon that was open to the community, and wouldn't you know it, there was even a ceramics kiln in the industrial arts shop. Between quilting projects with my home ec students and holding another after-school ceramics class I still had time to run my own household which included baking bread from scratch on the weekends, plus I had taken up my husband's hobby of long-distance running. I was pretty much the Martha Stewart of northern Saskatchewan, and with my cosmetology training I can confidently say that I looked damned good while I was doing it all.

In the next couple of years my husband was awarded another promotion and was soon the Principal of La Loche high school. He was progressing up the administrative ladder in leaps and bounds, accomplishing more than he ever would have while teaching in Florida. We were both building impressive work portfolios with everything that we were doing and I was starting to feel that our time to head for the city, any city, was drawing near. My husband didn't seem as concerned about this as I was, but I was hoping that giving birth to our son would be the incentive he needed to make this decision.

Becoming pregnant during our third year in La Loche was a pleasant surprise, but it was completely unexpected. For starters my husband was such a workaholic that he barely had time to acknowledge me outside of school let alone woo me into bed, but aside from that I had also stopped having a regular menstruation cycle. Between the constant workload and long distance running I had lost so much body fat in the past few years that I was as lean as an Olympic athlete, which can sometimes trigger a defense mechanism in the female body. Boobs and hips are a must where childbirth is concerned and I was currently lacking in both departments so my body wasn't quite sure if it was a good idea for me to be with child. I guess my genetics finally said it's now or never.

Despite my body's initial uncertainty about carrying a baby it soon took to the task like gang busters. By the fifth month I had to give up on running since I would've had to wear an adult diaper to go any meaningful distance, plus the advancements in athletic bras were nowhere near to what we have today. My girls were growing just as fast as the baby and I didn't feel like ending up with two black eyes from a quick jog. By February, one month before the due date, it was decided that I was done working. Despite all of the new buildings that had recently gone up in La Loche, a proper hospital was not one of them. An ATCO trailer staffed by a temporary, drive-in nurse was the extent of our medical facility, so you were either very lucky to get medical attention when you needed it or you had to plan your accidents very carefully. Having a baby in La Loche simply wasn't an option for anyone, so I was headed for Prince Albert where our Superintendent and his wife were more than happy to put me up at their house until the baby was born.

Having a child in the '80s wasn't like it is today. Educating first time mothers about delivering a baby was somewhere in between the medieval dark ages and today's highly commercialized and almost overly-informed generation. I had a handful of pamphlets and a few video tapes to review before deciding if I wanted a C-section, an epidural, or a completely natural birth. Today young parents are spoiled for choice with so many options to choose from, including the possibility of not having the mother carry the baby at all! Even Lamaze was considered New Age by some in my time if you could even find anyone to hold those classes, not that I would have been able to get my husband to attend with me. In contrast, a quick internet search on "pickles and ice cream" today will land you almost four million results in 0.2 seconds comprising of not only different recipes for that famous pregnancy craving but also cupcakes and an actual ice cream flavour with the pickles already in there! Truly mind-boggling.

My husband headed right back to work after dropping me off at my new lodging and I went about keeping myself busy for the next while. I had no intention of being an idle house guest, not that I think I would have been able to, but luckily there was lots to do. Aside from caring for their three children the Superintendent's wife had a greenhouse business as well, so I busied myself with a sit-down job of planting tomato seeds in their sprouting pots along with doing whatever I could to ease her domestic workload. In fact, I had things so well in hand that she took off to a retreat for a few days while I managed the house. Their children were a delight to be around, and one day after their mother got back from her trip we ventured out for a walk into town to pass the day. There and back was probably under ten kilometers, but it was just enough to do the trick.

I felt a bit of pain when I went to bed that night and I awoke early in the morning with some more pain. I quietly got up, had a quick shower, packed my bag, then knocked on their bedroom door.

"I think it's time," I told them. I stood there quietly as they shot out of bed and ran around the house getting ready. I would have thought that already going through this with their own three kids would have made it a bit less exciting, but I suppose the arrival of a new baby is always a big deal. The Superintendent stayed home with the kids while his wife drove me to the hospital, and once it was confirmed that these weren't false labour pains I called my husband and told him the news. He showed up just in time to go into the delivery room with me and our son was born in early March. An extra bonus was that my brother, who was teaching nearby, had managed to get off of work and visit me in the hospital before we headed home. No longer just a couple, we were now a family whether we were ready or not for the changes that came with it.

For the next four months, the remainder of the school year, I learned all about motherhood in the north which wasn't that bad for the most part. My mother came to visit for a month soon after I got home from the hospital, which was a true blessing, but she didn't know what to say when we first got back to La Loche. I had gotten accustomed to the living environment long ago, but to her it looked just like it did to me when I first arrived; a small, dirty, isolated town with drunks wandering the streets and animals on every corner. We may not have seen eye to eye when I was younger, but she still cared enough to see that these living arrangements were unacceptable for raising a family.

We made the most of her visit and she was that essential extra pair of hands that every new mother needs, but what I didn't expect was for her to fill another void in my life. Perhaps I had been denying it for all these years, but life with my hand-picked husband had made me incredibly lonely. Having my mother re-enter my life had helped me realize that hard work can only give you so much satisfaction. It was rewarding to have accomplishments, but it wasn't everything, or at least it wasn't everything to me. It was clear that my husband would have been more than happy to put all of his attention on the job and treat our marriage as an arrangement of convenience, and it was also beyond his comprehension why that wouldn't make me happy.

My mother's visit was good for me on many levels. Not only was she the calm guidance that kept me from freaking out whenever the baby would cry, but she was also the affirmation to my doubts about our current living situation. My mother had pretty much lived through hell and survived with flying colours as far as I was concerned, and both she and my father knew how to 'make do' when it came to life in general. They were gracious people who were thankful for even the smallest things, so complaining about hard work or less than perfect living accommodations just wasn't something that would cross their mind ever since they came to Canada. Those qualities were instilled in me, whether they knew it or not, so I fought those nagging feelings that had been building up inside for the last few years. If my mother could live through the holocaust then I could certainly make a go of it here. But when my own mother didn't approve of our living arrangements, and was not afraid to say so, I finally knew that I wasn't being ungrateful.

When my mother voiced her concerns, my husband gave his usual response.

"Just a few more years," he would say, "then we'll move."

I call this his usual response because it's the same one I had been hearing since we left Florida. It's what he told me when we moved to Turnor Lake, it's what he told his own parents when they visited us a few years ago just as we'd moved to La Loche, and here he was telling my mother the same thing a few years later. I didn't want to believe that I had married a liar, but it was also pretty clear that 'a few years' didn't mean the same thing to my husband as it did to everybody else whom he had said it to, including me. I also think he was realizing that nobody believed him anymore. You thought he was hardly home before? Well after my mother had confronted him on the issue he was avoiding her like the plague. We would only see him at dinner for the rest of her visit, and I wonder if that's only because she's such an amazing cook. Otherwise he'd probably have made an excuse to live at the school until she left.

Aside from luring my husband home from work every day, my mom's fantastic culinary skills also allowed us to pay off a few social debts. My husband and I had been invited to many dinners over the last few years yet we had never returned the favour as is customarily expected. You would think with all of the new people passing through our town on a regular basis that there would be a wide variety of culture in its midst, but it was kind of the opposite. We did have one Chinese food restaurant, but that was about it for ethnic diversity. My mother, on the other hand, had taken a great interest in ethnic foods when my brothers and I were kids, so we were treated to a wide variety of dishes throughout most of our childhood. It wasn't until I watched all of our dinner guests enjoying her cooking that I realized how we were spoiled back then, even though we didn't know it or know how to fully appreciate it.

By the time my mother returned home I was ready to face motherhood, and parenthood, on my own. Two of the most important choices I made were to breast feed, which was pretty much a no-brainer as far as I was concerned, and to use cloth diapers. Disposables were available at the time, but regular, curb side garbage collection was not. Most houses had a burning bin to get rid of paper and cardboard, but everything else was accumulated until you had enough garbage to justify a trip to the dump. There weren't any of those special, odour-eating diaper containers back then, only a diaper pail which could barely go one day before needing to be emptied.

My decision to use cloth diapers was two-fold. First of all there was no real excuse not to use them since I wasn't working, plus I had running water and a modern washing machine, but my other reason was that I had already seen enough disposable diapers to last me a lifetime. The disposable diaper craze had hit La Loche like any other community and earned our town the charming nickname of Diaper City, though not for the reason that you'd think. Most of the local mothers, who were also home all day, took to this new convenience like, well, flies on stink and they had the shelves picked clean every delivery day. Unfortunately they were not very diligent at disposing of them properly so it was not an uncommon sight to see a horse munching away on a used Pampers at the side of the road. Quite the mental picture, isn't it?

Of course I wasn't completely opposed to disposable diapers since they were a necessity when travelling with a baby, and they were probably my only saving grace on those trips. Every month or so we would make the eight-hour drive to Saskatoon to do some serious shopping for those necessities that you just can't get in a small town like La Loche or even Prince Albert. We would leave on Friday, right after school, and get to the hotel by midnight. Our usual routine was to get up the next morning, go for a run, and then take care of our business before heading back home on that same day so we'd still have one more day to relax, or work in the case of my husband. It hadn't really occurred to us, and when I say "us" I really mean "me", how much of a change that the baby would make in this routine.

My husband would always start off doing the driving, but I would have to take over at the half way mark because I'd catch him nodding off at the wheel. To this day I'm surprised that he didn't get us killed. This part of our routine stayed pretty much the same since our son was like most babies and slept through the car ride. We'd gas up in Green Lake and I'd make sure that he was changed and fed before taking over the driving. So far, so good. But when we got to the hotel guess who was all rested up from his eight hour sleep? I would be up with our son on and off for the rest of the night while my husband tried to sleep through it, but things really changed when morning came.

"You go do the shopping," he'd mumble from bed, "and I'll have my run."

It will shock anybody who knows me today how well I played the dutiful wife back then. Without arguing I packed up our son and went to do the shopping after driving until midnight and having a crappy sleep. This type of shopping wasn't just getting a few hard to find groceries; it was buying those hard to find items by the case-load and doing it while carting around a baby as well. After a lot of grumbling and yawning I had the back of the truck loaded and headed back to the hotel. Guess who was still in bed, sound asleep. Our return got him moving, and he'd give me the next line:

"Go gas up the truck and I'll have my run and get us checked out when you get back."

He said it as if he were pulling off a major accomplishment. What a hero. So off we went again, my son and I, to gas up the truck and get it washed while my Superman husband managed to go for his run, take a shower and get us checked out of the hotel *all by himself.* I caught up on my sleep while he drove all the way home and he would also help me unload the truck, but then it was back to the school for him, "Just to check up on things" while I put everything away. What could have possibly happened over night and couldn't wait until Sunday, if not Monday, was beyond me. And that's how the rest of our out-of-town excursions went for the rest of the year. It soon became apparent that, even though he was *our* son, the baby and household responsibilities were all mine no matter what the circumstances. After four months of blissful motherhood and housewifery (Surprise! That's a real word), something inside of me snapped. I'm not sure if it was postpartum depression or if I was jealous that my husband got to go to work while I had to stay home, but I was fed up with being the only parent in this relationship and I told him so in just as many words.

"Well," he replied, "Why don't you just go to your parents' for a while?"

In one response my husband had managed to shirk any of his husband or fatherly duties and placed them all on my parents, but by the end of June I wasn't rejecting the idea. He was heading to Oregon for the month of July to complete his course on Administration, so I headed in the opposite direction to visit with my family.

This was the first time that my father or my youngest brother got a chance to see the new addition to our family, and I have to say that the visit went well. As expected my mother had told my father all about the circumstances of living in La Loche and he had the solution to my problems. A new subdivision was being built just a few blocks from my parents' house and they also knew the contractor who was building it. There would be no question as to whether or not the workmanship would be good, which is getting to be the problem these days. Back then a man still had his reputation to live by, and to build anything that was substandard was a disgrace to their name. I looked at the area and liked what I saw. Even as a half-finished subdivision it looked better than La Loche ever would. I called my husband in Oregon and asked him what he thought of the whole thing, and he seemed oddly open to the idea. After finishing his course he flew to Ontario, checked it all out for himself and we put a two-thousand dollar deposit on the house of our choice. My parents were happy, I was happy, and my husband seemed happy. I couldn't believe that after running from home for all these years I was finally moving back, and it felt good.

I returned to La Loche with a renewed spirit knowing that this would be our last year in the north. My dad and brother spent the rest of the summer putting some finishing touches on the house before the actual finishing touches were done. Dad was concerned that the hardwood floors would squeak if the sub floor wasn't screwed down, so the two of them went through the entire house and re-secured the floor boards before my brother had to return to his own northern teaching job. Winter was made all the more bearable knowing that it was the last year I'd be making eight hour journeys to Saskatoon for items that were readily available just a few minutes from our new house. Or so I thought.

In the spring I got a phone call from my dad. His friend, the contractor, had mentioned to him that unless we put the rest of the money on the house he would have to sell it to someone else and we'd lose our down-payment. I forced myself to bury the panic that was creeping up and I told dad that I'd sort it out. Then I talked to my husband. It turned out that the Deputy Superintendent of our school division was retiring in one more year and my husband was inadvertently told that he would be a shoe-in for the job. In light of this new information he had decided that we would no longer be moving to Ontario, and I have to wonder if we ever really were. The fact that he didn't have the nerve to discuss this with me pretty much tells you what he thought of my opinion, or how scared he was of me by now. It was no secret that I wanted to leave the north, yet I had to find this out as if it were something that didn't concern me, like he'd decided to change from boxers to briefs. I called back to tell my dad what was going on, and he couldn't believe it. Was my family ever mad, and I couldn't blame them one bit. I knew now that unless I took matters into my own hands I would never leave this place.

I played the dutiful wife for one more year, all the while applying for teaching jobs that would get me out of the north. I didn't do this secretly, behind my husband's back, but instead brought up the possibility of each of us trying to find a job that would get us closer to city living. He agreed, saying that we'd move when one of us found a permanent job elsewhere. I'm sure that he only agreed because of two things: he was never going to look for another job, nor did he think that I would be able to get one on my own. By the month of May I had secured a teaching job in Beaumont, Alberta, just a few kilometers outside of Edmonton. To say that my husband was surprised is an understatement, though he hid it well.

As with all new teaching jobs, I was hired on a one-year probation. Permanency would only be granted after a full review of my performance, and I don't think my husband thought I could pull it off. It's clear to me now, at the writing of this book, that after eight years of marriage and all that we had been through he never knew me at all, or he just didn't want to. Nevertheless, after getting the job I secured myself a townhouse to live in and found a day-care for my son, and when the school year was finished we packed up the truck with some bare essentials and moved me to my new job.

Unlike our usual eight-hundred kilometer drives to Saskatoon, which I dreaded, the eight-hundred kilometer drive to Beaumont was like a drive towards freedom. When we crossed the provincial border at the city of Lloydminster, that peculiar place that is half on the Saskatchewan side of the border and half in Alberta, everything seemed to change. The sun was brighter, the sky was bluer, and yes, the grass really was greener on the other side of that line. We got to the townhouse and unloaded my things, which didn't take long, and then we were off to buy me a new car.

Our money situation seemed reasonable at the time. We lived off of my paycheque, using it to pay for everything from rent to groceries, and my husband was banking his for our future needs. Despite that I had still managed to save a substantial amount of money over the years and used it for down payments on my townhouse and my son's day-care, plus I had enough to buy a new car outright. Only after that did I request my husband to buy me some furniture which consisted of beds, a couch and a television. I was content to live with the bare essentials until I got my permanent Alberta teacher's certificate, of which I had no doubt. When my husband finally headed back to La Loche he still had me convinced that our agreement was good; if I was granted permanency in Alberta then he would find a job here and we would finally be out of the north. I went into my new home, nearly broke but with great expectations, and he drove off with a big, fat bank account, certain that I would fail.

Everything went as well as could be expected with my new job. The school was brand new, my Principal was a very nice man, and I was teaching the same courses that I had been teaching in La Loche. As far as work goes it could not have gotten any better, and the same could be said for my husband as well. I got a call from him in November about taking our son to see his mother. His father had died suddenly just before our son was born, which had been a huge loss to the family, and he finally had an opportunity to go for a visit. This was the first time that my husband was not in charge of a school since we had gotten to Canada and he was able to use some of his time off that he had been banking over the years. He was going to spend a month in the United States and I was going to get a month off of having to cart our son back and forth from day-care. It was a win-win, right?

I made regular calls to see how everything was going, and by the time December rolled around I was wondering when the boys would be getting back from the states, so I asked my mother-in-law when my husband would be returning.

"Oh, he's already back," she replied. That panic started to set in again, and I asked where my son was.

"Oh, he's still here with me," she replied again, and I could hear the nervousness in her voice. "I don't want to get in the middle of this, Annie. You'll have to call him about it."

I hung up the phone in disbelief. She was one of the most decent people that I knew, whom I thought I could trust, yet here she was holding my baby ransom but telling me that she didn't want to get in the middle of it. She was EXACTLY in the middle of it! Or, to be more accurate, she had gone a step further and chosen a side, and I can only imagine what lies or threats that my husband had used to get her there. A man lying to his wife is bad enough, but I was now dealing with a man who had no qualms about manipulating his own mother, who had just lost her husband, to meet his own ends.

I called him up and asked point blankly what the hell was going on. Apparently the school division was already grooming my husband, whom they saw as their new golden boy, to be the new Superintendent starting next year. Again, something that I apparently didn't need to know. The exact discussion was something of a blur, but it went along the lines of this: I reminded him of his promise to move here since I had been the first to get a job; he simply countered with "That's not going to happen"; I retorted with the fact that I liked Beaumont and didn't want to live in the north any longer; he replied that I'd have to return if I wanted to see my son again; I angrily shot back that I was sick of living in a teacherage, nor was I giving up a career to sit at home for the rest of my life; his attempt at justification was to tell me that he'd bought a house, was having it renovated, and would get a nanny so that I could keep working. I can't remember exactly how the conversation ended, but I do remember what I did next. I called the RCMP to report a kidnapping.

I'll spare you the lengthy and painful details of my communication with the RCMP, but the long and short of it is this: I gave permission for my son to go to the states, therefore I had no grounds to claim it as a kidnapping. This may sound surprising, but I'll lay it out again since even I had a hard time wrapping my head around this. I, the legal mother of my son, could not go to my in-law's house to take my son back because I gave permission for the visit in the first place. A Canadian mother could not reclaim her Canadian son from American soil because I hadn't filled out any documentation beforehand to state that the visit was meant to be for a specific amount of time. It all boiled down to a lack of paperwork, and because of that I was powerless to right something that was so incredibly wrong. The only thing worse than my situation was that my husband felt completely justified in doing it.

My next phone call was to my parents. Surely they would know how to handle this situation or at least give me some comfort. They were angry all right, but instead of being angry with my husband they directed their anger towards me! If only we had bought that house down the street from them then none of this would have happened, my father said as if that were my fault. It seemed that they weren't angry at what my husband had done, but they were angry that this situation had gotten out of control. I'll probably never know the exact reason for their behaviour, but I suspect that my husband had called them earlier and told them about the unacceptable behaviour that their daughter was displaying. Some well-placed lies about me running off with our son is all it would take to bring shame to my parents, which is the one thing that old, European people will not tolerate. They didn't want to hear my side of the story; they just wanted this to end. My mother's final advice was to swallow my pride and go back to my husband, stating that marriage can't always be about happiness. I slowly hung up the phone, realizing that every single person whom I thought I could trust had turned on me in a matter of hours. I drank a whole bottle of Vodka that evening, then spent the rest of the night vomiting in the bathroom. I didn't know how I was going to go on and I really didn't care if I did.

I will be the first to admit that all of this can be blamed on my persistent naivety, never wanting to believe that my husband would lie to me so casually on a regular basis, and certainly not go to these lengths to get his own way. After all, I had always been honest with him. I never pretended to love the life we were living in the north, but he was acting like I suddenly dropped a bomb on him when I'd had enough. It took much longer than it should have, but my eyes were finally open. He didn't want a wife by his side; he wanted a woman behind him at his beck and call, doing whatever was needed to make him look good. And that's exactly what I had been doing all these years whether I knew it or not. My husband was a fine administrator on his own, but with me by his side he was the complete package.

I can remember when I suggested that I should get my administrative papers as well, but he would respond that it wasn't necessary, that it was enough for him to have them. He would make it sound like he was carrying a great burden by being an administrator and he was sparing me from the ordeal, but I now knew that he simply didn't want me to have any more skill than I already had. I would have made a damned fine educational administrator in those days and he knew it, but he needed to keep me in control so he did everything in his power to keep me as low as possible while he shot up in the ranks. In ten years he had entered the Northern Lights School Division as a nobody from Florida and made it to the top spot of Superintendent. All eyes were on him, and everybody was wondering why his prize Mare wasn't trotting behind him.

I don't like referring to myself as an animal, but that's the best way to equate our relationship. I was the untamed mustang that he had been keeping on a short leash all these years, using every trick in the book to keep me from running, but in his overconfidence he had gone and left the gate open. It was starting to make him look bad at a time when his image was everything, so he had to take drastic measures in an attempt to finally break me. It didn't happen right away, but by April I couldn't go on any more. I cried whenever I'd see mothers with their own children, and those who didn't know what was going on in my life thought I was a blubbering fool. I told my Principal that I was done. I was an emotional wreck and I could no longer perform my job at an acceptable standard. He understood completely, and without making me feel bad or directing blame he told me to put in my resignation. I went back to my husband a broken woman and he couldn't have been happier.

The Truth About Submission

Back in chapter three I discussed how God hated lying and pride, and now you can see why. The two combined acts can lead to the complete destruction of a person's spirit, and that is the most fragile part of a human being. My husband had become the big fish in a small pond and he was never going to give that up. That in itself is understandable to a certain point, but his pride and selfishness lead to his twisted justification that my personal happiness was of no consideration whatsoever. He had attained his point of glory and he couldn't bask in its glow with me getting in the way, and he certainly didn't want to share the spotlight either. Perhaps if he had encouraged me to get my administrative papers then we could have ruled the north together, but that must have been a calculated risk that he wasn't willing to make. It was safer to keep me beneath his boot where he could control me instead of allowing me to flourish on my own and not being sure of what might happen.

Ephesians 5 has several verses that deal with marriage, but a lot of people don't like how it starts with verse 22:

Wives, submit yourselves unto your own husbands, as unto the Lord. ~ Ephesians 5:22

Gladly, this isn't the "make me dinner and fetch my slippers" kind of obedience that some would twist it to mean, but rather the type of loyalty that we show towards Jesus and God. They have both proven how much they love us, so when they tell us to do something beyond our understanding it's best to do it without question, for our own good, and understand why we did it later. A husband is supposed to have this same love for his wife, which can be summed up in the last verse:

Nevertheless let every one of you in particular so love his wife even as himself; and the wife see that she reverence her husband. ~ Ephesians 5:33

Men are supposed to love their wives *as themselves*. This means that, unless a man likes to be lied to, mislead, treated less than an equal, and the list can go on and on, then he should not treat his wife this way either. Only after the woman is treated equally, with true love and respect, should she "see that she respects her husband" as quoted above. The part about respect comes *after* the part about how the man should treat her, but it is equally important. There are many stories where the man has done everything he can to make his wife happy but she is still ungrateful, taking advantage of the husband's good nature or simply claiming that it isn't good enough. I'm sure that in his own way my husband thought he fit into this category, giving me everything he could while I refused to be happy, but what he gave me did not come about honestly. No matter how wonderful a life may seem, if it was built on lies then it can't bring forth happiness.

Chapter Eight

The Nanny

Returning to my husband was probably one of the most difficult things I had ever done, but thankfully I was doing it in a new town. With the retirement of our former Superintendent it had been decided that Prince Albert was not the best location for the school division's head office and it was moved three hundred kilometers north (by paved highway) to La Ronge, also known as the Capital of the North. While not a big place it was a big improvement from La Loche. La Ronge was the tourism centre of northern Saskatchewan, and it still is today, located on beautiful Lac La Ronge.

My husband had kept true to his word, for once, having bought and renovated a proper house for us to live in. The kitchen had been gutted and completely re-done, as was the family room downstairs, and the back wall was refit with patio doors that led out onto a large deck overlooking the lake. For a northerner it was a dream home, and a far cry from any teacherage we had lived in, but considering the circumstances it was just a big fancy cage for now. It would take a lot more than this for me to learn to trust my husband again.

He also came through on the promise for a nanny. The government had some sort of arrangement with immigration where new immigrants were welcomed into the country on two-year work visas. People with minimal skills were brought into the country with the understanding that they would be furthering their education or employment opportunities while performing some form of employment. If these conditions were not met then the work visa was not renewed. It was through this program that we were paired with a young woman from the Philippians who seemed nice enough, allowing me to take on some substitute teaching at the local schools. Though there was only one elementary school and one high school at the time I was kept busy enough during my first year, and I wasn't the only one who was busy.

During his first year as acting Superintendent my husband made his presence known throughout the division. If you thought I hardly saw him before, when he was only in charge of one school, you can imagine how little I saw him now. With the school division spread across northern Saskatchewan he would often be gone for days at a time as he took care of business on one side of the province or the other, and I can honestly say that it was a good thing. He got to focus on what was important to him, I got to focus on what was important to me, and I had the second adult in the house to help me out whenever I needed it. I still didn't consider this to be the ideal life, but it was better than the life we had earlier.

I spent the entire year trying to reprogram myself to accept this new situation, reviewing the pros and cons in my head over and over again. I was definitely being provided for, there was no question of that, nor was my husband an abusive man in any way. He had been misleading for the past several years, and technically was an outright liar that couldn't be trusted, but now that we had this "understanding" of me knowing my place there wasn't much to lie about any more. My biggest obstacle with this life was that it wasn't the life that *I* wanted. It wasn't even close. According to my mother, happiness and marriage were like two passing ships that could only be together briefly at times. To expect anything more was wasteful dreaming that took away from the sacrifices needed to make marriage work. Besides, it was no longer just about me anymore.

Our son was happy and healthy, being raised with everything that a child could want. It didn't matter to him whether we lived in a big city or here in the north. It didn't even seem to bother him that he hardly saw his own father, but that made two of us, so I did my best to put aside my dreams even though it still felt wrong. I was married to a successful and respected man, I had my own teaching career to keep me busy once in a while, I lived in a nice house that had a beautiful view, and we were even affluent enough to have a live-in nanny so that I would have that extra help which many mothers go without. Most women would probably see me as being spoiled, so I did my best not to seem ungrateful for what I had while learning not to focus on what I didn't have. Looking ahead, and not behind, was going to be my new motto.

Speaking of looking ahead, it was well into our second year at La Ronge yet I hadn't noticed our nanny making any attempt to further herself as per her immigration agreement. I got the impression that she wanted to stay in Canada, and she seemed to like it here in north, but unless she produced some documentation to show that she was at least taking some courses then we'd have to be looking for a new nanny by the end of the school year. It wasn't like she was being worked to the bone in our house, and she had enough time to spend with her local boyfriend so there really wasn't any excuse why she couldn't also keep up with her obligation. Not wanting to be the bad guy, and also because I spent the most time with her, I waited for my husband to get home so that he could handle this delicate matter.

He was diplomatic of course. These kinds of things had to be done properly, addressing the situation without sounding like we were accusing her of anything. Perhaps she had lost track of time? Perhaps she didn't want to stay in Canada after all. We just wanted to do the proper thing and bring the matter to her attention before it was too late. Without a hint of worry she just looked back at my husband and claimed that she wouldn't have to leave Canada because she was pregnant! "Great," I thought. We were looking for a new nanny no matter what happened now. I wondered if her boyfriend even knew yet. I didn't realize that she was still speaking to my husband.

"And I'm pregnant with *your* baby!"

What did she just say?

Without another word she stormed off to her room leaving me looking at my husband and my husband looking very unsettled. He insisted that he had no idea what she was talking about, that it was impossible for him to be the father since nothing had ever happened between them. For once I would have to agree with him on the matter, because he was never home. When would she possibly have gotten him alone? Needless to say, the next few months were very tense. We were obligated to keep her on unless there were more serious charges for her dismissal, and she was entitled to her side of the story until a paternity test would prove otherwise. I'll spare you the details of those horrible months and get to the conclusion that most of you have already made: she was indeed carrying his baby.

You would think that once this matter had been indisputably settled that my soon-to-be ex-husband would have enough dignity to admit his wrongs, but that just wouldn't be his style now would it? Once the test came back positive he accused the nanny of somehow drugging him and then seducing him without his knowledge. If this hadn't been happening to me then it would have been laughable, watching the desperation on his face as he tried to figure out a reasonable excuse for his sperm to find its way into her body without his penis being the culprit. Not that I'll ever want to know exactly how it happened, or even care, but I honestly feel that it wouldn't have taken much. She only needed to stroke his ego the right way at the right time, because I was years away from telling him how great he was at anything. With the way he kidnapped my son to force his chosen lifestyle on me he's lucky I came back at all.

I immediately secured another job for myself in Alberta, but this time I went alone. Since it's still a painful memory after all this time I'll sum up the atrocity that resulted in me losing custody of my son. The courts dictated that the divorce hearing had to take place in the province where we had both resided. I was now in Edmonton, so I attempted to secure a lawyer from there to represent me but I was told that I had to hire a Saskatchewan lawyer instead. During the long, drawn out affair that lasted about a year I learned some interesting, but dubious facts about divorce. I was told that I could not divorce my husband on grounds of infidelity (I don't know why), nor was this integral fact brought up at the hearing at all.

In the end they made me look like a disgruntled, single mother who would have trouble raising my son on my own while he was made out to look like the successful, hard done by man who loved his son so much that he had a nanny to look after him. I would have thought that the earlier allegations of that same nanny drugging and then seducing him would make her a liability in this case, but those facts must have been conveniently forgotten. My ex was good at twisting things to his advantage, how to get to my emotional side, and my lawyer didn't seem to care how the case went. He was getting paid no matter what the outcome and I wasn't there to make sure he did his job. By the end of it I just wanted the entire affair to be over with so I signed the papers to do just that, which resulted in me getting nothing. Not only had I lost my son to a man who never cared about him until now, but I also got no money in the settlement. I know that I was legally entitled to half of his big, fat bank account, but it's my own fault for letting my emotions rule my life at that time. It's also my lawyer's fault, of course, who did nothing to fight on my behalf, but like all dishonest people he will have to answer for his ways eventually if he hasn't already.

At the writing of this book I can tell you that my ex-husband is paying dearly for his actions, and has been for many years, but none of it was at my hand. His misery is his own doing that started with this very act of infidelity and escalated over the years due to his pride, greed, and arrogance. He had lost his prize show horse and traded it in for a small, braying mule that would nip at his heels for many a year to come.

Committing Adultery

You don't have to be a Biblical scholar to know that breaking one of the Ten Commandments is bad. "Thou shalt not commit adultery" is the seventh Commandment, and though it was near the bottom of the list it was still taken very seriously. How serious was this offense?

And the man that committeth adultery with another man's wife, even he that committeth adultery with his neighbour's wife, the adulterer and the adulteress shall surely be put to death. ~ Leviticus 20:10

This was a very big deal back then. Aside from the death part this law came into being before there were any official officers of the law to carry them out. It was everyone's responsibility to uphold these Commandments and also to carry out the punishment, so you can be darned sure that it didn't happen as often, or as casually, as it happens today. Something else to keep in mind: Malachi 3:6 states "For I am the Lord, I change not;" Even though our society has become lax and tolerant of this behaviour, God still feels the same way about adultery now as He did back then. I'm not advocating for this ancient death penalty to be brought back, but I am bringing to your attention the severity of such immoral acts in the eyes of God.

Incidentally, instead of calling this chapter "The Nanny" I was going to call it "Husband-stealing Filipino Gold-digger", but I didn't want to give away the ending. Besides, is it actually stealing if I didn't really want it in the first place?

Chapter Nine

Back to Square One

I started my new lease on life by teaching at the Hobbema Native reserve, just south of Edmonton, and by renting a townhouse at the southern end of the city to give me a shorter commute. To get my mind off of the divorce hearing I turned to one of my dependable distractions: my shoes. I had some expensive ones that needed a little TLC, and by asking around for a reputable shop to take them to I was directed to one particular Italian shoemaker. His main store was all the way downtown, but he also had a kiosk in the nearby mall, so I looked him up and asked if he'd be able to fix my shoes. He commented on their quality and agreed that they were definitely worth taking care of, then told me that I could pick them up in a week. Sure enough they were ready on time, and as I paid my bill the small talk followed.

It started off with the usual questions as to whether I was new to the area, what I did for a living and that sort of thing. He never did ask for my birth sign, but we did arrange to meet for coffee on the weekend. I used the same defensive protocol with the shoemaker as I did with my ex-husband when I met him; no personal info like phone number or address, only an agreement to meet again at a specified time. During the few months of coffee dates I learned that he was also going through a divorce, giving us some common ground even if it was something negative. Of course we had one other thing in common, and that was a love for shoes. He was a true, Italian-schooled shoe maker who had built his successful business on the premise that people will pay for quality. My love for shoes goes beyond the usual womanly obsession, extending to a true appreciation for the quality and craftsmanship that goes into fine footwear. It was almost as if we were meant to be together.

As winter was closing in he finally built up the courage to make a move. I was comfortable around my shoemaker now, and he had persisted to court me despite not having my address or phone number, so when I did divulge where my townhouse was located he displayed some concern. Apparently I wasn't living in one of the best neighbourhoods, which I was unaware of, but until my divorce hearing was settled I had to live within my means while paying legal fees. His solution was for us to move in together and my reply was that I would have to think about it. I was pretty sure that I wasn't on the rebound since emotionally I had left my ex a few years ago. Being in a serious relationship so soon could be considered a bit reckless, and in truth I hadn't been in a real relationship at all with my marriage, but being with my shoemaker felt different. Here was a man who seemed genuinely concerned for *me*, for my well-being, and who had also shared his current downfalls in life along with his successes. After everything I had been through, and was still going through, moving in together actually felt like a step in the right direction.

His divorce was just finishing up, and since neither of them wanted the house they sold everything off, split the earnings and went their separate ways. It was about as civil as you could get when a marriage fell apart. He and I ended up renting a beautiful little two-story semi-detached dwelling in a nice, gated villa that was nowhere near any of the questionable parts of Edmonton. We had two bedrooms, two bathrooms, and a cozy kitchenette that looked out onto the small, private yard. I thought it was perfect, but my Shoemaker considered it "Good enough for now." I should also verify that, while I claim that 'we' rented this place, I never actually paid for a single bill. I learned that no self-respecting Italian would even consider letting his lady help with the bills since that would insinuate that he couldn't provide for her. My money was for settling my own personal affairs and he took care of everything else. It took a little getting used to, but it was nice to be appreciated for a change.

Meanwhile, back on the job front, I was about to go through another change. Up until now all Native reserve finances were under direct Federal control. Even though there was a set, annual amount of money set aside for each reserve, no band had direct access to these funds. Every monetary transaction was carried out under the government's watchful eye, including education, and the bands had had enough of being treated like children with an allowance. For years they had been negotiating to be independent, meaning that they would be in full control of how they spent their yearly funds, and the Feds finally gave in to the request. Starting next year each band would be recognized as an independent organization that would be responsible for their own finances, which included the hiring and paying of teachers for their schools. This meant every teacher currently employed in such a manner had to make a choice; stay with their current school and work under the new system, which would be observed somewhat like a private sector, or stay with the public sector and get transferred to a public school. I wasn't particularly interested in either option so I came up with a third one and made my own proposal to the government to stay on as a Native educational liaison of sorts.

A common Native complaint, and justifiably so, was that they were constantly being told how to teach their children by a government official who knew nothing about education or Aboriginal culture, and I was very knowledgeable in both departments. Another concern was that the Feds couldn't just dump millions of dollars into the bands' laps and expect them to figure out what to do with it all, especially in the area of education. They would need guidance from a government employee who also understood their culture and their education needs, and I proposed to be the answer to all of these problems. As a result the title of Capital Planning Officer for Education was born. While technically still a teacher, I was also part of Indian and Northern Affairs with the Government of Canada, or INAC for short. This was definitely the most prestigious title I had ever possessed. I moved from the classroom to working at the downtown government building, complete with access to a secretary. What did I actually do? Here's the lengthy blurb on my resume that describes my responsibilities:

- Identified education capital requirements and analysis proposals related to the acquisition, operations and maintenance of education facilities and equipment in federal, provincial, and band operated schools throughout Alberta.

- Participated in the planning, prioritizing, development, and implementation of federally funded education projects in conjunction with Band Support, Capital Management, Engineering, and Architectural personnel.

- Developed 5 year Capital Plans in excess of $10 M for federally funded schools.

- Worked in conjunction with Alberta Department of Education for the purpose of setting and maintaining curriculum equivalency standards.

Simply put, all First Nations bands in Alberta wanted a new school, and it was my job to assess each request and see if it was realistic or not. I was part of a three person team, including an engineer and an architect, which would have to travel to each and every Native reserve to carry this out. As you can imagine it required a lot of travel and a lot of paperwork, even more so if the proposed school got approved. Aside from the structure itself I was also responsible for assessing each band's capacity to deliver an education to their current and future student population. I took into account every possible element of the classroom, from desks to books to the pencil sharpeners on the wall, ensuring that everything was there for both staff and students. While this might sound like common sense to you it was a ground-breaking concept for the government to have somebody who actually knew their way around a school to help design it and the teaching that would be going on inside, and all because I chose to think outside the box by not accepting either of their first two offers.

Thinking for Yourself

Any good minister will do two things: quote directly from the Bible during a sermon and then tell you not to take their word for it but to look it up yourself. By doing this they are getting you to be familiar with the Bible and also to think for yourself, both which are crucial to be a strong Christian. There are many churches and so-called religious 'leaders' that would prefer for you to be the complete opposite, to simply believe every single word that comes out of their mouth and never question their teachings. Unfortunately there are plenty of churchgoers who think that this is the ideal situation. A lot of people don't want to be burdened with the chore of having to actually read the Bible for themselves let alone figure out what the scripture actually means. They figure that being able to sit back once a week and have it all laid out for them is good enough, then they can get back to the regular routine of modern day life.

Why is this a problem, you ask? Firstly, it's been proven that for an idea or lesson to be most effective you need to hear it three times or else it's more than likely to be forgotten. Secondly, scripture from the Bible can impact different people in different ways. Thirdly, only by taking a bit of time to read the Word for yourself can you actually apply what it says to your life, and finally you may not fully understand, or even agree, with what you just heard, and that is perhaps the most important part. There are an increasing number of religious leaders who don't understand scripture themselves. They blindly believe what they have been told to believe by their own superiors or they simply interpret God's word to suit their own needs knowing that few people will challenge them. I know this makes me sound like a naysayer, but take into account the "Turn the other cheek" example at the end of chapter 2. We've always been told that turning the other cheek meant Christians should simply roll over during a confrontation, and deep down I don't think that anybody thought it was right, but if we blindly accept incorrect teachings and don't read anything for ourselves then we'll never really know.

As for my first points about reinforcing and applying scripture to your life, you would be surprised at how important this is. Not taking the time to properly learn scripture and then practice it in life is just like playing a sport and not knowing all of the rules. Sure, you may know all of the common rules, allowing you to participate in the odd weekend game, but without knowing the detailed ins and outs of a sport you are also less likely to be aware of when your opponent is cheating, plus you will never be able to play the game to its full potential because you don't know all of your options. This leads back to how I got my new government job.

If I had just blindly taken one of the two options offered to me then I'd still have been a teacher no matter what, but because I knew what I did about the situation I was able to go past what was offered to me. You could say that I knew the rules better than the rest of the teachers that were in the same situation, and because of that I was able to take what I already knew and make a play for a better job. My suggestion in itself was not enough of course. If I didn't have the proper skills to perform this new job then they might have thanked me for the idea and found somebody else to do it. Being a strong Christian is kind of the same thing. You're free to say that you don't agree with certain church teachings, but when somebody asks you why you don't agree with them then you had better have something to back up your idea or you're just wasting your time and looking bad while doing it. If you can approach a challenge with facts and a positive attitude then you'll have a much better chance of somebody listening to you and maybe even liking what you have to say.

Chapter Ten

The Thing About Natives...

Despite being a white girl there has always been this unavoidable draw to Canada's Aboriginals which I can't explain. It was never my intention to spend half of my career working on or with Native reserves, but I have always been able to have a good relationship with the people who live on them. My ample exposure to their culture and lifestyle has left me with a collection of experiences that rival many of the Natives that I meet to the point where I've usually taken part in more of their own traditions than they have, though I am always careful not to come across as being boastful about this. I don't view it as a contest to see if I know more than they do; it's just the end result of a very interesting life.

Without trying to stereotype Natives I can safely say that they have one thing in common: they like to laugh. I think it is part of their nature to smile and be happy, to share what they have, plus there is a genuine, child-like honesty about them which is probably what led to their present situation: they were easy to take advantage of. During the centuries that followed white man's claim to rule over this country the government seemed to continually make promises that they didn't intend to keep and strike deals that were never meant to be fulfilled to their entirety. More unfortunate, perhaps to the point of being disturbing, is how well some Aboriginals themselves have adopted these dishonest traits to use against their own people, many of them Chiefs. It's no wonder there is a general mistrust towards authority figures, but I did what I could to show that at least I was not going to be like that towards them.

For the next six years I addressed the educational needs of the fifty-five band-operated schools in Alberta, and no two were alike. They ranged from the small, isolated northern bands with a few hundred members to the large, central, oil-rich bands that had populations in the thousands. This meant that their needs were all over the map. Some of their schools were in good shape, only needing minor improvements such as portables to deal with population growth. Others qualified for additions to the existing building like a gymnasium or an extra wing of classrooms, but the ones that required a completely new school were always the most interesting to work on.

Once I had the feasibility study done it was up to the band to have their school designed. In the old days the Feds would just build a basic and unimaginative structure that was efficient and quick to put up, but with this new step towards self-government we encouraged them to get three designs submitted before progressing to the next phase. It was a good start to get the bands on the road to independence and some of the designs that came out of it were absolutely beautiful. Native architects have a way of translating their spiritual side into a structural work of art, but just like any other architect they had a problem with sticking to the budget. Their designs were so wonderful that they were destined for the pages of Architecture Digest but first we needed to trim it down so that the band could afford to build it. That's where my teammate the architect came in.

Luckily, most of the cost trimming could be done without affecting the actual outlook of the school. When the architect has gone to the trouble of designing a floor plan that looks like a turtle or an eagle's feather from an aerial view you hated to mess with it, so it was generally the building materials that were addressed. Did they really need to install that expensive, one-way glass that can only be bought from a single manufacturer in all of Alberta? Is the cedar siding going to look that good in a few years, and how easy or expensive will it be to maintain? Do you really need to spend half a million dollars to find and relocate the gigantic boulder in front of the school? Will that boulder look as nice when covered in graffiti? These were the hard questions that needed to be asked to keep a government-paid project on track and within budget.

Another important aspect to keep in mind with these schools was something that affected all small communities: this building wasn't just a school. Small community schools often become town halls, public libraries and after-hours recreational centers once the school day is done. I remember one particular school that wanted to incorporate an Elders' meeting chamber in their design and it took a bit of finagling for me to explain to my boss why this was a valid request. Despite not being directly related to education, denying the Elders' chamber would be like telling a Catholic school that they couldn't have a chapel. Eventually my superiors realized that I really did understand Aboriginal culture and they came to trust my decisions. If Ann said it was okay then it must be okay.

One particular contentious issue that came up time and time again was oil rights. There are several Alberta reserves that happen to be sitting on oil, and while you would think that this should be a good thing the Feds managed to turn it into another headache for everybody. You see, for some reason when a bunch of white guys find oil in Alberta they get to form a company and extract the oil while getting outrageous tax benefits, but when Natives find oil on their land, that was assigned to them by the government, it becomes a completely different game. The government takes it upon themselves to remove the oil and hold all of the profits "in trust" for the band, only doling it out allowance-style when the band can justify a need for the money (that the Feds agreed with). I'm sure there are plenty of government documents that defend and justify this decision, but that didn't keep one band from taking matters into their own hands.

They had put forward a proposal to get a bridge built on their growing reserve, and the Feds approved for the project to be funded with this trust money. The band did everything by the book, from getting a Native architect to design the bridge to finding a Native engineer to direct the band-employed crew. After the money had been signed off I happened to be in the meeting when the Public Works guy had to deliver the news to our boss—there was no bridge. The architect had gotten paid, the engineer had gotten paid, all of the workers got paid, but the money that was supposed to go towards materials was never used for that purpose.

This wasn't a wooden foot bridge built with pressure treated lumber; we're talking about a steel and concrete structure worth a few million dollars. Did the shit ever hit the fan on that day! Heads were rolling all over the place and I just sat there quietly, glad that it wasn't one of my schools that this had happened to. You see, every single government dollar MUST be accounted for when it goes towards a project like that, whether it's trust money or otherwise, and it's only supposed to go out in stages as that project gets further along towards completion. How the reserve got all of the money without ever lifting a shovel was the unanswered question and a serious accountability issue. When the band was confronted on the matter they just dug in their heels and said that they shouldn't have to go to such lengths to get some money that was technically already theirs. I have to agree (unofficially) with their reasoning. In the end the Feds managed to juggle a bunch of numbers around to hide their little oopsie from Ottawa, and the band held a big community meeting on the whole thing... in Las Vegas.

Needless to say this mistake only happened once, but there was another recurring issue that also had to be dealt with, and it also had to do with this oil trust money. Once a year, around spring time if I remember correctly, each band member that had turned 18 years of age would get a royalties cheque that was their share of this oil money. The figure was calculated with a formula that I know nothing about, and some kids got more money than others for some odd reason, but it was not uncommon for these cheques to be to the tune of one-hundred thousand dollars or more. Yes, you're reading that correctly; a six-figure royalty payment for turning 18 years old if you happened to be a member of an oil-rich reserve. So you can see that the Feds weren't being completely stingy with this oil trust money, and it would seem that quite a lot if it was finding its way back to the members of the community. Fair enough so far, right? Unfortunately it never occurred to the government that dumping a huge amount of money in a kid's lap was a bad idea.

Not every kid went crazy with their new-found wealth, but it was never a surprise to hear if any of them were flat broke by the end of the weekend. Some made sure that family members got a nice helping hand with the money, and if they had a big family then that would pretty much do it. There was also a nearby car dealership that just so happened to have a bunch of shiny, new trucks parked in front of the band office on this special day. How could they not buy one when it wouldn't even use up half of their cheque? The unfortunate ones, however, were the ones who had to pay back their party debt. If you had helped a buddy blow his money a few years back then he was there to collect with your money, and if you had helped a few guys to have a good time then you had that much more payback waiting for you. The one that takes the cake is the guy who got a huge cheque, but he also had a huge debt to pay.

He bought himself a truck, packed all of his buddies in it and drove to Vegas. They gambled away the money, gambled away the truck, and had to borrow a quarter so that they could call home by the end of the weekend. This was an extreme case, but similar spending sprees happened enough times that the government was trying to find a different way to give out this money without actually being controlling about it, though it hadn't been resolved while I was there.

I would have to say that the most prominent moment in my life at this time was personally meeting the Prime Minister in the mid-90s. Jean Chrétien was touring Alberta, making stops at any relevant locations that were media-worthy, and one of my schools made the list. It had just been completed so the Prime Minister's press manager set up a ribbon cutting ceremony to officially open the school. We only met for a few minutes, just long enough for me to brief him on all of the need-to-know facts about this project, and it went something like this: the limo pulled up, I was ushered into the car, I shook his hand and made the formal hello, we quickly went over the who-what-when-where-why facts, we both got out of the limo and I stood back while he did his thing (only men take part in these types of ceremonies in native culture), wave, wave, picture-picture-picture, then off he went to his next venue. Not exactly how I expected the event to go, but it's a good thing that he was opening one of my schools. Can you imagine if he had gone to open that bridge that was never built?

Money & Culture

If I came away with anything from my years at INAC I would have to say that it was a better understanding of the Aboriginal struggle to maintain their identity in this new age that they are trying to live in. Their traditional ways do not properly translate into the monetary society that is closing in around them.

I believe that the government was sincere to a certain degree when agreements were made over two-hundred years ago, but the magnitude of those promises was not fully realized until later. When both sides agreed that the Natives would need "enough" to practice their traditional way of life, one side was thinking of fixed areas of land that could be identified on a map while the other side was not thinking of a specific land mass at all.

The term "enough" is not a fixed amount that you can put a dollar figure on. You may as well point up to a clear, blue sky and ask what it is worth, when in the end it is both free and priceless at the same time. Aboriginal culture, perhaps even their whole identity as a nation, is just as hard to quantify. The government would like to be able to simply pull out a cheque book and be given a definitive amount that will solve all of the problems, but that will never work. Unfortunately as long as the Natives try to do the same thing by putting a price on their traditions then they are in an equally perplexing trap. As soon as they step into the world of money and commerce they are stepping away from their traditional identity. The two worlds just can't coincide as smoothly as everyone wants them to. In fact, I don't think there is a single traditional culture on the entire planet that is immune to this enigma. All culture developed around the need for people to exchange ideas and items, to progress in life, without resorting to the exchange of money. Many of these practices require great skill and a lot of hard work, but the end result is accomplished without the need for money. I'll illustrate this concept with a short story.

Just a few years ago a friend who was working as an Aboriginal liaison for a school board got an e-mail from a co-worker. The message was from a typical, uncultured white man who needed to perform some sort of Native project with his class, and he wanted a cured moose hide by the next week. I myself have skinned a moose (the traditional way with the thigh bone I might add) and also took part in the process of curing and smoking the hide with the moose's brains. Gross and fascinating at the same time, right? My point being that it is a big and lengthy task to do this, yet the request was worded as if my friend was able to produce this item in a matter of days just because he was Native, or as if there were a special Aboriginal Wal-Mart where he could go to buy this item. Sure, if you look hard enough you could find this particular item eventually, but to place a dollar value on it is completely unrealistic. By combining the expertise and man hours that it would take to make this item should give it a price tag of thousands of dollars, but you know that somebody would only want to pay a few hundred for this hide. The math doesn't work and it probably never will.

Is there a solution? Probably not, but I would suggest for any of Canada's Aboriginal communities to consider the following. Just a few short years ago in 2008 a bunch of greedy white guys tried to make a lot of money out of nothing, causing the infamous sub-prime mortgage crisis in the United States. They just about destroyed North America's economy and we will all be feeling the effects of that action for a very long time. My question to you is: if the economy had collapsed, and money suddenly became worthless or disappeared altogether, would you have been able to carry on? Are your practices of tradition and culture strong enough to get through such a catastrophe? Or would you be paralyzed without money and gasoline like the rest of the country? Money isn't strength or power; it is only an alternative to doing something for yourself. Those who only know how to use money to get what they need would have no alternatives if the economy failed because money can't replace traditional customs.

This same problem is plaguing Alberta's farming culture as well. The occupations of agriculture and livestock are demanding careers, yet many farmers cannot farm full-time and make a living. It too has been reduced to a simple financial formula that rarely equates to enough money for the farmers to support their career and their families. The end result? Very few of their children want to carry the torch and continue farming. I heard on a news report the other day that the average age of an Alberta farmer was 55 years old. That's an entire, crucial industry which is only years away from retirement with nobody prepared to carry it through for the next generation. I would suggest that this is the same problem that our Natives are having. Instead of addressing the issue for what it is really worth, and making it a priority, those in charge are only patching it up with money every year and hoping that the problem will sort itself out or at least not fall apart while they are in office.

There is a growing mentality in parliament that all politicians need to do is hang in there for five years, after which they can collect a full pension, and then pass the problem on to the next candidate while they sit back in comfortable retirement. Just like everything else it's a nice formula, but that's the mentality that some European countries were living with for centuries and now look at the mess they're in. When nobody is producing the food we need and half of the country is fuming because you won't address their needs, how comfortable is that retirement really going to be?

At the writing of this book, the Idle No More movement has just started across Canada. It comes at a time when the government's political integrity is at an all-time low as scandals and reports of improper spending crop up faster than they can be dealt with. Regular citizens with similar allegations against them would be fined or sentenced accordingly, but politicians seem to be granted more leniencies from the law. In the public eye it would appear that there is a different set of rules for those in Parliament, that if the trial can be dragged on long enough then it will eventually be forgotten and conveniently swept under the rug when everybody turns their attention to the newest moment of shame. Political leaders seem to get away with just about anything these days and the working class voter feels powerless to do anything about it, which is why I applaud the Idle No More movement to a certain degree, for they have been swept under the rug one too many times. If anybody can make the Canadian Government accountable for their actions it's the Natives of this land as long as they can go about it in a way that targets the government parties responsible and not the general public.

Chapter Eleven

Husband Number Two

At this time my personal life was just as interesting as my professional life and just as rewarding. Once my sham of a court hearing was over and paid for I was able to focus on my new life with my new man. After a year of living together in the villa my shoemaker and I knew that we were right for each other and commenced with the building of our permanent dwelling. We designed a bungalow-style home with everything that I had ever wanted in a house. Though not big it had everything that two people needed to enjoy it: a marble bathroom in the center of the house so the tub never got cold; a heated, two-car garage; a large master bedroom with my own walk-in closet; a stylish, open concept living and kitchen area. It was located in a nice neighbourhood on a wedge shaped lot which gave us a larger-than-normal back yard, and it was built by an Italian company that my shoemaker knew personally so you know it was built right. Every time I walked into that house I felt like I was at home, and as if to signify its completion we officially tied the knot and got married. To top it all off he still wouldn't let me pay for anything either.

To simply call my second husband a shoemaker was like calling Michelangelo just another artist. He was in fact *the* shoe maker of Edmonton to whom all of the well-to-do people came for any footwear. His most notable clients were the Ghermezian family; the billionaires who own the West Edmonton Mall. They would bring their father in to have custom shoes made. Of course they didn't just drop in for a fitting like regular people. They would call ahead for an appointment and my husband would close the shop for however long it took to deal with this prestigious customer. His leather sewing skills also brought business from the fashion specialist store Holt Renfrew, though not for shoes. They needed someone of appropriate calibre to fix their Louis Viton purses and he soon became their exclusive repairman for the luxury French product line. Quality was in high demand during the 90s and my husband had worked his way into their ranks. This meant that well-known shoe labels like Jimmy Choo, Manolo Blahnik and Christian Louboutin were also knocking at his shop door and asking to be part of the product line.

As you might imagine, having access to these high-end items was any girl's dream come true, but equally interesting were the people that came into the shop as well. One particular woman was a personal shopper for Holt Renfrew who was also the personal shopper for the wife of a famous Edmonton hockey player who we'll call Mr. G. Personal shoppers, for those who don't know, have the job of doing the high-end shopping for wealthy people who either don't have the time or can't be bothered to shop for themselves. It sounds like a cushy job at first, but after hearing some of her stories I could see how the career has its pitfalls as well. Dealing with the rich and famous is always a delicate situation, and having a client like Mrs. G was a good example of this. While she viewed her husband's finances as a bottomless bank account he was a bit more realistic. Mr. G was born a regular kid from Ontario (not far from where I grew up) who never seemed to lose his regular kid sensibility. Even though he was now a millionaire he would always keep an eye on his wife's spending habits by calling in and clearing a certain amount of money for the purchase, putting the personal shopper in between the man who was paying and the woman who wasn't getting everything that she wanted. Definitely not someplace I would want to be.

Another dangerous situation for a shopper was dealing with their clients' sizes. How do you tell a rich woman that she is no longer a size 8? That's actually a trick question, because apparently you don't tell them! No, you instead have to go through the tedious task of swapping out the size labels in their high-end clothing so that they can continue believing that they haven't gained an inch, even when they are probably a size 12. Oh, the power of denial. My favourite story, though, would have to be the one involving the opera singer Pavarotti. While in Edmonton for a concert he had made a call in to the luxury store Escada and asked for a selection of clothing for Nicoletta to be brought to his hotel suite. The shopper put together an ensemble of clothing to suit his wife and brought it to the hotel only to find out that Nicoletta was his personal assistant, who was 34 years younger than him, with whom he was having an affair. The singer was furious about the selection of clothing which was obviously meant for his older wife, to which the shopper apologized profusely and quickly returned with a more suitable wardrobe for the stunning 25 year old. I think that poor shopper probably aged a year by the time that night was finally over. Incidentally the two did eventually marry, but not until years later when Pavarotti finally divorced his first wife.

With all of this exposure to the upper crust of society I decided that I should look the part as well and explored the world of beauty salons. Paying a lot of money to get your hair done might just be a status symbol for some women, but for me it was mandatory. I was born with a head full of thick, wavy hair that has a mind of its own, and while many women would love to have that I was the one who had to live with it. I found out the hard way that my type of hair is difficult for many stylists to cut, especially inexperienced ones, and had been stuck with lackluster hair styles up until this point in my life. Even though I had been teaching cosmetology for years I had never had the opportunity to spoil myself at a salon since, a) I was always living in the middle of nowhere, and b) My paycheque had always been used for living expenses while my ex-husband was squirreling away his money "for our future". I had paid a big price for being naive.

Anyways, now that I had a *real* husband and found myself with an excess of income I decided to try out Bianco Nero, one of the premiere salons of Edmonton. It was there that I had the great fortune of having Eveline Charles herself cut and style my hair before she stepped away from the chair to run her expanding salon business that she reformed under her own name. Eveline was probably the best stylist I've ever had because of her skill, but also because she knew exactly how to handle my troublesome locks since she has the same problem. It hadn't really occurred to me to find a stylist with my type of hair, but now I roam the country in search of stylists with thick, out of control hair in hopes that they will be my next Eveline. To this day, after dozens of attempts, I have only found a couple that really fit the bill.

By now some of you are wondering what has happened with my son. Due to the distance between Edmonton and La Ronge it was not feasible to have weekend visits so I had it put in the divorce settlement that I was to get him for one month each summer, but do you think my ex would even give me that much? There were many occasions where I would call to arrange for my half of the summer vacation with him only for my ex to proclaim that it wouldn't fit his own schedule. He and the Filipino were going to be off somewhere with their love child and they were taking my son with them as well. That's the way it went for most of the time that I lived in Edmonton. I would call on weekends to talk with my son, only to have the u-know-what answer the phone and tell me that he was taking a nap or simply couldn't come to the phone. When I did manage to talk to him it was clear that the cards and gifts I was sending were not being given to him—*she* was giving the gifts to *her* son and throwing out the cards.

I was finally able to track down my ex at his office to confront him on the matter, to which he angrily replied that I should just take it up with the lawyers. I could tell by his tone that he wasn't completely aware that all of this had been happening, but he had to cover for her because she had his jewels in the proverbial vice and would take him to the cleaners if their marriage didn't go exactly as she wanted it to. One night I finally broke down and my Italian husband sat beside me, put his arm around my shoulders and said, ever so kindly: "You know, I can arrange for something to happen to him if you want."

I looked up, and though my eyes were full of tears I could see that he was not joking. I was honored, and a little scared, that he would go to the lengths of using his Italian connections to have my ex roughed up, but instead I shook my head. I knew that he was completely miserable with his nightmare of a wife and that was comfort enough. Besides, the following summer I did manage to see my son, even if it meant that I had to go to La Ronge to be with him. My husband came with me, and it was a toss-up to decide if we'd arrive in the silver Mercedes with the red leather interior or the metallic blue Jaguar. We took the Jag.

Every visit with my son was special since I hardly saw him, but my most memorable visit was during the summer that my parents flew to Alberta as well. My husband paid for a lodge in the Banff Mountains and I got to show off the pride of our province as we explored the whole area, including Lake Louise and Jasper. My son was absolutely fascinated with the mountain goats that could be seen clinging to the cliffs and sheer rock faces. We were never able to get that close to one so my dad bought him his own plush mountain goat at one of the gift shops which he named Timothy. My son never let that toy out of his sight for the rest of the trip, sleeping with his new buddy at night and carrying it everywhere by day. I guess that when you can't have a lot of memories it's good to have a few quality ones instead. My life finally felt like it was on track again, so those of you who have been paying attention know that something bad must be coming soon.

At the beginning of our relationship, just after we had moved into the villa together, my husband needed an operation for a bleeding ulcer. He came through without any complications so we put the matter behind us, but a few years after we had moved into the house my husband needed another operation for the same problem except things went a little differently this time. His recovery was not going as well as before and the doctors were suspicious that he had suffered a mild stroke during the procedure, but the signs were so faint that it was hard to tell. He was a little older than me, having just turned 50, and he had looked after me so well for these past years that I decided it was my turn to do the same for him.

The Government was looking to do some voluntary cutbacks at that time so I put in the request for my pink slip so that I could be with my husband more often. He hadn't become an invalid or anything like that, he just seemed a little 'off' as people sometimes do after a serious medical issue. Instead of quitting my career cold turkey I continued my job as a part-time consultant and spent the rest of my time at the family business. After several months of his new behaviour it was becoming clear that it was not a phase as I had hoped. My husband was now an entirely different person. At first I had thought that I was just being worrisome, but my son noticed it as well on his latest visit and even my husband's own brother, who worked with him in the shop every day, knew that my Italian's new behaviour was not like him at all.

Over the course of a year he had developed the habit of coming home later and later after work on the days I wasn't with him until the point came when he would be arriving well after midnight. I was worried that he was having an affair but I was also too scared to confront him on the issue. We became distant so I focused on my work and tried to think of a way to bring him back to his old self. He had always wanted a motorcycle so I secretly bought him a Harley Davidson plus matching leather jackets for the two of us. I felt it was my last chance to win him back but it didn't seem to do anything. I had also managed to save sixty-thousand dollars to pay off our house, but that was a special surprise that I'd been working on for a while.

Our anniversary was coming up and I was hoping that my big surprise would snap him out of this mood and bring back the man I had married, but I ended up being the one who got surprised. I found a withdrawal slip in one of the cars and the account total was off by a decimal place. Instead of showing around $60,000.00 it only showed about $6,000.000 left in the account! Denial set in immediately and I hoped it was an error until I found the rest of the ATM slips in the glove compartment. My husband had pulled out over fifty-thousand dollars during the past several months. Unable to ignore the issue any longer I confronted him about the missing money and finally got my answer—his mistress was the local gambling casino. Unfortunately I hadn't heard the worst of it yet.

During the past year, when the personality change set in, my husband had gotten into gambling. Nobody knew, and he certainly had the money for it, so it went unnoticed at first. Unfortunately he had started to borrow against his million-dollar company to fuel this new addiction, and after that was maxed out he turned to our joint bank account in a desperate effort to regain his immense loss. With that having now failed there was only one option left: bankruptcy. Actually there were two options left, and that was to decide which one of us would claim the bankruptcy to get us out of this mess. If my husband claimed it then we would lose everything, but if I claimed it then somehow it could be worked that we would not lose anything, or rather, *he* wouldn't lose anything. I don't know how that was arranged, but it really didn't leave me with any choice. Happy Anniversary.

That summer I made the difficult decision to inform my ex about my unfortunate financial situation. It put a damper on my son's yearly visit but by the next year he still decided that he wanted to live with me instead of with his father. Despite the efforts to erase me from his life there was no doubt in his mind that he had to get away from that miserable Filipino woman that was always trying to keep us apart. I made sure that my ex filled out all of the proper paperwork this time to state that I had full custody of my own child and we made the most of our new life together, as broken as it was. I wish I could say that things got better after that but it was not meant to be. After having destroyed my credit rating to cover his mistakes I asked my husband when we were going to start his addiction counselling, but he just looked at me and said that he wasn't ready to do that yet. I couldn't believe what I was hearing! I had just sacrificed everything for him and yet it wasn't a convenient time to deal with this extremely serious issue.

For the next few months I focused on my son and thankfully he couldn't get enough of the West Edmonton Mall. Free distractions were the best kind right now and this was a time when the Edmonton Oilers would practice at the mall's indoor skating rink. He was more than happy to watch the team skate around and shoot the puck which allowed me to save my money for the other attractions that the WEM had to offer.

For those of you who don't know just how massive the West Edmonton Mall is, picture every tourist activity possible and put it under one roof. Aside from the enormous, two-level shopping mall there are additional attractions built onto it that are all enclosed within the main structure. There's the Galaxy-land Amusement Park which has several of the standard rides that you'd expect at an amusement park including a full sized roller coaster; there's the glass-roofed water park with a tidal pool the size of a sports field and almost twenty water slides, some that are ten stories high; there's the multi-lane bowling alley complete with glow-bowling; there's the 12 screen Cineplex Odeon mega-theater that also has an IMAX theater, and those don't include the in-mall attractions like the interior skating rink, a mini-golf course and a full-size replica of the Santa Maria pirate ship that floats in its own marina resembling a Caribbean lagoon. Visiting the mall was a vacation in itself that my son couldn't get enough of and I was glad to be able to spend that time with him.

Something else that my son couldn't get enough of was watching the Edmonton weather on television even though he lived in Saskatchewan. He would tune in to watch Clair Martin whenever he could because he was fascinated with weather forecasting and because he knew that she was an Edmonton weather person. I suppose it made him feel a little closer to me by watching an Edmonton station when we couldn't be together, so when he finally came to live with me I arranged for a studio tour. I got to tour the television station with my son and I thought it would be a real thrill for him to be able to watch Clair present the weather live, but she had an even bigger surprise for us. When the time came for her to go on camera she let my son go on instead! Clair gave him a quick lesson on what to do and coached him from off camera, and I was pleasantly stunned to watch him up there on his own delivering the weather live to the city of Edmonton. I couldn't thank her enough for that magical moments with my son that couldn't have been bought with money. It was a bright moment in an otherwise bleak point in my life. With her personality it's no wonder that Clair Martin was awarded the honour of "Best Weather Presenter in the World" in 2000, 2001 and 2003.

We ended winter with the somewhat expected news that the house, my dream house, would have to go up for sale since my husband couldn't maintain the payments. I then told him that I couldn't live like this, that he had to choose between the gambling or me, hoping that such a choice would sober him up, but it didn't. He at least had the decency to move out of the house while I arranged the divorce.

Over the next few months I made several calls to my brothers and parents, completely distraught about my situation, and they told me to come back home with my son. If I would just move home then we could stay with them until everything gets sorted out. Since I was now completely broke I needed to sell off whatever things I could to scrounge up enough money for the move. Selling off the Harley would have solved a lot of problems, but I was genuinely frightened of this man whom my husband had become. He was uncaring and without feelings, and I didn't want to risk getting him mad at me, so I settled for selling off enough household items that would fund a move on a shoestring budget. I managed to find a cross-country mover that could haul items on the cheap by renting out space on transport trailers that were already headed to the customer's destination. They dropped of the trailer and my son and I packed up everything that we could. I had been so proud to finally have him back in my life only for him to get caught in this terrible situation. I returned to Ontario bankrupt and humiliated once more.

Living with Your Rewards

The book of Job is probably one of the most famous parts of the Bible. For those who are unfamiliar with Job, a very brief summary would go something like this:

The book starts off describing Job as a man with many blessings who also has great reverence for God. Job has a large, happy family, lots of land and lots of livestock. Fields and herds were a measure of a man's wealth in biblical days, and Job was considered to be one of the richest men around. Job is such a faithful servant that God even talks of him fondly to Satan. The devil replies to God with a challenge, saying that it is no wonder Job is so faithful since he has so many blessings, but if those blessings were taken away then Job would be like any other man and curse God to His face. God disagrees and the challenge is on. The devil creates one disaster after another that leaves Job with no livestock or children, then goes so far as to curse him with sores that cover his body, yet still Job does not curse God. Even his wife, who still lives and is healthy, tells Job to curse God for all that has happened, but he refuses to do so, claiming that the good Lord giveth and the good Lord taketh away. The rest of the book is a lengthy, philosophical debate between Job and three of his friends who come to visit him, but the summery of this particular scripture is that Job perseveres through his affliction without cursing God and is therefore rewarded in the end for his faithfulness. He is healed, blessed with twice as much as he had before, has another family and lives long enough to enjoy four generations of his new children.

Right now I was definitely feeling a lot like Job. I had already survived one bad marriage and rebuilt my life from nothing. I'd found a caring husband, created a new, successful career for myself and was all set to ease into an early and very comfortable retirement. I had the nice cars, the designer wardrobe and the stylish lifestyle, only to have it all disappear in a matter of months. Again, I suppose I am partly to blame since I chose not to confront my husband earlier on. I probably wouldn't have been able to stop the gambling, but I sure could have made arrangements that would have kept me from ending up homeless and flat broke again. Although Job didn't curse God for the hardships he did wish that he had never been born, which is about where I was in my emotional state, but Job's friends rebuked this complaint. They reminded him of all the good he had done up until now and all of the people whose lives he had enriched, which is a fair point. We can't measure our lives by what we have in hand but instead by what we have done. This leads into a well-known Bible verse from the book of Matthew:

19 *Lay not up for yourselves treasures upon earth, where moth and rust doth corrupt, and where thieves break through and steal:*
20 *But lay up for yourselves treasures in heaven, where neither moth nor rust doth corrupt, and where thieves do not break through nor steal:*
21 *For where your treasure is, there will your heart be also.*
~ Matthew 6:19-21

The moral of this particular verse is that a sense of security based on how much we have is a false sense of security, which I can attest to on two accounts now. Twice I had been living my life according to the rule that if you work hard and save your money then everything will be alright, which I feel that I did successfully and properly, but both times my years of effort were taken from me in the blink of an eye leaving me with nothing. I had definitely set my heart with those earthy treasures and I was now feeling the consequences.

It also needs to be mentioned that I was nowhere near the Christian that I had been in my younger years which could be the cause of my apparent blindness to the actions of my husbands. Though I had never stopped believing in God I certainly believed more in the power of money. So I had put my faith in the all-mighty dollar, twice, and now had nothing to show for it. My earthly treasures were gone and to be honest I didn't really feel that I had any treasures built up in heaven either. Sure, I had always been an honest and hard-working person, but that is something that God *expects* from us at all times. We aren't rewarded for behaving properly in our own best interest; we are rewarded for behaving properly while serving His best interest. Those are two very different things. When serving our Father's best interest we can be blessed with rewards here on Earth, but we are also building up some sort of treasure for ourselves where it cannot be stolen from us, and this is something that I needed to be working on although I didn't quite know it at this time.

While I'm on this topic there is something else that needs to be mentioned. When doing something that is in God's interest there is a right way and a wrong way to do it. Looking back to Matthew:

1 Take heed that ye do not your alms before men, to be seen of them: otherwise ye have no reward of your Father which is in heaven.
2 Therefore when thou doest thine alms, do not sound a trumpet before thee, as the hypocrites do in the synagogues and in the streets, that they may have glory of men. Verily I say unto you, They have their reward.
3 But when thou doest alms, let not thy left hand know what thy right hand doeth:
4 That thine alms may be in secret: and thy Father which seeth in secret himself shall reward thee openly.
5 And when thou prayest, thou shalt not be as the hypocrites are: for they love to pray standing in the synagogues and in the corners of the streets, that they may be seen of men. Verily I say unto you, They have their reward.
6 But thou, when thou prayest, enter into thy closet, and when thou hast shut thy door, pray to thy Father which is in secret; and thy Father which seeth in secret shall reward thee openly.
~ Matthew 6:1-6

To put this in simplest terms, those who make a big show of doing God's will are not really doing His will at all. Jumping up and down while yelling, "Look at all the stuff I'm doing for God!" does not only guarantee that there will be no reward for you, but it also makes Him look bad. Definitely not the proper way to go about it. When we do what is good and what is right in His name the only people who should know about it are the people you are actually helping, whether it's the elderly person you're helping across the street or the family who has suddenly fallen on hard times and needs a boost to get back on track. Words are cheap, but actions speak volumes.

Chapter Twelve

Forty-Five Year-Old Loser

It would appear that after running away from home for all these years my life had come full circle. I was back in my old room, in the same bed, only this time it was my son in the room across the hall instead of my brothers. My youngest brother had a finished basement that he wasn't using so I was able to store my belongings there until I knew what I was going to do next.

Both of my brothers now lived in the Toronto area near my parents so it was a bit of a family reunion for me to be home as well. We would do the brunch thing on Sundays and I kept myself busy with my new venture into the moving industry. The head office for the company that moved me back here was in Edmonton but they needed a representative in the Toronto area since their current guy just quit. When the owner saw that I was headed to that part of the country he offered me the job which I took without hesitation. If there was something I knew a lot about, it was moving. It was a decent little job with no overhead since I could work out of the house, and I had the use of my mother's car. It wasn't a permanent career move but it got me out of the house and kept me from thinking about the obvious decline of my life. Little did I know how significant a role this job would play in my immediate future.

Summer had arrived and I had just celebrated my 45th birthday a few weeks ago. I had only been home for a few months but everybody was eager for me to move on with my life. My parents were already fussing about how long it was going to be before I was out on my own again while my sister-in-law, whom I had always gotten along with, was trying to set me up with doctors from the hospital that she worked at. I know she meant well but my interest in a social life was not only non-existent, it was in the negative. A wall was up and I actively repelled any man that came near me, which was actually a bit of a chore.

You would think that with everything I had been through in my failed life of marriage that I would have aged prematurely, easily gaining an extra ten years after losing everything I had, twice. However, it would seem that the one thing my ex-husbands couldn't take away from me was my genetics. My parents were both strong survivors from strong races of people, and though I was closing in on the half-century milestone I easily looked ten years younger than I should. While I credit my parents' genes for most of my youthfulness I also did my best to look after myself with the nightly habit of caring for my skin. Genetics and proper hygiene kept me looking my best even though I wasn't doing it for anyone but myself. The plus side of this was that I still looked great, but the down side was that any men I was introduced to looked just like they should: past their prime. I'd lost more money than they were ever going to earn and I was far from being impressed by their job title after everything I had accomplished in my career. My only potential suitors had no potential at all.

There was a moving job that my predecessor had taken on just before he quit but it was in an area of Southern Ontario which was a few hours away. Not only that but the customer who had set up the move was not there either. She was already on the other side of Canada, on the West Coast, looking for a place to live and had left all of her stuff with a friend who was coordinating everything at this end. This meant that neither of the two people who set up this arrangement were around to finish it. Wonderful. While the long drive was inconvenient I was still glad for the excuse to get out of town for the day.

I had already spoken with the man whom I needed to meet when he called a few weeks ago to confirm the move. He had been told that the original agent was no longer with the company but their new representative, who was a retired school teacher, would be able to handle everything. When he spoke to me over the phone I got any extra details that I needed, but then something unplanned and unexplained happened. Instead of the conversation ending when it should have I began to explain why I was the new agent and that the guy I was replacing just took off without warning. That tidbit lead to me explaining how I got the job, and why I had to move, and from there it was like a flood gate had been opened.

I think I spent the next hour telling this complete stranger about my past life and everything I had gone through. It was probably his polite understanding that kept me going as he patiently responded with small talk which let me feel that I wasn't being judged. Maybe it was the fact that this person had no idea who I was which made it so easy to completely unload the emotional baggage that I had been carrying around. I apologized once I was done but he still insisted that it was no big deal, that everybody needs to talk. What I hadn't considered was that I would have to meet this guy eventually when it came time to move his friend's stuff, but I was hoping that he would have forgotten about it by then. Sure enough, when I called back on the day before we were to meet he treated me as if nothing had happened and I could get this over with as painlessly as possible. I knew it probably didn't matter since I'd never see him again once the move was done, but nobody likes to be remembered as a basket case.

We arranged to meet at the loading dock to fill out the paperwork, and when I walked through that door I think my heart skipped a beat! The unknown man on the other side of the phone was cute and young which would make this transaction that much more enjoyable. We exchanged the necessary info as I filled out the forms plus I managed to fit some small talk in there as well. I remembered from our previous conversation that he was going through a divorce himself after separating from his wife a year ago, and I could also tell that he was curious about me despite everything that I'd already told him. He knew my age and exactly what I'd been through to end up here but he was still checking me out in a discreet, non-creepy way.

He was polite, charming, and a little bit shy, but aside from all of his obvious assets there was something else about this man, this much younger man, that I couldn't shake. I brought up the fact that I had been to this area a few times already since the company had no agent here, suggesting that perhaps he might like to take on the position, and he agreed that we should definitely get together again to discuss the issue. Woo-hoo! It wasn't exactly a date, but the idea of seeing him again made me very happy. We exchanged phone numbers and went our separate ways but I couldn't stop thinking about this man I had just met which was strange since no guy had ever affected me that way before.

I found an excuse to be back in his city within a few days and phoned up this new interest in my life to see if we could meet at the loading docks again to look over the job paperwork. I also gave him his first test; I requested a Starbucks coffee if it wouldn't be a bother for him to pick one up on the way. To my delight he arrived soon after with coffee in hand. This was going very well. I felt like a school girl all over again except this time I was doing it properly. We spent the time engaged in small talk, even discussing the job now and then, but I was sure that he was more interested in me right now. He made no presumptions despite the subtle signals that we were sending back and forth, but when it was time for me to get going he found the courage to ask me over for dinner so that we could continue discussing the moving job. It was his last night with his kids before they went to the ex's place for the next week, and he warned me ahead of time that it was going to be vegetarian, but I gladly accepted.

All sorts of warning bells were going off in my head for the rest of the day. What was I thinking? This guy had to be around ten years younger than me, but I still couldn't help myself. I had built a wall to be protected against this exact situation yet here I was anyways! I can just imagine what my family would say if they knew what was going on. I was falling for someone that I didn't really know, obviously confused in my current, vulnerable state, and I was only setting myself up for another disaster. So what did I do when it was time for dinner? I went to the nearest grocery store to buy candy for the kids and a bunch of flowers for him. I know what you're thinking right now, and you are correct; I had no idea what I was doing. I knew almost nothing about dating, but I didn't want to show up empty-handed either.

As I knocked on his apartment door I couldn't remember the last time I had been so nervous. I'd been through plenty of the other emotions lately, but this giddy nervousness was something new. He greeted me with a smile and was immediately thrown off when I presented the flowers, but before I could feel like a complete loser he thanked me and rummaged around for a vase. His two kids were adorable and friendly. The six year old daughter and four year old son wasted no time in walking over and saying hello. She with her little blonde bob and him with his short blonde crop looked like they could have walked off of a catalogue page. I was starting to panic, but luckily candy solves just about anything. Jolly Rancher to the rescue! Of course they wanted some right away, but dad said they would have to wait until after dinner. He gave me a disapproving look for the sweets but he never stopped smiling at me either.

Dinner was pleasant with lots of idle chit-chat, then I sat in the living room and had candy with the kids while he cleaned up in the kitchen. The three of us seemed to hit it off well as they introduced me to their three pet cats, but I don't remember much else besides looking around the apartment. It was tidy, but not to my standard of clean, and sparsely furnished. It certainly looked like half of the stuff was gone, and what his ex had left behind looked like left-overs from his student days. I had nicer pieces of furniture sitting in my brother's basement, but who was I to judge? His son and daughter were an absolute delight to be around, obviously happy in their life, and he was just as obviously devoted to them. Strange as it may sound I had never seen a man so happy with his kids, and for some reason this made him even more desirable. Shame on me for having such thoughts with the children in the room, but that didn't last long. Soon it was bath time, so while he attended to his duties I watched TV by myself which helped me cool down.

I listened to their interactions from down the hall and kept wondering what I was getting into. It looked like he was barely providing enough for himself and his kids, so how could I possibly be happy in a relationship with a poor man? None of this was making any sense, but before I could solve my mental crisis the kids were back, bouncing into the room all squeaky clean and wearing their pyjamas. His daughter's hair was still wet so I asked for a hair dryer and showed her how to dry it while bending over as it hung down, making it all poofy. She thought that was the coolest thing ever and her dad looked at me as if I were the coolest thing ever. We finished the evening with a Veggie Tales movie, then I bid the children good-night as they were whisked off to bed.

With the room to myself once more I finally put together a few pieces of the puzzle. Besides the undeniable attraction that I had towards my new crush he wasn't trying to impress me with, well, anything. He was just being himself, unafraid to show me who he really was, and that open honesty was something that I must have needed in my life. There were Christian books around the room and the Christian-based Veggie Tales video meant that he wanted his kids to have the same values. It was obvious that his life was a bit upside down but there was still this aura of calmness about him that kept a part of me calm as well while the rest of me wanted to bolt out the door in a mad panic. I was somehow relaxed when I was with him, so relaxed that he found me dozing off on the couch when he came back! How embarrassing is that? He didn't seem bothered and just smiled at my embarrassment, then we talked a bit more about life in general. I commented on his books and he asked if I was Christian at all, to which I answered that I was. Then I asked him if he wanted to know more about the moving job and got the answer I suspected; he only showed interest in that to get another chance to see me. I finally had confirmation on where we stood, or at least I thought I did.

"You look tired," he said. "You should probably get going."

I felt like such a fool! After all that he was kicking me out! He didn't try to make a move on me or anything! "Oh, I see," was all I managed to say before getting up and heading for the door. How could I have been so wrong? Then things got even more confusing.

"What?" He said, seeming confused himself. "No, wait, that's not what I meant..."

Before I knew it I was in my car and down the road. I didn't know what was going on, I didn't know how to deal with this, but one thing for sure is that I certainly was tired. By the time I made it to the other end of town I was physically and emotionally drained, and I certainly wasn't up for a few more hours of driving. That's when my phone rang. I knew it would be him, so I pulled into a parking lot and answered the call even though I wasn't sure what would happen next. He was very apologetic, not meaning for me to take what he had said the wrong way. He was just worried because he knew that I was tired and had a long drive to get home. He also felt terrible that I was so upset. He didn't think I was crazy or anything like that, he was only concerned for me right now and wanted me to come back so we could talk some more and sort this out. I looked out my car window and saw that I was in a hotel parking lot. Maybe it was the fatigue, but I felt it was time to get everything out in the open.

"I can't come back." I said. "If I come back to see you then I'm worried something will happen."

He wasn't expecting that, but it didn't scare him off either. I told him that he shouldn't worry about me because I was checking into a hotel and that I would see him tomorrow. I had some other business that I could finish up in the morning and then I would be over to see him in the afternoon. He was relieved, I got some rest, and tomorrow couldn't come fast enough.

The next day I was knocking on his door again and I was still just as nervous. I had opened my heart up to this guy that I hardly knew which is something that I swore would never happen again. One side of me knew that I wouldn't survive another emotional let-down, but the other side of me couldn't go on without attempting this relationship. When he opened the door and smiled at me I could feel the calm coming over me again. We didn't hug or do anything like that but I could see that we had established something over the phone last night.

Without going into any embarrassing details I will say that 'something' did happen. We ended up looking into each other's eyes and thinking the same thing: What the heck just happened? This was something that neither of us would have done with anybody else in our entire lives. Shameful, I know, but we finally broke through the barrier of uncertainty that was keeping us apart. More importantly, though, was that there was no regret because we had finally connected. We hardly knew each other but felt as if we had been together for ages. Our previous lives were a distant memory, and as long as we were together then the pain and hardships of our marital failures were all but forgotten. As corny as it sounds, I knew that Chris was my soul mate and he felt the same way about me, but it would have been nice if it hadn't taken forty-five years to find him. While my insecurities still struggled with our fourteen year age gap it became clear that I would have to quit worrying about being the older woman in his life and learn to enjoy having a younger man in mine.

Recognizing True Love

First of all I would like to address the apparent double-standard of Chris' and my values that seemed to have been left at the door during that moment. Neither of us condones the behaviour that we displayed on that distant day, fourteen years ago, nor do we encourage anyone to take our personal actions as an excuse to use the 'soul mate' card to justify careless fornication. We were both living by our strict values of sexual abstinence even though we were no longer committed to our spouses. He did his best to continue doing so with me in spite of our feelings for each other, but the love that we felt was simply too much for me to cope with at the time. Both of us thought we knew what love was with our previous partners, but we were confusing it with dedication.

I had stuck by both of my husbands until there was nothing left to love, and his wife had moved out after confessing that the woman he had married was not the woman that she really was. Back when they had met she had hidden her real self to win him over, pretending to be someone she was not, but couldn't keep up the charade when the stresses of life piled up. During the last few years of their relationship it seemed that nothing he did could make her happy since what she really wanted was for him to change and be more like her, or at least to accept her for the person that she wanted to be again. It became apparent that neither of those things were going to happen because Chris felt that he would have to lower his values and personal standards. Resentment quickly set in and dominated their relationship which ended up with her moving out. It was her idea to find her own place, but the feeling was mutual. Saving the marriage wasn't an option in Chris' eyes since it was based on a lie in the first place, and though the separation was difficult for the children it was better than the constant arguing that they were being exposed to. He never claimed that his ex was a bad person, she was just bad for him.

Recognizing true love is a tricky thing, especially when we are younger and have no real experience with the emotion. Love and lust are easily confused when we are first learning about relationships, and with today's general acceptance of casual sex, even amongst teenagers, I doubt that anybody thinks there is a difference between the two. While I can't tell anybody how to determine if love is true, I can describe to you how Chris and I knew it was true for us.

As you've read about my life, I think the closest I'd ever been to feeling love was the crush I had on the student minister back in university. If it had been true love then I would have gladly changed my plans and gone on to be a preacher's wife, but that wasn't something I considered for a single moment. After that I graded my men on how well they could provide for me because that's what I thought marriage was supposed to be, but you know how that went. Now I found myself overwhelmed with emotions that I hadn't felt in forty-five years, and they were towards a man that was in no position to provide for me at all in the area of finances. I think I was able to overlook that because Chris provides for me abundantly in the spiritual and emotional areas of life, loving me unconditionally and admiring my qualities that other men feel threatened by. He loves having a strong woman with strong values that equal his own, and the fact that my 45 year-old husband still gets butterflies when he sees me, even though I'll be 59 years old at the printing of this book, is a testament to that love. He also says that it's easy to be in love with me since he thinks I look better than most of the women that are half my age.

Chris didn't know how to describe his feelings for me when we first met. He had been told that a retired school teacher was handling his friend's move, so he was expecting to meet an old lady with glasses, wearing a shawl and her gray hair up in a bun. I'm glad that I was a pleasant disappointment. He had definitely been overcome with something when he first set eyes on me all those years ago but he says that the sheer magnitude of those emotions were beyond words at the time. That sounds like a lame line from a dating manual, but he was finally able to clarify those feelings to me a few years later. He hadn't been outside the province of Ontario too many times before he met me, so on a road trip to Vancouver Island, when we were about to pass through the Rockies, I took over the driving. This was going to be his first time through the mountains and I wanted him to be a passenger so that he could experience it properly. As we were going through the heart of the Rocky Mountains range and surrounded by the largest of those majestic, snow-capped wonders he turned to me with a look of revelation.

"This is how I felt when I first saw you." He said.

I didn't understand right away, but he explained it like this: the way I made him feel on that special day we met could only be matched by the overwhelming feeling of awe and wonder that he was feeling right now while experiencing the mountains for the first time. He couldn't explain it back then because he didn't have anything to compare it to until now. I don't know about you, but when a man tells you that your only comparison is a breathtaking view of the most incredible, natural attraction on the continent then that's pretty special. That's true love at first sight. Is it any wonder that I couldn't keep my hands off him?

What really mattered back then wasn't so much how we felt about each other, though that was a huge part of it, but that we could be ourselves. Neither one of us pretended to be somebody we weren't. Chris knew that I saw myself as a forty-five-year-old failure but he also knew that there was a lot more to me than that. Both of my ex-husbands knew that as well, but my first husband was threatened by the fact that I could do anything that he could do while my second one wanted somebody who needed him to look after her, which technically I didn't need. I had succeeded on my own and would have continued to do so if not for my misguided dedication to him and our marriage. Chris, on the other hand, loved me for who I was despite my current situation and I could say the same about him. Too many people try to change themselves for somebody else, worrying that if they don't then they won't get the person they want. What they don't understand is that any relationship based on a lie is doomed to failure one way or another. Before you can even begin to get to know somebody, make sure that you know who you are first.

Chapter Thirteen

The Third Time's a Charm

One would think that my life would even out now that I was united with the man who would love me for the rest of my life, but that was not the case. Even though I had hit the jackpot in the area of companionship, I had difficulty accepting Chris' love while dealing with everything else that I was going through. A healthy relationship is an important aspect of life, but it is still only one part of it. For the next couple of months I made as many visits as possible to see my new Darling, but I was also trying to cope with my current financial, employment and living arrangements which I saw as a complete disaster, not to mention an embarrassment. Moving into Chris's two-bedroom apartment with my son wasn't an option but I certainly wasn't able to get my own place either since personal bankruptcy sticks with you for seven years. It doesn't matter if it was a heroic attempt at saving your last marriage; nobody wants to touch you. Moving back in with my parents was an easy way to get out of Alberta, but now there was no easy way to get out of their house.

I found myself re-living that last year of my life, running it through my head over and over again. It was an endless collection of "What if?" scenarios that would have given me a handful of different outcomes with any of them being better than where I was now. What if I hadn't quit my Government job? What if I hadn't claimed bankruptcy? What if I hadn't left Edmonton? What if I'd fought for alimony instead of leaving with nothing? My mind was like a broken record that played the same tunes of regret while I tried to dismiss the "What ifs" and deal with what *was*. Unfortunately my current state of insecurity almost sabotaged the one thing in life that I could rely on right now.

Many women at the age of forty-five would have difficulty seeing a down-side to being with a thirty-one year old man. I won't go through the list of obvious benefits since that would be bragging, but here are some other ideas that went through my head: when I was starting high school, he had just been born; when I was learning to drive, he was learning to walk; when I was entering university, he was entering kindergarten. Do I need to continue? When I thought of it that way it was weird on so many levels. I couldn't help but wonder if others would think about it that way as well, so it's understandable that I tried to run away from this relationship as it was just getting started.

Chris was the assistant Superintendent at his apartment building which gave him the duties of looking after things every other weekend. Normally this was a low-maintenance job but some new landscaping had just been planted around the property and the lengthy chore of watering needed to be done every day. It was on one of those days that I had managed a visit, and as he was out doing his thing I gave in to a moment of doubt. Something inside of me said that it could never work between us, so while Chris was busy outside I went to my car and decided it would be best if I left. I didn't even leave him a note. In the end it didn't matter because as I was heading out the driveway there he was watering the last of the plants and chatting with a few of the tenants. He saw me leaving and walked over to my car. He knew what was happening but he played dumb for my sake.

"Where you goin'?" He asked playfully. He knew this was a delicate situation, especially with on-lookers.

"I'm leaving," I said quietly. I wasn't able to say any more and Chris saw that.

"No," he said with a smile, immediately formulating a plan that would allow me to drive away while still retaining my integrity. "You're going down to the grocery store to get a few peppers for dinner. I'll be finished up by then."

It worked, of course. Ordering me to turn around would have gone very badly, especially with other people watching. Instead I was able to drive away as I had wanted to do, but using it as an excuse to run an errand helped me to collect my thoughts once more. When I got back we had a wonderful dinner, an even better evening, and I never tried running away again despite still having issues with our age difference.

Mind you, nobody was ever aware of the drastic age gap between us. Chris knew I had issues with it and understood completely, always telling people that I was simply a bit older than he was. Even his parents have no idea what my real age is, but they will now that this book is out. It was our own little ruse that wasn't difficult to pull off since I easily passed for thirty-five and I certainly didn't act my age either. Being young in love kept me young at heart, and an up-to-date wardrobe did the rest. Even to this day Chris insists that I have an ageless beauty which keeps anyone from knowing how old I really am, but I'm sure that having him in my life makes all the difference.

One particularly memorable visit during this time was the weekend that I brought my son. He and I hadn't done anything special since we moved from Alberta so I wanted to have a little road trip to give us some quality time together. Instead of taking the main highway to Chris' place I planned a day trip through some of the more scenic areas of rural Southern Ontario, specifically to make a stop in the beautiful town of St. Jacobs. I was glad to have this time with my son as we walked up and down the town's Main Street. We explored the multitude of quaint artisan shops, complete with an authentic blacksmith, and the only thing missing was having Chris by my side to enjoy the moment with us. As much as I wanted this experience to continue I wanted to be with my Darling even more, so we bid the town farewell and hit the road once again. I called Chris to let him know that we'd be there in about an hour and a half and he said that he was looking forward to meeting my son. Ninety minutes later I picked up the phone again and told him that I was lost.

There was no straight line from where I was to where I wanted to be since the rural region of Southern Ontario is a zigzag patchwork of gravel roads and secondary highways. All it took was a missed left turn and we ended up traveling away from our intended destination without even knowing it. I started to worry about an hour into the drive when I realized that I hadn't seen a directional sign for at least thirty minutes, but the last thing I wanted to do was look stupid in front of my son so I just kept on driving. We finally did pass one of those green signs telling us how far it was to the next town but our destination wasn't even on it, and that's when two things happened: I learned to swallow my pride and Chris learned that I can't read a map.

"You're *where*?" Is all he could say at first, unable to believe that I had gotten so far off the mark. For some reason I was an emotional wreck at this point. I'd had enough of country driving, I felt like an idiot, the day was getting late and I told Chris that I just wanted to turn around and head back to my parents' house. Now it was Chris' turn to panic. He'd been looking forward to seeing me for a while and wasn't about to let me off the hook so easily. Besides, while I wasn't really that close to him it was a lot closer than heading all the way back to Toronto. He calmed me down, got out his own road map and figured out the best route to get us back on track. Now that I knew what towns I needed to pass through it was easier to navigate the maze of farm fields and side roads until we were back on the correct highway. Dinner was ready when we finally walked through the door and I didn't realize just how happy I would be to see him. He got the chance to meet my son, even if it wasn't exactly how I had planned for the day to go, and we ended the evening with a movie to help me wind down.

By the end of the summer it was clear to both of us that we shouldn't be apart. The moving job had served its purpose by bringing us together but now anything that took me away from him was an inconvenience and an extra stress that I didn't need in my life. There was a neighbourhood on the other side of town which Chris thought would be more suitable for us where we could rent a townhouse big enough for him, me and my son, plus his kids when they visited. It was a nice area that backed onto a large green space with three schools, one of which was his old high school. His rationale was that I could start substitute teaching while he continued his second job as a graphic artist. It made sense so we took the tour and I had to admit that it was exactly as he said. The area was clean and established; the three-bedroom townhouse we saw was very nice; there were two elementary schools and his old high school just outside our door, but it was more like living at the edge of a large park. It seemed like the perfect place to get back on my feet. With my younger brother's help to co-sign my half of the lease we were ready to move in for October and start something new together.

When moving day came, Chris took the Greyhound to my neck of the woods since he would be driving the U-Haul truck back to our new home. I picked him up at the bus station and hid him away from my family for the day. It wasn't a secret that our relationship was serious or even that we were moving in together, but I knew that if we made a social occasion out of this then somebody was going to bring up a piece of my past that I didn't want to deal with right now.

Chris had already put up with enough of my emotional baggage over the past few months, and while he had a general idea of what happened with my last two marriages there were still a lot of details that he didn't need to know. Not yet. Even though I was with my soul mate I still felt like I was living on the edge of a knife. Trust was a huge issue for me as you can imagine and I honestly thought that if my new Darling discovered every single embarrassing detail about my past then he might have second thoughts about us. I know now that he never would have left me, and it could very well have made this part of our relationship easier, but that was a risk I wasn't prepared to take. I was perfectly capable of scaring him away on my own; I didn't need my family's help.

By now you're wondering just what kind of relationship I had with my parents, to which I can only answer that it was complicated. In their hearts they always wanted what was best for me but they could never truly understand what that meant. I'll have to admit that it must have been confusing for them when I'd had my second divorce in less than ten years. They couldn't understand why I was unable to stick it out through the rough times of either marriage, especially since these challenges were a pale comparison to what they had survived in their earlier years.

My father had grown up on a farm in a house that was half-way up a mountain. They were so poor that he would have to share shoes with his brothers, meaning that he couldn't go out until somebody else came home. Now compare that to my mother's childhood of being raised in a German concentration camp and my father's life could be considered luxurious. Fast-forward a few decades to their one and only daughter who can't seem to put up with the little issues of adultery or a gambling problem. Both men still would have taken care of me for life *as long as I knew my place*, which brings us to the complication; I may not have known where my place was, but I certainly knew where it wasn't.

Perhaps what my parents saw as foolish pride is what I view as dignity, and it's quite possible that we will never see eye-to-eye in that aspect. There's also the difference in concept of what "being looked after" meant to them and their generation of survivors. Having three square meals a day and a roof over your head may have been the very definition of providing for your family after the war, but that was half a century ago. It's possible that if I had walked in my parents' shoes then I would have been able to overlook the behaviour of either of my husbands by chalking it up as a lapse of judgement, but I can't equate that to being looked after. I was capable of paying my own bills so why would I let somebody else do it for me as an excuse to treat me badly?

Besides, I did try to turn a blind eye towards each incident that ruined my marriages but in my opinion that only made things worse. I let my first husband have his power trip in the end, but it wasn't enough to emotionally dominate me so he had to have the nanny as well. I also tried to live through my second husband's sudden personality change and gambling problem by sacrificing *everything* for his sake, but when the house had to be sold then that was the sign for me to get out. I had never asked to be treated as any more than an equal throughout my entire life, which I felt that I had proven to be worthy of over and over again, yet nobody wanted to give me that simple decency. Perhaps that's why it was so hard for me to accept that Chris was different.

Aside from the incredible soul mate connection that we had my Darling also treated me with the simple respect that I had been looking for. We were different in many ways but we were equals as well. Chris' mannerism balanced with my own, but one thing we did share was our inability to excuse bad behaviour. That trait is what ended both our marriages when we could no longer endure what other people thought we should put up with. He was also very protective of me at this point and knew that my parents had a double standard when it came to me and my brothers. I didn't want a heated family debate to erupt in front of him because I knew he would come to my defense and it would get messy. Chris found my brothers' favoured treatment throughout high school and university confusing enough, and he also knew that they had been given the down-payments on their houses which they could repay at their leisure.

I had asked for a similar favour from my parents when I moved back in, but after all I had been through I was still flatly denied any financial support. I didn't like to badmouth my family in front of Chris, but when this happened I couldn't keep it inside. I had only asked for half of what each of my brothers had been given, and I promised to pay it back, but something inside of them just couldn't do it. To ask for the money was hard enough, but to be denied this help from my own parents felt like betrayal. It was no longer a case of not having the money like I had been told during school. It was almost as if there was some invisible force at work that kept them from crossing that line. It had been *their* idea for me to come back home until I sorted myself out, but it wasn't long before I started hearing how much more the water and electricity bills were going to be with my son and I in the house. It was *their* idea to help me out until I could get back on my feet, but I was constantly asked when I would have a new job and my own place once again. Deep down I think they wanted to help me, but like everybody else they had their own ideas about how I should get through this part of my life and they didn't consider asking me what *I* needed. If I had known that this was my parents' idea of helping out their daughter, perhaps I would have been better off staying in Edmonton.

Now that you have a clearer picture of my family relationship you'll understand why the only help I had to move everything out of my brother's basement was Chris. He had been expecting a traditional moving party where everyone from my family was going to be there, but without complaining he just got right to work hauling everything into the truck. There was no packing to be done since everything was still in the boxes but it still took us the entire day.

On our way out of town the next morning we did make one stop at my parents' house since it was only right that they met the man I would be living with. I never even brought him into the house, but instead met my parents on the driveway to make the introduction. It was pleasant enough as he shook their hands and said hello, then I told them that I would come back for my son once we were settled and I had him enrolled in school. The sun was just rising as we hit the highway and I gave a sigh of relief to be out of my family's hair once again. We made one detour on the way to our new home to grab Chris' stuff from his apartment, then it was non-stop to the next chapter in our life together.

Trusting in God Through Hardship

Near the beginning of the Bible, starting in the book of Genesis at chapter 37, the story of Joseph tells about a man's life that is a roller coaster ride of blessings and tragedy. He is born as Israel's favourite son but his step-brothers despise his favoritism and conspire to kill him because of it. He is spared from this fate and instead sold off as a slave and taken into Egypt, but the ups and downs continue. Joseph's new master likes him so much that he's put in charge of the entire household, but then the master's wife had Joseph put into jail because he won't sleep with her. Next the jailer thinks that Joseph is a great guy and puts him in charge of all the other prisoners where he interprets some dreams, carefully proclaiming that God is the interpreter while he is only a vessel. Instead of being recognized for this gift Joseph is forgotten about for a couple of years until the pharaoh has a dream that needs interpreting. After every wise man in the court fails to explain the dream somebody remembers Joseph, so he is finally brought out of jail to interpret the dream through God's grace. The explanation of the dream is so profound that pharaoh makes Joseph his right hand man putting him in charge of the entire country of Egypt. To top it off Joseph finally meets his brothers from the beginning of the story, and after giving them a hard time for what they had done to him he finally forgives them.

While this rendition of Joseph's life is extremely condensed it illustrates that sometimes we must go through hardship to finally get to the greatness that God has planned for us. Chris and I both believe that we were meant for each other and that it was always God's plan for us to be together. Many people would argue this belief, stating that if God really did want us together then we would have been born at the same time as next door neighbours instead of spending half of our lifetimes apart. That would have been nice but if we had met as kids then it's possible we wouldn't have gotten along. He was afraid of girls until late in high school and I would have just beaten him up anyways for trying to steal a kiss. We both had a lot of growing to do before meeting, and I guess I had more growing to do than he did.

There are many verses in the Bible that depict this important fact: we grow by enduring hardship. There are probably entire books written about this very subject, but I'm just going to apply it to my life for now. From a physical point of view it is well known that the human body can only grow stronger when it is stressed to some degree and the same goes for our spiritual walk with God. Many people want this part of their life to be problem free, but a Christian life without conflict is just like a human life without exercise. Imagine a baby's life if his parents loved him so much that they carried him everywhere and never put him down. He'd never learn to walk. In fact, nothing makes a parent more proud than watching their child take those first steps, and that's how our spiritual walk with God should be seen. Unfortunately for us, spiritual growth is not as easy to gauge as physical growth. Sometimes it only takes a few weeks of regular exercise to notice a difference in our bodies whereas spiritual growth is almost impossible to measure. We are also able to control our physical exercise to the smallest detail but our spiritual challenges will come and go when we least expect them and usually when we feel the least prepared. This can seem a bit cruel if we don't understand why.

Physical growth is all about us, from what we eat to how we exercise. Our bodies are our responsibility and nobody else can do the work for us. Our spiritual growth, however, is meant to be done differently. We are meant to look to God, to lean on him during these times instead of tackling every challenge by ourselves. This is how we build our faith in Him and it is through these trials that two very important things happen: we learn to trust in God while he proves Himself to us. Always remember that our spiritual walk with God is a two-way relationship. He will meet us half way as long as we are brave enough to take that first step towards Him. Our spiritual lives aren't meant to be a non-stop test of faith that keeps us guessing the whole time as to whether or not God is real. He will meet you along the way with proof that is only meant for you, so don't be expecting a sign that you've read about in a book or seen in a movie.

Was it necessary for me to go through all that hardship so that I could find my way to Chris? It would certainly seem so, otherwise I wouldn't have moved back to Ontario after all these years. But that's only half of the equation since our meeting also relied on his friend moving and setting up her move with the guy who would later quit and whom I would replace! If I had only met a nice guy through this chain of events then I might consider it a coincidence, but to be united with my one and only soul mate can only mean that it was a meticulously orchestrated miracle. But instead of being distracted by the hardships of my life we need to look at what I learned from them.

I had become a materialistic person who valued what I had, or what somebody could give me, over anything that God could do for me, but if we look to Psalms 118:8:

It is better to trust in the Lord than to put confidence in man.

I also thought that by controlling every aspect of my life then I would be guaranteed happiness, but Proverbs 28:26 says:

He that trusteth in his own heart is a fool: but whoso walketh wisely, he shall be delivered.

In the end I had brought about my own hardship by living according to my desires instead of living a Christian life of wisdom, but we should never feel that we have wasted our life up until this point since Romans 8:28 reads:

And we know that all things work together for good to them that love God, to them who are the called according to his purpose.

God can take all things that we do and make something good out of them as long as we lovingly follow Him. By enduring those hardships and learning from them I was also strengthened and was now ready to begin my walk again, this time in the proper direction. I just needed to learn how to truly love and trust God instead of always trusting in money and relying on myself. It was going to be a rough start but now I had somebody to do it with.

Chapter Fourteen

Searching for a Sign

When we arrived at the townhouse Chris' dad and brother were waiting to help us unload. It was my first introduction to his family and I was glad that we were starting small. Meeting two members at a time was just about the speed I was capable of at this point since my outlook on family relations was a little shaky. It would be safe to say that I was officially shell-shocked when it came to relationships in general, but meeting Chris' family while pretending that I was fine would be one of the hardest things I would ever do.

To sum up my life so far from my point of view would make it a collection of trusted relationships that took advantage of my trust and used it against me. The men whom I thought were supposed to make me a priority in their lives ended up destroying my life instead, and when I turned to my parents both times they seemed to be more interested in keeping the whole thing quiet as if I were an embarrassment to them. In order for me to be any more jaded about people my skin would have to turn green. What's truly unfortunate about the whole situation is that Chris' parents are two of the most wonderful people that

I would ever meet. His mom is a small woman who is always smiling and always nice, while his dad is the gruff jokester who always puts family first, even if it means complaining about it. It was impossible to *not* like them unless you had something seriously wrong with you, and that's where I fit in.

To be fair it wasn't that I didn't like Chris' parents, it was that I couldn't bring myself to get close to them. Keeping Chris in my personal space was hard enough, and only possible through divine intervention, so the thought of getting close to the rest of his family would result in a lifelong struggle that continues to this day. I always put on a brave face for his sake, knowing that to completely avoid his family was not an option, but I'm pretty sure that they saw past my efforts to be social and knew that something was wrong. I guess it could have been passed off as shyness if I hadn't connected so well with his dad. For some reason his mildly coarse personality brought out the sarcastic side of me and we hit it off quite well. Despite my standoff-ish nature mom and dad welcomed me without hesitation. I have never met Chris' ex-wife, but from the way his family accepted me I could only assume that I was an approved replacement.

We spent the next week getting our house in order. Putting the furniture in place was easy enough but it took a while to sort through all of my other stuff and decide what I was bringing out and what was staying in boxes. Being well organized was the last thing on my mind when I had packed everything up since I was really just trying to get out of the house before the foreclosure date. I equated my life's success with material objects, so in my mind I thought that the more items I could take with me the less of a failure I would be. I suppose it was a form of denial, and my life certainly could have been easier if I'd been able to calmly look around the house and only take what I really needed instead of burdening myself with every knickknack and widget. Luckily our new home had a big basement. I didn't need everything that was packed away but it seemed that the few things I wanted were buried under everything else. Most of you will relate to the idea that physical objects trigger memories, so going through box after box was a mental torture session. Instead of being happy about what I had managed to keep I was only reminded of what I had lost. I treated my possessions as a lifeline when they were really an anchor that was keeping me from moving on, but that was a realization that I needed to come to on my own.

My poor Darling had no idea this was going on in my head. Men aren't generally materialistic to start with unless you're talking about tools or sporting equipment and Chris had neither of those. He didn't really have much of anything and it didn't seem to bother him. It's hard to say if our special bond was a help or a hindrance at this point in our relationship since I would view it as close comfort one day and an inescapable chain the next. To sum it up neatly: I was a mess. I wasn't ready to talk about it either, and since he was busy with his own divorce settlement I was able to coast along in denial for a bit longer. I suppose I was waiting for a sign to hit me on the head and say "Now is the time to deal with your issues!", but until then I would simply avoid going into the basement and take everything one day at a time.

By the end of the week I was ready to register my son for school. Autumn was starting to make its presence known and I was grateful for the long, pleasant stroll through the park-like setting of the three school properties. Chris' old high school was the building closet to us with the Catholic and public elementary schools at the far end of the block. All of them were relatively new and I could tell that my son would like it here. It didn't take long to get the paperwork in order and the secretary gave me a shiny, new agenda for him as well. I enjoyed the walk back home even more and had a strangely optimistic feeling about everything. Being outside on my own had done me some good by getting me away from the house where I was surrounded by my past. It was time to start a new beginning.

When Chris got home he asked how it went and I told him that it went fine. He smiled at me and left it at that, knowing that a small bit of good news was better than no news at all. He was learning how to give me my space even though he still didn't fully understand my current disposition. I engaged in what small talk I could over dinner, telling him about the school, and once the dishes were done I called my parents to let my son know that everything was ready, but he told me that he didn't want to come.

I suppose I should have expected that, because this *is* my life after all, but I still wasn't ready for the rejection. He told me that he liked where he was and that it wasn't fair for him to switch schools right now. As soon as he said "wasn't fair" I knew that he hadn't come up with those words on his own so I asked to speak to my parents. Sure enough, they too were concerned about exactly how "fair" it would be to force my son to switch schools right now. A few weeks ago they couldn't stop complaining about the utility bills going up because of us, and they seemed overly concerned as to how soon I'd have my own place, but now they had completely changed directions. Is it any wonder I had serious issues? We ended the conversation by agreeing that perhaps Christmas would be a better time to do this. Somehow it would be more "fair" by that time, but I wasn't holding my breath. Chris didn't know what to say at this point. He had just experience first-hand what it meant to have my parents in my life.

The next day, on a hunch, I went to check my bank account to see if my ex's child support payments had been deposited. Nothing. It should have been in there by now so I called him up for an explanation. He was all too eager to tell me that he knew our son was with my parents and not me, so he was sending the money to them. I'd thought that this arrangement was a spur-of-the-moment decision, but my ex knew about it before I did! How could I NOT think that my parents were purposely conspiring against me? They knew how my son's other grandmother had held him hostage when he was a baby; they knew how that had affected me as it would any mother; they knew that my ex had traded me in for an uneducated, domestic servant because he couldn't keep it in his pants; they should have known that by taking his money and keeping my son that they were doing to me what had been done over ten years ago. Thankfully, instead of breaking down into a complete mess I simply went numb.

It amazes me to this day that this situation did not send Chris packing. That support money was going to be my main source of income meaning that I could not pay my half of the rent, or utilities, or *anything*. The thought of being around other children all day made me queasy, so substitute teaching was out of the question for now. I was essentially dead weight in our relationship with absolutely nothing to offer. I even asked Chris to sleep in the spare room when his kids weren't visiting because I couldn't be around anybody at this point. I wanted to die.

It was at this time that I had my dream. Normally I don't have dreams when I sleep, or at least I don't remember them, which Chris thinks is a little strange. On this particular night however, I had one of the most memorable dreams of my life. All around me was empty and dark which makes sense considering the circumstances. Then I held out my hands and I felt God take my hands in His. There were no words spoken, and I did not see God in my dream, but I knew without a doubt that my Father was reassuring me. The touch was so profound that it woke me up, and the notion did not fade as dreams usually do. I did not simply dream about being touched, I *was* touched while I slept. God took my hands in His for a few moments and I knew that my life was in His hands. This was the one and only sign that I would receive to give me hope and help me to carry on. In the morning I went into Chris' room to tell him what had happened and I even had him hold out his own hands so I could demonstrate exactly what I'd felt. He was very happy for me and shared his own moment of confirmation.

Last winter, before he met me, Chris was leaving for work early in the morning. It was still dark, there was a gentle snow falling, and while walking to his car he found a five-dollar bill on the ground. Money was tight for him then, as it always was, and he was struggling with his faith in Christianity. "Father," he said, "if you're really out there then give me a sign. Let me find more money today." It was a doomed test, of course, because how often do you find money twice in one day? He put it out of his mind and drove to work, but when he was walking from the parking garage to the office what do you suppose he found? There on the sidewalk was another five-dollar bill, neatly folded and sitting on the fresh snow. There were no other footprints on the sidewalk, so it must have blown there from somewhere, but he insists that the "how" isn't important. With God it's all about timing. Even though it was still snowing the bill was clean, so it had just been put there, and if Chris has shown up a few minutes later then it would have been covered up. The timing was perfect and Chris took that one instance as God's confirmation to him that he was being looked after.

I regained a bit of my composure after that and put some effort into letting Chris back in my life. The next few months were very lean with my Darling paying for just about everything while also paying his own child support. I asked why the kids didn't spend half of their time with us so that he could forgo the payments altogether, but his ex wouldn't go for that. At the beginning of the separation they did have the kids equally but he thinks that she was hoping the separation was temporary. Once he made it clear that they weren't getting back together she decided that the arrangement was changing and dared him to do something about it. He didn't want to put his children in the middle of a legal tug-o-war so now he was seeing them every-other weekend and paying support.

Christmas rolled around and can you guess what happened? That's right—absolutely nothing. My son didn't even come for a visit since my parents thought it was better that he went to see his father for the holidays. How nice is that? Chris' parents made up for it though with a huge gathering. Family members even flew in from the other side of the country for this event so it was quite the special occasion. Due to my current state of mind I viewed this evening as a social nightmare that I would have rather avoided altogether. My heart was beating so fast that I'm surprised I didn't have a heart attack. I kept looking for a reason to leave early but they were all so damned nice! Chris insists that I was a hit with everybody but that must have been some sort of auto-pilot because the entire evening was a blur. I guess I pulled it off but I was glad when it was finally over.

Thankfully our New Year's Eve was low key. Chris isn't an out-on-the-town kind of person and was content to sit in front of the TV and see if the world was going to end. This was the infamous Year 2000 that everybody had been hyping for the last twelve months or so, with the media getting everybody worried that the Y2K bug was going to destroy the world as we knew it. The only official glitch I witnessed was when the millennium clock on the Eiffel Tower quit working a few hours before midnight. For those of you who don't know or have forgotten, France put this huge digital clock on the Eiffel Tower a few years earlier that displayed a count-down to the Year 2000, only to have it quit working on the final evening. These days kids would call that an Epic Fail. My life may have been a mess, but that was embarrassing on an entirely different level.

Once it was clear that my son would never be living with us I needed to find a way to help with the rent. Chris was very good at not pushing me into teaching even though he still wasn't sure what the problem was so he started hocking anything and everything that he didn't need to get the extra money, right down to his old wedding ring. That still left us short after a while so I resorted to selling the two pieces of furniture that I kept from Edmonton: a beautiful wardrobe-style entertainment unit and my rosewood lingerie dresser. It was my first attempt to separate myself from my past, and as difficult as it was it was a good first step.

Another big step was letting the cats out of the basement. Had you forgotten about those three cats? I certainly wanted to, so while I was going through this phase of my life they had the spacious, subterranean floor all to themselves. When Chris' kids came over we would let them out and play with them on the main floor, but it soon became apparent that their companionship would also be a form of therapy for me. I would sit on the couch for hours with a cat on my lap and it wasn't long before they had integrated themselves into my life. Besides, having the cats out of the basement gave me an excuse for my second type of therapy, which is cleaning. It was pretty tough to justify running the vacuum cleaner every day when it was just Chris and I in the house, so having our three furry companions out and about was the perfect excuse. If I wasn't going to be working then I'd have the cleanest house on the block. It would seem that the healing process had started once I remembered how entertaining cats could be and by the springtime we had gotten a harness and leash to take them outside for walks in the yard.

By June it became apparent that I couldn't avoid employment any longer so I scoured the world wide web for a job in my comfort zone: teaching on a northern native reserve. Despite my gradual, emotional recovery it was still too difficult for me to remain in Chris' home town. Under different circumstances it would have been the ideal situation, but without my son I just couldn't make it work. I found a job in the Kenora area, also known as the Lake of the Woods, and I fully expected Chris to let me go my own way. It wasn't fair to make him choose between me and his family, especially his own two children whom he loved to death, but I had underestimated his dedication to me. As hard as it would be to move away from his kids, losing me was not an option for him. He knew that I wasn't trying to wreck his life, but he also saw how hard everything had been during this year we were together. He knew that I was getting ready to run whether he was with me or not. I had put our relationship through the baptism of fire and it survived.

Everything was a bit of a whirlwind after that. We would have to leave at the beginning of August, during the civic long weekend, in order to get to the job on time. It was a waste of a month's rent but what else could we do? Getting out of our lease one month early was also going to be a sticky situation. The agent told us that she would show the unit as soon as possible but couldn't make any promises. After the first showing we got a call. Apparently the agent had never seen a lived-in townhouse look so clean and the family that viewed it said that they could move in right away, on the August long weekend, without the usual in-between cleaning that was normally required. Not only had we just gotten out of our lease two months early but we were refunded our last month's deposit as well! Who says obsessive cleaning doesn't pay off?

The hardest part of the whole ordeal was when Chris had to tell his kids that he was moving far away. He had asked his ex to bring them over one Sunday because he had something important to tell them. I stayed upstairs when they arrived because I still hadn't met his ex and I didn't see a reason to ruin a good thing. Besides, I had an idea how this would go and I really didn't want to be in the room. Judging by the reaction he got from his ex-wife I think she was expecting this to be a good news kind of announcement. That's the only thing that could explain the shock when she learned that Chris was moving a few thousand kilometers north, with me, in a few weeks. His son was still a little too young to fully understand what this meant, but his daughter started crying immediately. I felt terrible. Chris was understandably upset after they had left and was sitting on the stairs when I finally came down. I sat beside him and asked if he was absolutely sure that he could leave his kids. He just kept looking straight ahead and said that he had made a deal with God.

“I’m going to look after you,” he told me, “and He is going to look after them.”

We didn’t speak about it anymore until he realized how guilty this was making me feel. My Darling explained to me that his ex-wife would continue controlling him through their kids for as long as he lived here, just as she had done since their separation. She was obviously angry about their failed marriage and would do whatever she could to make him miserable even if she didn’t realize it. He also reminded me that Jesus had told his disciples to leave everything behind in order to follow Him, so this act of commitment was not only to me but towards our Lord as well. Besides, if we really intended to start a new life together then we couldn’t very well do that while constantly surrounded by our old lives. The explanation didn’t make me feel any better about leaving his kids but now I understood *why* he had made it.

With the U-Haul packed solid, right to the back gate, we were ready to roll once more. It was the largest one you could rent, and with the car strapped down to a full-length trailer we were almost as long as a transport. The route was planned and the weather was good, but I could tell that Chris’ dad was a little concerned. He had been a transport driver long ago and knew how tricky a big load could be but Chris wasn’t worried. A part of him was born to adventure so we drove away that morning with no regrets, only looking ahead to this new path that we were on together.

Becoming a New Christian

Waiting for a sign from God can be a frustrating experience since it can come at any time and be nothing that you were expecting, with the “expecting” part being the main point here. The prophet Elijah was going through a bad time during the first book of Kings where all of God's prophets had been killed except for him. He made the journey to a distant mountain to commune with God and expected to see a mighty sign of vengeance in retaliation for the killings, but instead he heard this:

[11] And he said, Go forth, and stand upon the mount before the Lord. And, behold, the Lord passed by, and a great and strong wind rent the mountains, and brake in pieces the rocks before the Lord; but the LORD was not in the wind: and after the wind an earthquake; but the Lord was not in the earthquake:
[12] And after the earthquake a fire; but the Lord was not in the fire: and after the fire a still small voice.
~ 1 Kings 19:11-12

God wanted to demonstrate to Elijah that He didn't always manifest His signs in terrible and mighty acts, but also in subtle, less obvious ways. I think it's also fair to say that nobody should be demanding or expecting any kind of a sign from God, just as Chris didn't really expect to find more money. Every one of us is unique which means that we all have a different and very special way for God to get our attention, plus it's all about His timing, not ours. Proper timing can make all the difference between making a memorable impression and getting completely ignored, not to mention that we get to work on our patience as well.

Chris' idea about leaving everything to follow Jesus stems from the book of Matthew:

[37] He that loveth father or mother more than me is not worthy of me: and he that loveth son or daughter more than me is not worthy of me.
[38] And he that taketh not his cross, and followeth after me, is not worthy of me.
[39] He that findeth his life shall lose it: and he that loseth his life for my sake shall find it. ~ Matthew 10: 37-39

These verses aren't a demand for everybody to abandon their families in order to follow Jesus, but instead they tell us that we shouldn't love anything *more* than we love Jesus. Why? Because the moment we care for something more than our Lord we are capable of making exceptions to the rule for that particular love. Examples of this would be people who justify stealing, cheating, lying or worse, and then claim that they had no choice because they were doing it for somebody. That type of love has clouded their judgement to the point that they turn away from God and our Lord's teachings and rely on themselves instead. Chris also knew that he wasn't abandoning his kids. They were surrounded by his family and his ex-wife's family, all who loved those two children whole-heartedly, not to mention that he also entrusted them to God. He knew that they were in good hands and to this day I can attest that both of those children have grown to be two of the best young adults that you will ever meet.

The idea that we had to leave our old lives to start something new together can be found in this obscure passage in the book of Matthew:

16 *No man putteth a piece of new cloth unto an old garment, for that which is put in to fill it up taketh from the garment, and the rent is made worse.*
17 *Neither do men put new wine into old bottles: else the bottles break, and the wine runneth out, and the bottles perish: but they put new wine into new bottles, and both are preserved.* ~ Matthew 9:16-17

Verse 16 refers to the fact that cloth shrinks over time, especially those older textiles from the biblical era. To patch an older garment with a new piece of cloth, that will eventually shrink, will end up making the hole worse than it was before. Verse 17 is a little harder to understand until you realize that they used leather "bottles" made from animal skins, usually goat, to hold wine back then. "New" wine that was put into these leather bottles would not have gone through the fermentation process yet, but since the leather was also new and strong it could handle the expanding pressure. By the time this process had run its course the bottle was still strong enough to carry the wine but not strong enough to go through the process again if more new wine was put into the old container. A second round of fermentation would always rupture the worn out leather.

All of this eludes to the difficulty that Christians have when they want to start a new life with Jesus while trying to retain older parts of their life that don't really fit any more. Beginning a new life while hanging on to old habits or old acquaintances will always lead to frustration and compromise that threaten the new life you are trying to build. In other words, using Christianity as a patch to mend your old life will only work for a short while before the problems that you are trying to cover up only become worse or more noticeable. Becoming a new Christian requires growth that your old life can't handle, so you must start a new life or else any growth that you do manage will be lost, spilled out like a ruptured wine skin. This isn't to say that Chris' children would have compromised our new life together, but being around his ex and my entire family certainly would have. We were left with little choice if we truly wanted this to work.

Chapter Fifteen

Retracing My Footsteps

Chris and I weren't completely sure how long it would take to make the two-thousand kilometer drive so we planned on three days to be safe. The first leg of the journey went well enough and we managed to drive to our half-way point, the city of Wawa, by 11:00 that night which made for a very long day. We were up and off again by 6:00 in the morning with the goal of finishing our trek on this second day, but little did we know that was easier said than done. The second half of our drive was definitely the most scenic but this hilly stretch of the highway was extremely challenging for the U-Haul which couldn't build up enough speed to make it up some of the steeper areas. There were a few times when Chris had to shift the old standard back down into first gear and crawl up the highway with our four-way flashers on. He had a few choice words to say at those times which can't be printed in this book, and the fact that this was using up more fuel than planned put a big dent in our travel expenses. The U-Haul had terrible mileage on the flat parts of the road, but this semi-mountainous region of northern-Ontario had us gassing up at every town we came to. By mid-morning we asked somebody how long this went on for and we were informed that we had a few more hours to go. By lunch time we had made it through the gauntlet of rock to Thunder Bay and by dinner time we were in Kenora. It had only taken us two days, and six-hundred dollars in fuel, to get here.

Like most people we fell in love with the city of Kenora immediately. The struggling drive had been worth it and we took a bit of time to look around the picturesque, lake-side community before continuing to the reserve which was just another hour away. This too was a scenic drive that had us weaving our way past small lakes and huge rock formations that northern Ontario is famous for. It was like travelling through a Tom Thompson painting in real life. When the pavement ended and the gravel began I knew we were getting close. After ten more kilometers of bouncing along the washboard roadway we finally arrived at our destination.

I had definitely seen worse communities while working in Alberta, but it was Chris that I was worried about. To go from living in a large city for your entire life to the remoteness of a northern Aboriginal reserve can be a lot of culture shock for most people, but thankfully he isn't like most people and took everything in stride. As we drove in the school and the teacherages were some of the first buildings we saw. The school was in decent shape and there were two sets of row-houses beside it; older ones that were looking their age and a row of two-story townhouses that looked to be quite new. We were greeted right away and given the choice of where we'd like to live since there was an empty unit in each row. I did the polite thing and viewed both of our options while already knowing that each would need a serious cleaning. I opted for the newer unit, got our keys, then took a proper look around. It's a good thing that we got there a day early because it was going to take at least a day of cleaning before being able to move our stuff in.

There was a bed in one of the upstairs bedrooms but the condition of the mattress was questionable. I must have had that "What have I done?" look on my face because Chris started to reassure me immediately. We still had the U-Haul for a few days so we weren't in a rush to move our stuff in; everybody seemed nice enough so far; the townhouse was nice, just a bit dirty, and would look great once all of our stuff was moved in, but best of all, he pointed out, was the view. While the front of the housing faced the school and the gravel parking area the back of the housing had a spectacular waterfront view of the Winnipeg River. Stretching out before us was a few hundred meters of water that sparkled with the evening sun and was complimented by the far shore of rising granite cliffs that were dotted with rustic pines. To me, of course, the scenery was old-hat, but I was grateful for my Darling to be so enthused despite the circumstances.

When we went out to the truck it became apparent to Chris why I had insisted that the sleeping bags and a bucket of cleaning supplies were some of the last things to be packed. I could put up with most of the mess for one night but I needed to start somewhere before calling it a day. I assigned him to the kitchen while I tackled the bathroom which held some promise under the layer of filth. With my rubber gloves on I opened the four-litre jug of Pine-Sol, poured half of it into the sink to be used at full strength and started scrubbing everything down with my toilet brush. I was splashing that glorious, golden liquid everywhere and felt like the pope blessing the masses, but our efforts paid off. By the end of the night we had a clean bathroom, sterilized and pine fresh, and a clean kitchen which included every cupboard being scrubbed out. With that done we could now wash away our day of work and travels, lay out the sleeping bags on the bed and curl up for a well-deserved night of sleep. It had been a long time since I'd been serenaded by loons but hearing them that night was a purely magical moment for Chris. He was able to take in all of the good and dismiss any shortcomings of life on a reserve. Nothing seemed to faze him when it came to our life together, and even though the drive had pushed his patience to the limit it was all but forgotten now that we were here.

The next day Chris got to witness the full extent of my previous reserve experience. In no time at all I had the school janitor get a crew together to haul out all of the furniture that was currently in our teacherage, find me a working washing machine and dryer for the basement, and also see if he could find something to clean the carpets with. Thankfully they had a proper steam cleaner and Chris spent the rest of the day cleaning the carpets of the now empty rooms while I washed down the walls and coordinated some boys to move most of our stuff into the basement which thankfully was clean and dry. I don't think they could believe that we came here with so much stuff.

Normally teachers move to a reserve with the minimum of possessions since nobody plans on staying for long, but our truck had more stuff in it than some permanent residents had in their homes. We even brought house plants! By the end of the day our teacherage was clean from top to bottom and properly furnished to my satisfaction. Nothing quite says "home" like having your own couch to relax on and bed to sleep in. Even the cats were happy. We had tried to find homes for all three before we left but only managed to relocate one of them to a neighbour of Chris' parents. The other two had to suffer through the journey while hiding under the U-Haul's bench seat for the entire trip. A reserve is no place for domestic pet, but there was little we could do aside from abandoning them at an animal shelter. There was still plenty of unpacking to be done, but for now I could breathe a sigh of relief. The loons sang to us again that night and this time I gave in to their song and allowed myself to relax in our new northern home.

It was now the last day of our truck rental so we unloaded the car and drove back to Kenora to have a better look around the small city. Though it only had an official population of around fourteen thousand people that number easily doubled during the summer when all of the tourists and cottagers would flock to the camping haven. Locals would describe the event as a swarm of locusts descending to pick shelves clean in the grocery stores. The town youths would wear T-shirts with catchy phrases like, "If it's called Tourist Season, why can't we shoot them?" The two-month invasion may have been frustrating for the town regulars but the restaurant and shopping businesses that they enjoyed for the rest of the year depended on the massive influx of vacation cash. Without this yearly population boom they could say good-bye to most of the nicer restaurants and specialty shops that locals couldn't possibly support on their own for the other three seasons, so suffering through summer had gone from a hassle to a way of life. We pulled into the gas station/U-Haul dealer to settle up our bill, but when Chris brought up some of the vehicle's issues the owner just shrugged them off.

"It doesn't matter what's wrong with it," he said with a smile. "It has to go out again today!" Apparently the intermittent oil light, lack of power and kicking out of gear the odd time while going uphill were of no concern to the man who couldn't see past the dollar signs in his eyes. The truck had gotten us here so it must be good enough for the next sucker. Chris just shook his head and signed the papers to verify that we returned the vehicle "in good order", but rest assured the moving company's lax maintenance regime would soon catch up to them. Only a few years later, in 2005, multiple reports were made by both American and Canadian news agencies about the dangerous conditions of the aging U-Haul fleet, forcing them to take a serious look at fixing the vehicles or replacing them with new ones.

With that out of the way we drove to Kenora's downtown harbour front and had a proper walk-about. It was easy to see why the old trapping town turned tourist gem was a big hit during the summer months. A lot of the old architecture was nicely preserved to hold a variety of shops which included a few decent clothing stores! The surrounding lake side ambiance was enhanced by the sound of float planes taking off and landing in the background, and everything was tied together by that characteristic, northern backdrop of rocks and trees. Somehow that combination of pink and black granite formations decorated with just the right amount of jack pines made everything look better. It's no wonder that my Darling was completely smitten by our new home and I had to admit that while it was a lot of effort to go through for a teaching job, even I could handle living here.

Before returning home we had one last bit of vital business to take care of, and that was to purchase our satellite TV equipment. It hadn't occurred to us whether or not everything would even fit in our car but thankfully they had just changed over from the large, circular dishes to the newer, elliptical signal receiver which just managed to fit into the back seat. I breathed a sigh of relief once I knew it would fit, otherwise we would've had to wait a week for a technician to drive out to the reserve and complete the installation. My ideal way to wind down at the end of the day is to zone out in front of the TV, so with the denial of that simple pleasure for the past few days I was beginning to feel some symptoms of withdrawal. We made it home in time for Chris to have enough daylight to set up my digital life-blood and I was finally able to relax. It had been a while since I'd watched satellite TV so I spent the first hour channel-surfing through my new domain and getting my bearings. It was now official that everything was going to be alright.

Day number four started off normal enough but there was a knock on our door shortly after breakfast. It was one of the women who had been helping us out since we got here and she had some news of sorts; the new Principal had arrived with her husband last night and they decided that they wanted our townhouse. Chris looked a little worried about what might happen since this was my new boss making the request, but I straightened things out right away.

"I don't think so," I replied right away, remembering that she was only the messenger. "We just spent two days cleaning this place ourselves, plus we're completely moved in. If they wanted a better choice of housing then they should have arrived earlier." The woman smiled, looking relieved that there was no serious confrontation, and returned to deliver the news. From that one incident I already knew that our new Principal had never been on a reserve before, nor was she brave enough to address this situation herself. It was going to be an interesting year.

After that I gave Chris some pointers about conducting ourselves on a Native reserve. First off: don't go around trying to tell people what to do. That's kind of a general rule of politeness that everybody should follow, and one that our new Principal had already disregarded, but it's especially important in a community that feels excommunicated in their own country. If you take the time to learn how to get along with everybody then life can be so much easier. Second: don't say anything about anybody. You never know exactly who is related to who when you first set foot on a reserve, or any small community for that matter, and if you get on anybody's bad side right away then you may as well pack up and leave. You're not trying to make everybody happy, but you definitely don't want to make anyone unhappy. I learned these things from my early teaching years with husband number one. We had to figure out very quickly that the title of Principal didn't grant somebody the power to run a school *for* the community, but *with* the community, and those who don't know the difference won't succeed. I suspected that our new Principal was already headed down this path.

With the arrival of our new leader the school was officially open for us to have a look around. I was assigned to the Junior High section of the school and given the science room to teach my classes. My first order of business? That's right, cleaning the room. While it wasn't completely filthy, the room wasn't clean either. I left that task to Chris while I headed to the office to get my class info, a key for the locked storage closet, and to introduce myself to the new Principal. I didn't really want to meet her so I stalled by introducing myself to our secretary instead.

I don't remember our exact conversation but I breathed a sigh of relief when she laughed with me at my first attempt to break the ice. She was a local who had been the school secretary for a while now, so at least the year wouldn't be a complete nightmare. Few non-educators realize that the true success of a school depends on the secretary, not the Principal. A good office administrator who knows the school and the community can put a new Principal on the right track if they want to listen to the advice, but even the best Principal can't succeed if they have a terrible secretary. By now I could no longer stall my office visit without looking like I was avoiding my new boss so I bit the bullet and knocked on the door. She invited me in with a smile and I did my best not to judge her right away. She was short, very white, and French.

Without going any further I will first explain the double-edged danger of being a French Canadian outside of Quebec, at least from my experience. I find the Francophone mannerism to be a type of character enhancement that for some reason intensifies a person's personality. Kind of like being drunk, I suppose.

They can either be an enjoyable Francophone, always quick with a joke and ready to help, or an annoying Francophone who thinks being French is special in itself and therefore they do not need to have a personality of their own. I had a bad feeling that our new Principal was the latter. Our introduction was brief because she was rummaging through her desk while looking for the forms that needed to be filled out before starting the school year. The secretary didn't seem concerned and claimed that she wasn't sure what the last Principal had done with the required documents, making it clear to me that she wasn't sure if she liked her new boss. Before I realized what I was doing my experience kicked in and I informed them that everything should be in a specifically marked binder, probably on a bookshelf. I looked to a large, unmarked binder that was sitting nearby but the Principal interjected immediately.

"Oh, that's mine," she announced proudly. "Would you like to have a look?"

"Uhhh..." was all I could manage, not knowing what was going on. She quickly opened the binder and started leafing through pages of certificates, documents and letters that she had collected over the years as if it were a scrap book of every single accomplishment from her teaching career. At first I had simply thought that she was insecure about her achievements and needed to prove to everybody and anybody what she had done for the past few decades, but apparently this is what they were doing now in Ontario. A résumé was still used to get an interview and then the binder was the next step to justifying your ability to do the job. I had never heard of anything so ridiculous or unprofessional. She ended the show-and-tell with her new certificate of Administration which she was obviously very proud of. It was clear that officially being a Principal on paper made her think that she was fully qualified to run this school despite having no administrative experience as a Vice Principal. Yikes. We soon found the elusive papers and then

I helped her to understand how to properly fill them out. She expressed her gratitude for my help as I excused myself to check up on Chris.

I was greeted by the smell of Pine-Sol as I walked into the room, to which my Darling asked if I'd gotten what I needed. While I had managed to get my class list I was also told that the key for the storage closet was long gone. It was too bad since there was bound to be some science equipment in there to help me with my classes. Oh well, at least we could get the desks arranged and set up the text books now that I knew what was going on in my class.

We were just finishing up when the Principal had dropped by with her husband whom was introduced as the Vice Principal and computer teacher. I found this odd since a Vice Principal position hadn't been advertised for this school otherwise I would have applied for it. They hadn't advertised for a computer teacher either, which lead me to a conclusion that I had seen before; she wasn't the *best* candidate to apply for this position, she was probably the only one. When some people know that they're a ringer for a job like this they push it to their advantage by demanding a job for their spouse as well. I consider that sort of thing to be unscrupulous but most will agree that it's a fact of life up here in the north. I could write a few chapters about the antics that this couple used to fill their pockets for as long as they could stick it out up here, but to single them out for this type of behaviour would be unfair. Besides, this is a book about my life, not theirs.

The first day of school finally rolled around and I got to meet my new students. I introduced myself but it's always awkward for kids to meet a new teacher, especially when none of them want to be there, so I decided to lighten the mood. I walked over to the storage closet door and jiggled the locked door knob, then asked if anybody knew how to pick a lock. That got their attention. After waiting to see if this was some kind of trap one of the boys decided to give it a go. Cheering from the class began immediately with some giving him encouragement while others telling him that he didn't have a chance. He soon gave up but everybody had fun for a few minutes. Then I really got their attention.

"Who's got the biggest feet?" I asked, already knowing which boy I wanted for the task. It was obvious that we had a young giant in the room but I let the kids call him out by name. He stood up with a timid smile on his face.

"Think you can get it open?" I asked.

"Really?" He asked back, eyes wide.

"Sure!" I said. "Give it a shot."

This was no ordinary closet door. It was a full-sized metal door in a metal frame that was cemented into a cinder block wall. He walked up to it and only hesitated for a second before planting his size 13 foot squarely beside the door knob. BAM! The door didn't stand a chance. With one kick he had it open and for a moment the room was silent.

"Yeah!" Exclaimed one of his buddies. "Just like an Indian!"

The students all laughed as their friend returned to his desk grinning from ear to ear, and now that the mood was lightened I had a much easier time getting everyone to introduce themselves. After going around the room I let the kids ask me anything they wanted, knowing what one of the questions would be—had I ever taught on an Indian reserve before? I gave them a brief description of my earlier teaching days to let them know that I was no stranger to their world, and they accepted this with mild surprise. They certainly hadn't expected their first day to start like this but I think I earned the "cool teacher" status at this point. We finally got around to handing out text books before they had to move on to their next class but I was glad to have made a good impression right away.

At the end of the day the Native Studies teacher came up to me and introduced herself.

"The kids say that you've skinned a moose," she said right away as if it had been on her mind all day. I just shrugged and gave a smile, then told her what I'd told the kids except with a little more detail this time. She listened intently then nodded her head.

"Oh," she replied with a smile. "Even I haven't done that." I learned that her husband was one of the last true trappers in the community, and while she had witnessed plenty of skinning in her life she had never actually taken part in the act of skinning a moose. I could tell that I had piqued her curiosity and we went on to become close acquaintances during the next few years.

On my way out of the school I met up with the janitor, Alex, as he was getting ready to start his evening duties.

"How are you?" I asked.

"Okay." He said quickly. "It's always a good day with Jesus!"

I had met plenty of Natives in my lifetime, but none had been as enthusiastically Christian as Alex. I don't remember our exact conversation that day but we had many more from that time on. He was my age and had been raised in a Residential School but still managed to retain his heritage, including his Ojibwa language. He also confessed to having been a heavy drinker and smoker, but at the age of forty something inside of him snapped and he quit both habits cold turkey. Ever since then he had done everything he could to find his way closer to God despite not being able to read. Alex was generally shunned by the community because he refrained from the native spiritual practices such as drumming and dancing, but he was strong in the traditional ways of hunting, trapping and fishing. He loved the world that God has given us and thanked Him every day for the blessing of living off of the land.

Alex had been a large influence to my spiritual growth during our years in Kenora but he had made an even bigger impact on Chris' life. Their friendship started when Alex asked Chris if he'd like to help him with a house he was building. There was an area on reserve land where his grandfather had lived back before everyone was relocated to the current community location. It was only accessible by water, which was something that Alex liked about it, and over the next three years the two of them built the two-story house completely by hand. Lumber and materials were brought by boat, or by truck in the winter, but Alex had cut every board by hand and every nail was pounded in by hammer. They had salvaged some large, picture windows from derelict houses on the reserve and installed everything on their own. There were a few times when Alex had a couple of others to help with the big parts like raising the walls, but it was usually just the two of them heading off across the water to cut boards and pound nails for the day. For a man who couldn't read it was an impressive accomplishment.

That house was only one part of Chris and Alex's adventures on the Lake of the Woods. During our stay in the Kenora area Chris experienced more of the native traditions than most people do in a lifetime, from touring Alex's trap line in the winter to learning how to string a fishing net under a frozen lake to hauling 100-pound sturgeons into a boat and carving them up on the rock shore. One of their biggest adventures was an all-day journey by canoe that consisted of three portages in order to get to a traditional wild rice field. Chris got to be the mule for the next day, pushing through the field while

Alex knocked the rice into the boat, then it was another full day excursion to get home. Even to this day my Darling has never looked so tired, or smelled so bad, in all the years we've been together, but the pillow case full of wild rice was a definite pay-off and that was just his share of the harvest.

Despite that, I would have to say that their most memorable endeavor was when the two of them rescued a wolf from an illegal snare. Somebody had used heavy wire where they shouldn't have and a young wolf had gotten caught in the trap near the end of the winter. Alex had said that the wolf was only born that spring but she was bigger than any dog that Chris had ever seen. The poor creature had worn a rut into the ground by going back and forth while trying to escape the snare and she was completely exhausted by the time they got there. Alex held its neck down with a forked stick just in case it got a sudden burst of energy but it was so tired and so scared that Chris was able to cut the wire without it even budging. There was water nearby so they left it alone and hoped for the best, saying a prayer on their way back home. While it's hard for Chris to single out any event from those years as being the best memory, that one was definitely the most rewarding.

The second person to be most influential on Chris' and my spiritual journey was a dear friend by the name of Flo. We can thank Chris' hobby of gaming for the chance of meeting her, otherwise it's possible that we never would have crossed paths. Hidden at the end of a street, at the top of a hill, in the middle of a residential area was Flo's house out of which she had been running her hobby store for the past few decades. She was a missionary to the natives in this area before I had even been born and eventually started up her hobby shop so that the kids of Kenora would have someplace to get arts and craft supplies, amongst other things. Flo had just about anything you could want from a hobby store, from train sets to models of all sorts, both plastic and wooden, to an array of art supplies that would make any school envious. She even had an impressive collection of board games and role-playing game books along with the ever-elusive dice that were needed to play such games. What made her little operation that much more admirable was that she ran it all day long while confined to her motorized wheelchair.

At this point in her advanced age Flo's body was afflicted with many ailments. Osteoporosis had given her a pronounced hump while arthritis had set heavily into her hands; a fluid build-up in her lungs left her dependent on using an oxygen tank; whatever it was that had her confined to the wheelchair left her with almost no use of her legs; add to this the regular problems of needing glasses to see any meaningful distance and the need for a hearing aid and you have a debilitating collection of health problems that would dishearten most people. Despite all of this, Flo's mind was still as sharp as ever and she always had a smile for us when we visited.

"Hiya kids!" She would say when we came through her door. For the next three years we would fellowship together, discussing biblical matters while exchanging stories. She was always keen to hear about what was going on in our current lives while she would recollect her adventures and struggles in this same area over half a century ago. There were many times when Chris would make special trips into town just to check up on Flo if she was having more problems than usual with her health, plus he dedicated time to re-organize her two back rooms where she could no longer get to since being confined to the wheelchair. She was worried that the roof had started leaking back there, which it had, so my Darling re-arranged everything to keep her stock from being ruined while moving as much of it as possible to the front room where she would have access to it. It was rare for a week to go by when we wouldn't have dropped in on her at least once.

The relationships with Alex and Flo were enough to be grateful for, but the icing on the cake was having Winnipeg only a three-hour drive from the reserve which allowed for weekends of high-end shopping and spa treatments. Chris and I found a few favourite restaurants to have dinner at, and there were several downtown stores for him to browse through while I was at the salon. Although I would never again spoil myself as I had when living in Edmonton it was still nice to be able to leave some of my worries behind for a few days.

While I had a good feeling about being on the reserve, it became official that we were welcome at the end of October. Devil's Night, the night before Halloween, was renowned for being the night that teachers' cars got targeted by the local kids. It was usually only the non-native teachers that had to worry about this particular evening but I decided to ignore the whisperings that were floating around the school that day, as did the Principal. Besides, the car was due for a good wash anyways. Lo and behold, Chris and I awoke to a clean car the next day much to our surprise, but who do you think was out trying to wash their car on that cold, October morning? While our car had been untouched the Principal's car got the works: eggs, soap and a healthy dose of syrup, all hardened by the overnight frost.

Her husband didn't say much as we walked past on our way to the school but it was clear that it would take more than a bucket of hot water to deal with that mess. I didn't mention anything to my class that morning but some of the boys were eager to talk. Apparently some little kids were out causing mischief last night, but when they approached my car the older boys warned them against it. It would seem that I was unofficially under their protection whereas the Principal was not despite her efforts to get everybody to like her. It just goes to show that you can't fake sincerity.

For the next three years Chris and I did everything we could to support that group of kids at the high school end of the building. Community bingo was the major fund-raiser and every school group had to take turns so as not to monopolize this local event, but whenever our turn came I would make sure that I was available to give them a hand. I would find any chance I could to get them off the reserve for a day, whether by school trip or to a job fair, just so that they would have something to look forward to once in a while, but I might be remembered best for the Yu-Gi-Oh card tournaments that I held on weekends.

Yu-Gi-Oh is a collectible card game that had just come out and was very popular with kids. When I noticed them playing the game I made a point to buy an entire box of booster packs when in Winnipeg to sell back to the kids at cost instead of trying to make a profit from them. If I hadn't already been popular then that would have sealed the deal right there. Once I realized just how much the kids liked this game I would hold Saturday afternoon tournaments at the school every few months with packs of cards being the prizes. It was a small thing to most people but for them it was a huge deal and something that they always looked forward to, so imagine how it made them feel to organize a day trip to Winnipeg for a *real* Yu-Gi-Oh tournament. It was a very long day, and some people thought Chris and I were crazy to sacrifice a day of our free time for these kids, but they clearly showed their appreciation. They were the best-behaved kids in the building, and even though none of them won any big prizes they still treated the trip as a once-in-a-lifetime experience.

At the end of the first year I was faced with the question that is all too common in small community schools: Are you coming back? It's a shame that some students have to think about this every year, especially when they find a teacher that they really like, but that's one of the drawbacks to living in an isolated community. I assured everyone that Chris and I would be returning after our summer excursions. For the first half of the summer we drove down to visit Chris' family, then for the second half we drove west to visit that friend of his whom we had moved two years ago. It was during this trip when Chris could finally relate his feelings towards me as we drove through the mountains, and it was also on this trip that I overcame my fears and doubts about our relationship and married husband number three even though he was clearly my number one husband.

Our second year on the reserve was a little more interesting since there was a large teacher turnover from the previous year. The need for a new Principal was no surprise, but what wasn't expected was the chief's latest power trip. He had decreed that, starting this year, all teachers must live on the reserve. This affected the school greatly because there were five teachers driving in from Kenora every day and they weren't about to move from their homes and relocate to the reserve at the chief's say-so. The real shame was that these teachers had been here for a few years so they knew the kids and got along with them. They car-pooled for an hour each morning, and an hour to get home, because they *wanted* to be here. That is a huge asset for any isolated school. They were comfortable around the students, the local staff and the community which is always a good thing, but I don't think it was a good thing for the chief himself.

It was no secret that the reserve didn't think much of their current leader since the community's needs usually came after his own needs were satisfied. Upon his election band jobs were reallocated to his siblings and children to make his family richer while putting other band members on welfare. He had also given himself multiple jobs that would normally be allocated to several people, thus ensuring that as much band money as possible was streaming into his household. Now, it wasn't unusual for a newly-elected chief to claim some perks for himself with his newfound title, but this man was taking things to the extreme. What made matters worse was that, according to the grape vine, his father had been chief and a good leader until he passed away unexpectedly, so it was a big disappointment for his son to be the opposite. Nobody really took him seriously but he used his sons as goons to keep people afraid of him and to remind everybody who the boss was, but he had no real power over anyone who didn't live on the reserve. There was a new election coming up next year and while the commuters weren't actively against this current chief they knew that he was a joke of a leader and weren't afraid to say so in subtle ways. By making a demand which he knew these teachers wouldn't comply to he managed to get rid of them without telling them to leave, sacrificing the needs of the kids for his own selfish, insecure motives.

The new batch of recruits were naïve and unfamiliar with life on a Native reserve, and it wouldn't be a stretch to suggest that they were a little bit scared as well. It was exactly what the chief wanted. The school year itself was generally unimpressive aside from the fact that the kids directed their frustrations towards these new faces. By the time Devil's Night rolled around again they had every new teacher, and the new Principal, worried to the point that they all left the reserve to stay in Kenora overnight, returning to find that my car was just as clean as theirs. Even though they had only been here for a couple of months it was already clear that none of them would be staying on for another year.

One particularly memorable event from this year was when the windmill salesman came. A representative for a renewable energy company was making an offer to the band at a big meeting and somebody had asked me if I was going. I hadn't planned on it but I certainly didn't have anything better to do either. There was a large turnout at the community centre to hear the spiel so I just stood at the back of the crowded room and listened to what he had to say. The presentation started off by informing everybody about the increasing interest in wind energy and that this reserve was being given the opportunity to have one of those new, hi-tech wind turbines build on their land. Once it was constructed the band would be able to sell the electricity for themselves with the potential of making millions of dollars each year. This got everybody's attention. He rambled on for a bit more before concluding the information session, and while everybody saw it as a win-win situation I knew a sales pitch when I heard one.

"How much will this windmill cost?" I asked from the back of the room. I can't recall the exact figure but it was in the millions which also got everybody's attention.

"And who has to pay for this?" I continued. He could see that I was starting to ask the questions which he hoped would not come up.

"Well, the band would be responsible for paying it off," and now the murmuring started, "but the sales of the electricity would make this possible."

"Who's going to buy all of this electricity?" I think it worried him that I didn't even hesitate with my questioning. "Is *your* company going to buy it all?"

"No," he said. I could tell he didn't like me at all. "The band would be responsible for selling it."

"And how does that work? Is somebody going to help them out with that? Who's going to show them how to sell this electricity?" He didn't know what to say now.

"So really," I concluded, "you want to build a wind turbine here that *you* get paid for, then everybody here has to figure out how to sell the electricity to pay it off." Nobody spoke, but all eyes were on him as I asked my last question. "What if they can't sell it?"

What was meant to sound like a great deal was in fact a pitch to get the band to buy a multi-million dollar wind turbine without being fully aware of the details or the debt that they would incur. More importantly though was that I had been the one to act in the band's best interest, bringing up the questions that should have been asked by their leaders. I certainly wasn't planning to represent the band in this situation but I guess old habits die hard. Nobody thanked me or even mentioned it again, but that doesn't mean that nobody noticed.

At the end of the second school year our Principal was gone and we didn't have a replacement in sight. I was asked to fill in for the summer since there was a lot of work being done inside of the school during these next two month and somebody needed to overlook everything. I agreed and bought Chris a plane ticket home that year so that he could visit his family while I manned the school. It was during this month, while I was on my own, that the chief paid me a little visit. It would appear that he no longer wanted me working for the school, so he managed to get me alone and tried to fire me on the spot without any witnesses. I was taken completely by surprise but I wasn't off my guard. The fact that he was trying to intimidate me without anyone else knowing made it clear that nobody else knew. He was hoping that I would simply leave with my tail between my legs. He really didn't know me at all.

"Did you have a quorum?" I asked.

"What?" Was all he could muster, unable to believe that I wasn't obeying him.

quo·rum *noun* \ˈkwȯr-əm\
A select group: the number (as a majority) of officers or members of a body that when duly assembled is legally competent to transact business.

It was now clear that this man was simply a bully, not a leader.

"A quorum," I repeated. "You can't just fire me like this. You need to have a quorum and get the Elders to agree with you." He left without saying a word while I got in touch with the band members whom I'd gotten to know over the last two years. None of them knew about the chief's little scheme nor did any of them like it. A proper meeting was soon held where it was decided that not only could I keep my job but it would be a bad decision for Chris and I to leave. Later on the chief tried to make light of the whole thing by laughing it off and pretending that he wasn't really serious about trying to fire me.

When I finally picked up Chris at the airport I told him all about my bit of excitement. We had talked almost every day while he was visiting but I avoided telling him what was going on since he couldn't do anything about it and I didn't want to spoil his trip. Besides, it was all under control. While my Darling wasn't happy that he hadn't been able to protect me during this incident he was proud that I was able to stand my ground. Unfortunately it was becoming clear that I should probably start looking elsewhere for future employment. As much as Chris loved it here and would miss his adventures with Alex, he also knew that we couldn't stay much longer if the chief was going to make our lives difficult. In an ironic twist of fate, however, it would be me who made his life difficult for a change.

Knowing that this was going to be my last year teaching on the reserve, and possibly in Ontario, I decided to look into the teacher's pension that I had accumulated so far. I couldn't be bothered to add up the deductions from three years' worth of pay stubs but I knew the band had taken out over ten-thousand dollars since I had started here. I called the people at the Ontario Teacher's Pension to get an exact figure and found the answer to be most surprising.

"We don't have you on record." The girl told me. "In fact, there are only two names on the list for that reserve."

How's that for interesting? None of the money that was deducted for pensions was sent in, and this had been happening for a very long time. I kept quiet about my new discovery and went straight to the Kenora law offices to solicit a lawyer, but he told me that I was wasting my time. Because the band was independent from the government they were also pretty much immune to most laws. You simply can't sue a reserve for this kind of wrong-doing. Now I was mad, but I still kept quiet. If I couldn't settle this in a court room then I would have to go above the reserve's head, so I arranged to meet with the head of the area tribal council. He listened intently as I pleaded my case but he didn't jump to a solution as quickly as Chris would have liked. My hubby point-blankly accused the band of embezzling the money and suggested that it would make an interesting news article. That picked up the pace of our discussion since the tribal head certainly didn't want that kind of publicity. We resolved for me to be repaid the 'misplaced' funds in three installments, and it would be greatly appreciated if I kept quiet about this problem. I agreed that it would look very badly for the band if I told every member about this, so I settled for only telling one. It didn't take long for the rest of the community teachers to catch wind of this, and before the end of the year the band was dangerously close to losing their independent status and reverting back to being a Federally-controlled reserve.

It was also around this time that the election for chief was coming up and some of the band members were worried about a repeat of the last few years if the current chief got re-elected. Their solution? I was approached to run for chief. Right now everyone who is reading this is thinking the same thing that Chris asked—how can I run for chief if I'm not Native? The truth is that anyone can run for chief if they are sponsored by enough band and council members. This was the last thing that I was expecting, and despite it being a great honor I still needed time to think it over. To win would be a huge commitment not to mention controversial. Unless I pulled off a landslide victory, which was highly doubtful, I would be in for constant conflicts with those who didn't like the idea of me leading the band. Chris and I talked about it all night, finally deciding that I would run and we would leave it in God's hands. All of my supporters were happy about the decision, especially Alex. Flo thought that my running for chief was a complete hoot! She wasn't all that concerned with me winning, she was just glad that I was shaking things up.

Chris got right to work making my pamphlets and my election platform was the simple idea of bringing honesty to the band. While that may not seem like much to go on it was more of a jab at the man who was currently in power. My full intent was to give the band back to the people by making everyone accountable for the money that was spent. The books would be wide open for everyone to look at whenever they wanted with no more secret spending and hushed-up deals that only the chief knew about. Of course this is how a native band is supposed to be run so my ethical ideas weren't all that radical, although from what I gathered they were becoming a little uncommon in this area. Election Day finally rolled around and once the votes were tallied many people's fears came to light: the current chief was re-elected. It did not go over well.

Accusations of bribes and bought votes raced through the reserve. While it's a serious offense to accuse somebody of such a thing the stories were supported by anyone who had visited the chief's house immediately after the election. Apparently he wasn't even answering his own door but instead had trained his grandson to open the door, repeat the phrase, "No more money!", and then promptly shut the door without even bothering to see who had come to visit. It's little wonder that I received some government papers in the mail a few months later informing me, and all of the election candidates, that an investigation was being performed to address the issues of a rigged election. It turned out that not only the re-elected chief was being investigated but the two men who finished behind him had also been reported to have bought their votes. I had initially tied for fifth place out of fifteen candidates, but if you disqualified the first three candidates then I was suddenly tied for second place. Who knows what would happen with a re-election? I could very well become the first non-Native woman chief in Canada. That might have been the course I would've taken if these documents had come to me sooner, but by that time I had put the rigged election behind me and we had made a decision about our next move—Chris and I were going to live with Flo.

I felt bad for those who truly wanted a positive change, but at this point it would be easier for them to break away from their own band rather than try to save the existing one. It was clear that the majority of the reserve could be bribed or bullied into voting for a bad chief so we took it as a sign that our time there was done, and that's when Flo approached us about moving in with her so that she could claim to have live-in health care. As strong as she was in spirit and mind, Flo was always worried that the government would place her in a retirement home because of her delicate health condition. She currently had a nurse visiting on a regular basis, but it was often suggested to her that it would be much easier to provide for her needs if she were in a facility that was designed for constant medical care. Flo didn't trust the idea and was determined to do whatever possible to stay in her house, and if she could show that she no longer lived on her own then the government would have to back off. Despite everything that she had against her, I would have to say that Flo still had spunk.

The full plan was to have a massive sell-off and get rid of her stock, have the leaky roof fixed and renovate the back rooms for Chris and myself to have our own apartment. She was a little sad to close her shop after all these years, but sales had been down for a while with her business just breaking even. I could supply teach in the area until finding a permanent position and Chris would have no problem finding work once everything with the house was taken care of. The decision couldn't have come at a better time since she was experiencing some recurring issues that forced her to spend a few weeks in the hospital. While Flo was away from home Chris organized and oversaw the store closing and arranged for somebody to come and check out the roof. Everything was on track by the time the end-of-year school trip rolled around and we reassured Flo that we'd get back to it once we returned.

It was a school tradition for the senior kids to raise money throughout the year to pay for a week-long trip in June. Two adult chaperones were required to go with the ten or so kids and I had done it for the past two years already. During my first year the phys-ed teacher and I flew the kids to Calgary and then we drove up through the mountains, camped out in the West Edmonton Mall for a few days and then returned to Calgary for the flight home. The year after that one of the other teachers helped me take the kids to tour the Niagara Falls area. A last-second luggage change resulted in me leaving all of my underwear at home (Chris' fault), but it wasn't realized until later that day after a canoe-tipping accident sent me and a few other girls back to the hotel early. I had plenty of dry clothes to change into but no extra undies. Chris felt terrible when I called him that night, so the next day he arranged for a Bernard Callebaut gift basket to be sent to my room. How could I stay mad at my Darling after finding a basket of my favourite chocolate on my bed at the end of the day? For our last trip the kids had decided on the Alberta tour once again and asked specifically for Chris to be the second chaperone this time. He was touched that the kids wanted to include him and we had a grand time exploring Banff, Jasper and the mountain passage that connected them. It was a very special trip since the kids knew it would be my last, and also because I got to enjoy it with my Darling hubby. We returned from our trip with a positive outlook, only to find a message from the hospital on our answering machine. Flo had passed away during the few days we were gone.

We couldn't believe that this had happened. She seemed her usual self when we left for Alberta, so how could she now be dead? Chris phoned the hospital right away for an explanation and was told that Flo's health had simply deteriorated over the course of the week. Flo had always said that the idea of being in the hospital for too long made her nervous because she knew that she'd die there, and she had been right. We hadn't seen any indication that her condition was that severe, but perhaps Flo had been hiding her pain from us so that we wouldn't worry. Not only had we just lost a close friend but we knew that she had willed everything to the church, meaning that we were also homeless. When Chris hung up the phone I fell right to the floor and cried my heart out. I couldn't believe that so much had been taken from us in a matter of days. I cried out loud, asking God why he had let this happen. Even Chris was speechless, and he usually had an answer for everything. I had already resigned from the reserve, not that I could work under that chief for another year, so there were only a few short weeks left to find a job and a home that we could afford. Neither of those happened. What did happen was a ray of hope shining from an unexpected place.

During the recent year we had become friends with Melody, the new Gym teacher who was also leaving the reserve. She was heading back home to her mother's house and they had a finished basement apartment for rent. I wasn't keen on living in a basement but she assured me that it was only a partial basement with plenty of windows. I thanked her for the offer and said that I would have to discuss it with Chris. He felt the same as I did about living in a basement but it didn't seem like there was much of a choice at this point. Then I told him that it was in Sudbury.

Chris' only experience with Sudbury was when we were passing through on our way here. At the time there was no bypass around the city so we had to follow a hap-hazard "follow this route back to the main highway" obstacle course. We filled up at the first gas station we found, but to get back on the main road we had to navigate the U-Haul truck and trailer through a five-way intersection with multiple sets of lights and a set of train crossing gates. He learned much later that this particular collection of streets and train tracks is affectionately known as Killer's Crossing due to the number of accidents that occur each year, and that's just a touch of Sudbury's charm. After hesitating at the confusing intersection, resulting in much honking and yelling by some locals, Chris resorted to driving through a red light to get back on the main road and yelled, "If I never have to come back to this God-forsaken hick town it will be too soon!" And now it would seem that we were moving there.

Being Shaped by Hardship

One of Flo's favourite sayings was that God had a sense of humor, which was evident when considering that of all the places He could have sent us at this time, it was Sudbury. Losing Flo was an unexpected tragedy that had turned our world upside down, but in time I came to see it for what it truly was; she had been a good and faithful servant, even through the hardships, and was finally rewarded with her rest. God also needed Chris and me to move on because if we had gotten comfortable in Kenora then it's quite possible that we never would have left that beautiful place. Sudbury wasn't going to be our last stop, but it was a necessary one.

While writing this book I remembered that Chris had approached the executor of Flo's estate and requested to have her bible as something to remember her by. The woman knew that we had become a close friend and had no hesitation in giving us the small book. Written on one of the inside pages is a poem that Flo had composed almost fifty years before her death, yet it reads as if she had written it especially for me at this difficult time in my life:

God's Grace

We thank the Lord for daily food,
We thank Him for the birds that sing,
But for the rain, a different mood,
We turn our backs & curses fling.
Have we lost sight of God's great plan,
Which we may read all of our days,
Of how He made us and the rain,
Of how He with us yet still stays.
For every leaf & bird that falls,
God in His way has had the say,

So that when He upon us calls,
Stand still & listen, do not stray.
He has a reason for all things,
We here on Earth cannot conceive,
Until before the throne He brings,
And for our sins shall we then grieve.
Unless we now accept God's gift,
Of Life Eternal through his son,
If we say yes our burden lifts,
And Life Eternal we have won.

~ Flo MacKay, Aug/55

One of my greatest challenges is to remember God's plan during the rainy days of life. Sometimes I feel that I've had more than my fair share of hardship, but then I suppose anybody reading this book could say the same thing for themselves. Hardship is a personal journey that shouldn't be compared to anyone else's life. There are many references in the Bible about God being the potter and we being the clay:

Woe unto him that striveth with his Maker! Let the potsherd strive with the potsherds of the earth. Shall the clay say to him that fashioneth it, What makest thou? or thy work, He hath no hands? ~ Isaiah 45:9

While a little obscure, this verse directly refers to people who want to shape their own lives. The idea that we know how our life should go, that we know best, is related to the clay telling the potter how it should be formed. We all imagine a splendid life for ourselves but none of us want to go through the pains of being squeezed and shaped on the spinning wheel. We can't become a ceramic work of art without going through the time and discomfort of getting there, not to mention the time in the kiln! In truth, if we avoid the trials and tribulations of God's plan to shape us then we wouldn't be much to look at when finished. We want to end out lives as the tall, elegant vase with the intricate detail and fancy glazing, but this takes pounding to soften the clay, then the many stages it takes to finally put us to shape, and don't forget the time in the fire to make our form strong and our finishing glaze shine. By avoiding all of that we barely have the potential to become the simple, air-dried bowl or ashtray that children bring home from school, only to get broken from the first bump.

The master potter sees the potential in each lump of clay and strives to bring out the best from such a basic material. I had been resisting this process for most of my adult life and it was now time to make up for that. I had to quit being that difficult, resentful lump of clay and learn how to go with the flow and trust in the potter's hands, but at least I wasn't alone any more. Chris saw the potential in me, and while it wasn't his job to shape me he did his best to encourage me through the hard times. I knew that it wouldn't be an easy process but I was starting to realize that the more I resisted the longer it would take.

Chapter Sixteen

Into the Valley of Darkness

Considering the last-minute nature of our move it was a bit of a miracle that we could get a full-sized U-Haul and car trailer at such short notice. We took it as a positive sign that we were doing the right thing even though we were still unsure about it. Packing up the house wasn't a huge ordeal since we had only unpacked the necessities three years ago. Most of our things were still boxed away in the basement so it was just a matter of moving it all up the stairs and out the door. Hauling my life around the country in cardboard boxes was getting to be tiring, but that's the price a girl pays for having an extensive wardrobe. Alex had shown up to give us a hand and by noon we were loaded and ready to roll. I could tell that Chris felt like he was leaving behind his best friend but our time here was done. It was time to move on.

Our goal for the day was to reach Thunder Bay which we managed with plenty of daylight to spare. We could have gone on for a few hours more but the road ahead was uncharted territory for us. Instead of taking the same hilly route which had brought us here we were going to try a different way. Everybody we had talked to told us that the truckers take the number 11 highway to avoid the scenic part of Ontario that had tried our patience three years ago. It looped north around the worst of that treacherous terrain and was relatively flat for the entire way. It was also relatively sparse where human settlement was concerned so we decided to tackle that stretch non-stop on the second day. We called it an early night and awoke just as early the next day to get a head start on what we knew would be a very long drive. The town of Nipigon was two hours away where we would be turning off of the main highway to take the road less traveled.

Driving on a flat highway can be a little boring but it allows you to enjoy the scenery that you come across. Shortly after turning onto Highway 11 we skirted around the small mountain range that formed the northern shore of Lake Superior. It was a lot easier to appreciate the rustic beauty from down here as opposed to when Chris was cursing the roller coaster ride over top of them. We rounded a bend in the road and came to some of the most majestic cliffs that this area had to offer. The dark granite loomed ahead in the early morning light, green with age and as straight as a skyscraper, their tops lost in the low clouds. As the cliffs passed by on our right it felt like we were passing through a mythic gateway, leaving the region of rock behind us and entering a land of trees. Lots and lots of trees. About eight hours' worth of trees to be precise. We only stopped once for gas in the logging town of Hearst because it is pretty much the only town to stop at along that road aside from Kapuskasing. It seemed like the kind of place where somebody would live if they wanted to disappear for a while.

Late in the afternoon we finally broke the monotony and turned south, and by dinner time we were in Timmins, the last big population center before Sudbury. I was so happy that we ended up driving past the mall. I kid you not; without trying to sound blasphemous I honestly thanked God that Timmins had a shopping mall. We parked our rig and went inside to walk around for an hour, grabbing a meal at the food court before calling Mel and letting her know where we were.

She was concerned that we weren't closer and said that she'd set up an air mattress for us since it would be too late to unpack anything by the time we got there, but I told her not to worry about it since our bed was the last thing we had put on the truck. We were only three-hundred kilometers away and should be there in no time, but that was before I knew that the highway between the two cities was one of the worst I had been on. To call it a highway was being generous since the single lane roadway was barely wide enough for our truck and trailer. Chris was driving off of the crumbling shoulder in places to avoid oncoming traffic. Over four hours later we had finally arrived at our new home, safe but severely rattled.

It was after eleven o'clock at night by the time we parked in the driveway and were greeted by Mel and her mother, Mary-Joyce. We took a quick tour of the apartment and had to agree that it was as nice as you can get with basement living, but best of all it was clean. Mel had even set up the air mattress despite my earlier protest, for which I was very grateful at this point. We got the cats set up in their new home and called it a night.

Despite the spacious accommodations of our new apartment we were left with a pile of boxes that had no home. Since we also had no dining set the boxes lived on that part of the floor until I could figure out what to do with them. It wasn't until Chris took a careful look at what was written on their sides that a solution presented itself.

"Tupperware?" He asked, almost sounding surprised. Then he gave me a "Why are we hauling boxes of Tupperware around?" look, to which I really had no answer. In my Edmonton packing frenzy I had boxed everything and anything I could until

I ran out of time, and it stood to reason that if I hadn't needed it after four years then I probably didn't need it at all. I was having trouble letting go of that part of my life but it was time to take a hard look at what I really needed and what I could let go of. I asked Mel if she thought I'd have any success with a yard sale.

"Are you kidding me?" She responded in a way that only Mel could. "It's like a national sport around here. They can't get enough of yard sales."

So it was decided—I would start to lighten the load. Mind you it was like pulling the Band-Aid off very slowly, but it was a start. We didn't get rid of all the extra boxes but I managed to clear the space on the floor and redistribute the leftovers. We didn't even make enough money to pay for the fuel it cost us to get here, but in the grand scheme of things I had made an enormous step away from my past. All that was left now was to find a teaching job and get on with my life.

It turned out that Sudbury had four school boards: French, Catholic, French Catholic and English. It also turned out that Sudbury was *very* French. Yippee. Since I was neither French nor Catholic I was limited to the last school board on the list, and their cut-off date for applying for any job at all was back in June. Of course it was. I would have to wait until February before being graced with the privilege of applying for any type of teaching job. I'd only been here a week and I hated this city already. Thankfully we had some savings, and Sudbury had just built a Silver City movie complex plus an outlet mall with a Starbucks, so I did my best to enjoy a bit of the summer before going into full panic mode. My first order of business was to do something that I'd never had to do before, which was to apply for unemployment benefits. This was an all-time low for me, having to resort to social assistance so that I could pay rent, but at least I knew that it would be temporary.

Thank God that Chris found work almost immediately. He had felt drawn to a company's advertisement for hiring school bus drivers, and what started off as a part-time job driving a school bus soon became a full-time job working in the garage that maintained those same buses. They needed a shop attendant which was somebody who did everything around the shop that the mechanics didn't do. While it included the menial tasks of sweeping up after the mechanics and fueling the school buses in any weather, it also required him to maintain the basic shop needs such as re-stocking and maintaining anything that wasn't driven in for repairs. It started off as a simple job but my hubby tackled it with the motto that the only shame in a simple job is not being able to do it well. It was shift work, it was dirty work, it could be exhausting and frustrating work at times, but he was always grateful for that work and the steady pay cheque that came with it.

Over the next several years he gained many skills pertaining to basic mechanics and metal fabrication, such as welding and using cutting torches, and despite the occasional complaints when he'd had a bad day I knew he liked his job. I think what made that possible was the group of people whom he worked with. Though they could be a rough bunch at times it was unusual if he didn't come home with a story about one of those guys which he always told with a smile on his face.

For the next few months I felt like a complete failure but it didn't bother Chris to live pay cheque to pay cheque. He'd claim that God would always make sure we had enough. Not too much in case we felt that we didn't need Him any longer, but not too little so that we were struggling. It was a true test of faith and for me it was a very hard test indeed. Mel had found herself another teaching job up north and was gone until Christmas but Mary-Joyce knew that I was stuck at home for a while and asked me if I'd like to work with her. She had a little part-time job handing out samples at major outlet stores and had asked her boss if she needed any extra workers. It was only a few hours of minimum wage but how could I turn down such a thoughtful gesture? Talk about humble beginnings. Just a few years ago I was a major player in the INAC government offices, and I probably could've climbed higher on that corporate ladder if I hadn't quit the job for reasons that we won't go back into, and now I was handing out candy samples while wearing a red and yellow stripped apron and the matching elf hat to boot! I still have a picture of me in that outfit as a constant reminder of what can happen when we rely on our own faulty wisdom instead of letting God direct our lives.

It was during this year, when Mel was away, that Mary-Joyce and I became close friends. While I had initially seen my unemployment as a position of failure it would turn out that I may have been kept home so that I could be of better use. Aside from our occasional stints as product distribution associates there were a few times that MJ had become ill and I was able to drive her to the doctor's office. It may seem like a small thing from the sidelines but from a sick person's point of view it can be a huge deal. Once winter was done and springtime was beginning to blossom she had decided that she needed to sell the house and move into something more manageable for Mel and herself. House shopping entailed a lot of driving that MJ wasn't up for so I willingly became her touring buddy and roamed the area with her in search of a more suitable abode. We used her car so it didn't cost me anything and she would often treat me to lunch at an interesting restaurant that I never would have taken myself to. I didn't mind the change of pace. It was time well spent that couldn't be equated to a dollars per hour figure. I was starting to see that making money wasn't the be-all and end-all which was a foreign concept to me.

In February I was finally able to apply for a teaching position. After submitting my résumé and getting an interview I felt pretty good until I walked through the waiting room door. It was full of young, inexperienced (and inexpensive) teachers, and everybody had one of those ridiculous binders on their laps. I was easily the applicant with the largest price tag, but at least I looked the part as well. The room was quiet except for the sound of pages flipping back and forth as everybody tried to look interested in their own accomplishments. I found out later that this *portfolio* was the latest brain child of the education industry.

All new teachers were encouraged to keep an on-going collection of their endeavors, proving once again that the people training these kids weren't in touch with the actual teaching world. It would take hours to go through a single applicant's binder and verify that everything was legit. Time only warranted a casual glance at best during an interview, and how long do you think it took before those doing the interview weren't even looking at the pages as they flipped through them?

It was finally my turn and I'm not sure if it was a look of surprise or a sense of relief that they gave me when I walked in empty-handed. The interview consisted of a standard set of questions but I know now that these questions are only a formality. With the shaky condition of education budgets these days and everyone crying poor my experience put me out of everybody's price range. My single salary would pay for two new teachers, so even if I'd entered the room juggling fire while walking on water I didn't really have a chance. I did, however, get a letter in the mail informing me that I would be placed on the substitute teaching list for next year. I *really* hated this city.

By the month of May, MJ and Mel had found a house more to their liking out on Manitoulin Island, two hours away, while Chris and I had found ourselves a trailer to rent on the outskirts of Sudbury. Normally we wouldn't have even considered moving to a trailer park but this one was a bit different. Unlike the crowded trailer parks that you usually see on television sitcoms, this was only a single row of trailers set back from the highway. Most of the tenants were retirees, so it was quiet, and this particular trailer was at the end of the row on an extra-wide lot. Because of the way it was situated we had nobody directly beside us on either side and nothing but forest behind us. The trailer itself was only a few years old with three bedrooms and a large deck out front. As far as trailers go, this one was a winner. Once we saw it for ourselves we had no reservations about moving in. Add the fact that Chris' boss let him have one of the older mini-buses for the weekend, allowing us to move for free, and it was quite possibly the best moving experience I've ever had. In fact, I liked that little trailer so much that I started to feel happy about my life once again. Not extremely happy, but I could see that my new life with Chris was slowly getting better. Of course we all know what happens when Annie starts to feel happy, don't we? That's right! Something bad is about to happen.

It wasn't long after we moved into our lovely new home that I got a letter from ex-husband number one. He was claiming that I was $30,000 in arrears for child support and was taking me to court. The claim itself was utterly preposterous since my son had been living with my parents for the past four years at his own choosing, but he had moved back to Saskatchewan last summer so my ex was sniffing around for more money. The joke was on him since I hadn't been working since my son moved back there but I would still have to prove everything in court. My anxiety levels were at an all-time high as I was being forced to re-live everything that man had put me through so long ago, but at least I had Chris to help me through it this time. Once I had calmed down from reading that letter my Darling just shook his head and looked at me.

"How you managed to make it this far and still look so good is a bloody miracle." Then he took my hand and assured me that we'd get through it. I gave him a weak smile and hoped that he was right.

Since we only had one car we would have to deal with this while working around my hubby's work schedule. He had alternating shifts, working mornings one week and evenings the other, so going downtown to the courthouse was only possible when he was working the evening shift. This meant that he'd work until midnight each day, then we'd get up early, drive for a half-hour to the courthouse, talk to the free lawyer on duty, fill out paperwork, then get me home so that he could drive all the way back to the city to start his three o'clock shift. By the end of the week he'd be a bit edgy when grocery shopping was added to the list but he never blamed me for all of the trouble. Our saving grace was my legal training in mediation which I used extensively when working for the government. I knew *what* needed to be done, allowing me to do my own paperwork and represent myself, but family law wasn't my specialty so it wasn't an easy task.

As we were nearing the trial date I met the lawyer who was representing my ex. I forget exactly why we met but she informed me that he had retained her to be his representative, to which I replied that I would be representing myself. She seemed nice so I asked her if she had actually gotten her retaining fee before accepting the job. She admitted that he hadn't paid her yet and I just bit my tongue while quietly wishing her luck in that department. When the trial date finally came she approached us and let me know that my ex hadn't paid her at all. Why was I not surprised? Not only did my class act of an ex-husband jilt this lawyer but she made sure to tell the judge how he had misled her. That set the tone for my report that his claim for child support arrears was bogus since our son hadn't been living with either of us during those years and I had been unemployed since last July.

The judge was quiet for a minute then dismissed the case, adding only that I should make sure to address this matter again once I was employed. I just smiled and promised him that I would even though I could tell by the look on his face that he really didn't care if I ever sent some money to the man who had so casually wasted everybody's time except for his own. I made sure to thank the lawyer for her part in this since she wasn't obligated to do anything for me and she responded by saying that she had been more than happy to do it. Another trial of my life was over so Chris and I celebrated our victory with a trip to Starbucks before he had to whisk me back home and get to work.

It was also around this time that another burden had been lifted from me. My seven year sentence was finally over and the bankruptcy blemish was removed from my credit rating. How was I going to celebrate this personal milestone? Why, the same way that any credit-deprived woman would: I was getting my own credit card. Up until now I had only been allowed to have a secondary card on Chris' Visa but I was determined to become an independent credit card holder once again. I'd gotten one of those junk mail bank promotions inviting me to call in and get my own card. The process would only take minutes, so they claim, and this was just as good a time as any as far as I was concerned. I made the call, got put on hold, then spoke to a polite young man about setting up my very own credit card with them. I don't recall the exact conversation, but it went something like this:

"Ma'am, there's a problem with your credit application."

"What's that?" I asked. Perhaps I was a bit premature with this and the bankruptcy wasn't quite done.

"It shows that you were in arrears for thirty-thousand dollars." He replied.

"No, that's wrong." I responded. "That was a false claim and it's been dismissed."

"Oh, it shows that it's been paid in full," he continued, "but the fact that you were in arrears in the first place is a bit of a red flag."

It turns out that even though my ex's claim was unfounded the arrears would not be immediately removed from my credit rating but instead show that it had been paid in full. How long would this new smear to my name be in effect? I think you know the answer to that: seven years. Even though he didn't get what he wanted he still managed to leave me with some lingering damage. The words that I had for my ex-husband at this point cannot be printed on these pages. Once again I will say that my only comfort, no matter how un-Christian it may be, is that his life choices have driven him to be a very unhappy and insecure man.

While the arrears was definitely a bad thing to have on my record it was not as bad as the bankruptcy. By using my secondary cards exclusively from now on instead of using Chris' I would be able to build up a credit rating normally, but that red flag would still be there as a warning that I was some sort of risk. It seemed that no matter how hard I tried to leave my past behind it had a way of latching on, forcing me to drag it along. It's little wonder that I was soon stricken with a life-changing ailment.

I distinctly remember it being a Saturday morning because Chris was home. It was a beautiful, sunny morning, we had just finished breakfast, I was mulling over my most recent tribulations of life, and then I thought I was having a heart attack. The pain that was suddenly building in my chest was immense and before I knew it Chris had me in the car and we were zipping into town. I couldn't even sit still in my seat! I removed the seat belt and was on my knees while clutching at my chest, which is not a safe thing to do when travelling down the highway at a hundred clicks. My Darling was worried but he also managed to stay calm and asked exactly what I was feeling. Maybe it was hopeful denial, but he insisted that it wasn't my heart and more likely to be anxiety. We kept on driving as he tried to calm me down, but instead of going to the hospital he instead took me to the health food store.

The worst of it had passed by the time we got there and we asked the store owner what he had for my problem. This was one of my favourite stores in Sudbury and I had come to realize that the owner was a very knowledgeable man whom I trusted more than any doctor. He listened to my description of what I was feeling and he suspected that I was suffering from sort of acid reflux. He recommended a few different ways to treat it and we were soon heading home with several natural remedies to reduce stomach acidity and activity.

I immediately started researching my problem in detail and tried just about everything that I could, from cherry juice to freshly juiced ginger root concoctions. While everything helped a little bit, nothing was solving the problem. Some days would be good, but on most days I was unable to perform the most menial task without having to pause until the burning sensation subsided. I was unable to climb a large staircase without stopping at every landing, and on the bad days I wouldn't even be able to walk from our parked car to the store we were shopping at. I resorted to chewing on Gaviscon tablets several times a day and when I finally decided to seek medical help it was no surprise that doctors only wanted to prescribe the latest prescription antacids which were no better than anything I was already trying for myself. There was little doubt that my problem was stress-related, but stopping me from worrying about everything under the sun was seemingly impossible. I felt that I had become an invalid without even knowing why.

We had only been living in our new trailer for a few months and I already felt completely useless. Thankfully, when September rolled around, my Darling was able to remedy that. It turned out that his company was suddenly in need of a school bus driver for a route that ran through our distant edge of town and he knew that I was perfect for the job. There was enough room for us to park the bus at our new home so all I'd have to do was take the company's training course to upgrade my driver's licence. It was a two week course, and the driver was needed immediately, so Chris also took on the route until my training was complete. It was a little rough for him to do the morning run when working evenings but he knew it was temporary. His boss was very happy with the arrangement since it solved a problem for him and I was happy that I'd feel useful once again.

It was during this time that I finally got to know Jeannette. She was the lead instructor for school bus training and had trained Chris a year ago. When she realized that Chris was Christian they formed a bond of fellowship, though it wasn't unusual for anybody to get along with her. She was the heart of the training program and there were very few drivers who didn't adore this woman by the time their session was done. Chris had mentioned her several times before we met briefly at the company Christmas party, and he had helped her through some parts of the bible that are vague to many people. Once she knew that I was coming for training she couldn't wait.

Jeannette and I were of a kindred spirit; young at heart and almost mystically ageless from the outside. She was friendly and cheerful by nature, so being able to see her on a regular basis for the next little while was a spiritual recharge for me. We managed to spend some lunches together when we'd talk about everything *but* school bus driving and it was refreshing to finally connect with such a genuine individual. I truly believe that God was working through Jeannette at this point in my life, and while I wouldn't see her much after training was finished it was exactly what I needed to break out of my slump. It's amazing how a bit of positive energy could offset everything that I was going through.

Of all the careers that I would have expected for myself, school bus driver wasn't on the list. Nevertheless it was a small step to regaining my self-confidence. I had my own pay cheque once again, I felt like I had some independence with my new set of wheels, even if it was bright yellow and forty feet long, plus I would stop by to see my Darling when I needed to fuel up my bus and that was probably the best part. At first I wondered if I was bothering him when I visited, in case he was busy doing other work, but he put an end to that worry right away. He assured me that no matter what he was doing, having me drive in for fuel was always the best part of his day. It sounds like a mooshy line from a romance movie but no matter what kind of day he was having it always put a smile on his face when I showed up. He would greet me with a "Hello my SweetHeart!" not caring if any of the guys could hear. The genuine sincerity in his eyes is something that can never be faked, and I would leave for home feeling like the luckiest girl around.

I had a few adventures that year while driving my bus (remember that I can't read a map), but the most significant event was finding our next home. There was this small, secluded house that I would pass every day which had a special feel to it. It was a few hundred feet away from the road and its spacious yard was surrounded by trees and rock. I told Chris about it one day and he remembered it from the time when he had driven the route. He also thought that it was a perfect, little house for some reason, but that was the last we talked about it until a few months later when I saw that it was for sale. It was the end of my afternoon run and on my way past I saw a man putting up one of those hardware store For Sale signs on the front porch. Chris was on day shift that week so he was home before me, and I couldn't wait to tell him. It was only a few kilometers away from our trailer so he hopped into the car and drove right over. It turned out that the owner had bought the house with the intention of fixing it up but suddenly ran into hard times. He needed to sell the house and the acre of land as quickly as possible for forty-five thousand dollars which was something that even we could manage.

We went back the next day to have a look inside. It was basic, and it was January so everything outside was covered in snow, but it had potential. We went home to talk about it and Chris could see that I wasn't too thrilled with the inside of the house. It had too many walls for such a small house and the kitchen was in the wrong spot. It was on the side of the house where it looked out onto the gravel driveway through a small window when everybody knows that the kitchen should look out onto the yard.

"If the kitchen were on the other side of the house, where the large bedroom was, then it would be perfect," I said, thinking out loud.

"Well," my hubby replied, "why don't I move the kitchen then?"

"Really?" I asked. I wasn't sure if he was being sarcastic.

"Sure!" He said, then thought about it for a few seconds more. "I'll knock out those walls, put up a few posts and make the whole thing open concept." I just looked at him.

"That sounds like a lot of work." I had a hard time taking him seriously. "You're going to move the entire kitchen to the other side of the house? You could do that?" He just looked at me and smiled.

"I'd do it for you."

We talked and planned for the rest of the night, making sure that it was a realistic dream. If we took possession a month early then Chris could get the renovations done before moving in, and with such a small mortgage we would be able to afford a loan to pay for everything. It seemed too good to be true but I took a chance and dared to dream

The next day we hit the bank for a mortgage and filled out all of the paperwork. I decided to keep my name off of anything since we didn't want any red flags popping up during the credit check. If we couldn't make this happen on Chris' wages then we'd call it off. About a week went by with no news, so Chris called to leave a message with the agent. This went on for a few weeks and it was looking like we didn't make the cut, so Chris left a final message asking her to call us whether it was good news or bad. Shortly after that the phone rang. The agent had returned every one of our calls and left her own message, and she didn't understand why we weren't getting them until this day when somebody picked up the phone; the old lady at the other end told her that a "Chris" didn't live there. She'd been dialing the number incorrectly all this time and only just figured it out. She had been trying to tell us that we were approved for the financing and could come in any time to finalize the paperwork. I couldn't believe that Chris was buying me my own little house.

Understanding Faith

Hebrews 11:1 states: *Now faith is the substance of things hoped for, the evidence of things not seen.* To break this down to its most basic meaning: only by believing that something *will* happen *can* it happen. After moving to Sudbury my faith in God was at an all-time low but Chris had never given up. He had faith that

God was working in our lives and by looking back it's hard to argue. His simple, part-time job led to a full-time job; the full time job led to my part-time job; my part-time job led to a beautiful house that we could unexpectedly afford. Chris didn't know *how* things were going to go well for us, but in less than two years we went from being jobless to buying our own house. If somebody had told me that was going to happen I never would have believed them, especially if they had said it would all stem from a part-time bus driving job. In addition to our own lives God had paired us up with Jeannette. Our fellowship and friendship allowed us to support each other during the rough patches which is also something that I never would have expected.

Faith is the hardest path to travel for somebody like me because the key element to faith, as mentioned in the above verse, is hope. I was fifty years old now, and this was the checklist that went through my head almost every day:

- I'd had two divorces and lost everything to my name both times.
- I'd had my son taken from me twice, and when he finally came to be with me I failed to give him a stable home. It's no wonder he thought he'd be better off with my parents.
- I'd suffered through seven years of bankruptcy shame only to be burdened with another seven years of bad credit, neither of which were my fault in the first place.
- My health was deteriorating to the point that I couldn't be physically active at all.
- I was married to wonderful, younger man who loved me like no other, yet I felt like I had nothing left to offer. I considered myself to be a burden in his life.

I'd worked hard for the past thirty years, and did a damned good job at it as far as I was concerned, but it all seemed to be for nothing. There was no reward or respect for everything I had done and been through. All I had was a part-time job driving a school bus. I should be planning the retirement which I'd been working so hard for but I always managed to end up with nothing. Right now the prospect of any retirement was zilch. I was destined to muddle through the rest of my life taking piecemeal work and hoping for the best, but the honest truth was that I had no more hope in me. I didn't dare to hope for anything since it would only get taken away sooner or later. I had been beaten down too many times and fought severe depression every day, and it made me feel even worse that I couldn't be happy around Chris. There were moments when I could put on a brave face for him and pretend to be happy, but how could I possibly have faith? I did my best not to blame God for all of my downfalls but I certainly wasn't praising Him either. It's a good thing that my Darling had faith because he would need to have enough for the both of us.

Chapter Seventeen

Green Acres

Anybody who has renovated a house knows that it never goes according to plan, and my hubby had never renovated a house before. His troubles weren't from lack of experience, just the unexpected surprises that he found along the way. The areas that he thought could be covered up or patched ended up needing to be completely removed, so in order to do the kitchen properly the walls, ceiling and floor were completely gutted. We moved in to a half-finished house, but the end result was the most beautiful and cozy little home that I could have hoped for because it was everything that I had asked for. Please bear with me while I gush about the perfect country home that my Darling hubby made for me.

The kitchen had a wide, natural plank floor with a white-washed, tongue & groove plank ceiling; oak cupboards had come with the house but I got to choose new counter tops and one of those black, granite sinks; two decorative wood posts replaced the wall that separated the new kitchen from the living room; our bedroom was directly off of the living room, separated by double doors, and one entire wall was converted to a custom, double-tiered closet that held a huge portion of my wardrobe along with a full-length, extra deep shelf for most of my shoes; the bathroom was gutted and completely redone around the original, antique claw foot tub with dark, hardwood flooring and a marble top vanity; the back room, which was also the main entry, was converted into my laundry area complete with linen cupboards. I got the stainless steel, high-efficiency clothes washer of my dreams and a new clothes line out in the yard to hang my laundry in the fresh, country air; we ripped out the baseboard heaters and replaced them with a single, propane space heater and a decorative, cast iron wood stove; but most of all I loved the back porch.

At the back of the house was an 8' x 10' covered porch that had seen better days. The roof was rotten to the point of caving in and the screening was ripped to shreds. Not only did my Darling re-roof and re-screen the porch but he also ripped off the yellow, vinyl siding from the two walls and replaced it with some barn board that he had gotten his hands on. While doing this he found that an old window into our new kitchen had been covered up, so instead of doing the same he installed a large, glass window that he scrounged from somewhere else and I picked out some decorative, metal shutters that looked like miniature gates. The end result was the most serene and relaxing spot that anyone could hope for, completely protected from the rain and bugs while also being surrounded by the natural elements of the yard. Behind the house was a massive rock face, which Sudburians refer to as mountains, with plenty of mature birch and spruce growing at the base. If not for the occasional vehicle traveling past us on the secondary highway out front then you could think that you were the only people for miles around. Sitting out on that porch could be the answer to anyone's problems, whether during morning coffee or sitting under the stars.

Chris was also an experienced landscaper which he had learned over the summers during his college years. The front garden was cleaned up and expanded with a large rock border, plus he brought in a tree spade to move a bunch of evergreens around. For some odd reason the original owners had planted a small forest at the south side of the house which would have soon grown to be a green wall that blocked out the winter sun. He found somebody with the equipment to relocate the ten-foot high trees all along the fence line at the front of the property with the two largest spruce trees on either side of the lane way entrance. He had even gone so far as to make me a Jumping Jack garden at the beginning of the driveway. When spring arrived and I realized that Violas were growing wild in the lawn (which Chris insisted was not a lawn but a meadow that was continually mowed flat), I mentioned that they were one of my favourite flowers. From that moment on my Darling transplanted every one he found into a couple of large pots and then re-planted those into the new garden the following spring. The result was a large bed that was overflowing with my favourite violet and yellow flower. The entire transformation took a few years but there was no doubt that Chris had taken a diamond in the rough and polished it up especially for me. I still had mixed feelings about the city of Sudbury, but I simply loved my new home.

Despite the apparent turn of events I was unwilling to put my complete trust in God though it would have been foolish for me to ignore the signs that He was indeed working in our lives. Soon after moving into the house I got the chance to fill in for a maternity leave. The teaching position was at a correctional institute, which may be why nobody else wanted it, but I didn't mind. The kids had standard outfits that were similar to what prisoners wore, and there were guards to deal with them if anything happened, but I didn't have any problems for the few months that I was there. In fact I would have been more than happy to keep the position as a permanent job but that wasn't meant to be. Still, getting my full teacher's salary for five months was a real bonus which allowed us to finance a second car. It would have to be used, of course, and my request for it being owned by neither a smoker nor pet owner narrowed the options, but we managed to find a '98 Toyota Corolla in pristine condition. To this day I can safely say that my little car has rarely let me down.

With the end of the school year came summer and a surprising new discovery with our home. The entire region around Sudbury is known for its bounty of blueberries, and when Chris went for a wander on our little mountain out back he found it to be covered with blueberry bushes. He was busy enough around the house but with this new discovery he would be up on that rock almost every day and return an hour later with a small pail full of the freshest wild berries you'll ever have. The growing season was only a couple of months long, but for those two months we ate blueberries by the handful until our poop was black. "Just another gift from God" he would say. I wouldn't get to enjoy this natural bounty for the entire summer since I had been hired for another teaching job, but this one would come with a test of faith.

A reserve on nearby Manitoulin Island was looking for somebody with Native experience and curriculum development experience, both for which I was qualified. I would be able to earn my full teaching salary for a year but it was two hours away. I would have to live on the island during the week and only see Chris on weekends. It wasn't that hard of a decision to make but it was a bit harder to live with. I managed to find somebody with a room to rent so it didn't cost an arm and a leg to live there, and the two hour drive was scenic enough to be enjoyable when the weather was good. I would leave bright and early on Monday mornings and be home by dinner time on Friday. It was a long five days living away from my home and my hubby, and by the time Friday afternoon rolled around there wasn't anything that could keep me on that island even though the devil gave it his best shot.

Winter driving could be especially bad in the north, and on one particular Friday the worst storm of the season was rearing its ugly head. I prayed that it would hold off until I got home but I guess I couldn't expect special treatment all of the time. By noon I had heard that the highway off of the island was closed due to the severity of the weather conditions. By the time school was over the storm hadn't let up but I still headed for home in denial. I couldn't stand the thought of being snowed in on this island for the weekend, and that part of the highway was an hour away so I prayed that it would be re-opened by the time I reached it. Everybody thought I was nuts to drive in this storm and after a scary drive to the edge of the island I was wondering if they were right. The town of Little Current was the island's gateway with an antique, iron bridge being my sole means of escape. I could get a hotel room if there were no other choice, so I left it up to God. If He wanted to keep me here then the road would still be closed, but if the officer ahead of me let me pass then He would have to get me home. I rolled down my window as he walked over to my car.

"Is the highway open?" I yelled over the wind.

"We just re-opened it," he shouted back while looking over my vehicle. "You're no leaving in THAT?" It wasn't what he saw that bothered him, it's what he *didn't* see. My little car had no four-wheel drive, no chains on the tires, not to mention no winter tires. "You may as well be driving a metal coffin!"

I thanked him for the warning and headed into the blizzard before the fear could set in. My wipers were covered in ice, my stomach was in knots and I could feel the snow packed up into my wheel wells with every bump I hit. I was popping

Gaviscons like breath mints to keep the burning down to a minimum and I prayed the whole way home. It took almost twice as long to reach Sudbury but I had never felt so relieved when out of the dark I saw the sign for Chris' work.

He was on the evening shift and had been worried about me for hours. The garage where he worked was on the main road through town so I always dropped by on my way home from the island. Being almost two hours behind schedule had made him fear the worst so the smile I got on this visit was extra big. To get me out of the snow he brought me directly into the garage where I was the center of attention for a few minutes. The guys couldn't believe that I had driven from the island in this storm and a few of them helped Chris to completely de-ice my Corolla. Water hoses and air hoses made short work of the blizzard's frozen grip while my Darling put new winter wipers on my car and re-filled my washer fluid. For five minutes I had my very own pit crew without needing to leave my car. I was invited in for coffee but I just wanted to get home so they opened the garage door once more while my hubby stole a kiss and said that he'd see me soon.

The remainder of my drive was a walk in the park compared to what I'd been through, and before I knew it I was in my own driveway. The cats greeted me as I came through the door but this time their meows felt extra special. There were still some hot coals in the wood stove so I tossed on some fresh logs, got into my jammies and crashed on the couch. The wind howled as the fire crackled and I washed away the threat of the storm with blissful satellite TV.

It turned out that I wouldn't need to endure those long drives for much longer. By the middle of February my boss informed me that they had suddenly run out of money and would no longer need my services. It would appear that the contract I had signed to be employed until the end of June was merely a formality. Remembering from my Kenora experience that reserves are pretty much immune to legal obligations I decided to go a different route to extend my employment. In a politically correct way I informed my boss that there were two students who were very close to obtaining their school credits and the band was going to pay me for two more weeks so that I could help them complete what they'd been working towards all year. I don't think she liked being told what to do but she also knew that I was right. Students should never suffer just because the people running the show have mismanaged their funds and that goes for all school boards, not just the Natives. If it were the upper management who were first to be affected by budget shortfalls then perhaps they would do a better job of allocating the financial resources that they are responsible for.

There's an old saying: when one door shuts, another opens. Not having to spend my weeks on the island any longer gave me the opportunity to make a life-changing decision and find a doctor who knew that my stomach problem wouldn't be solved with pills. It just so happened that this doctor was the foremost leader in the field of gastroesophageal reflux disease, and he happened to practice in Sudbury.

After my diagnostic session I was outfitted with a device to detect how sever my condition was. A tiny sensor on the end of a wire was fed through my nose and down my throat until it was at the lower esophageal sphincter, which is the flap just above the stomach. If the flap wasn't working properly then this would detect it. The wire was plugged into a small data recorder that I wore on my hip and I needed to carry out a typical, twenty-four hour day while the device kept track of how many acid reflux episodes I had. I felt a little self-conscious walking around with a wire coming out of my nose but Chris went out with me for a Starbucks breakfast and a day of shopping as if nothing were different. It was worth the awkwardness, of course, because it turned out that I was having about forty acid-reflux episodes *per hour.* Even the doctor was a little alarmed at those numbers and arranged to have me scoped right away. I had thought the tiny wire was uncomfortable but at least the scope was only down there for a few minutes. The bad news: my flap was lose and partially deteriorated from the acid. The good news: it wasn't damaged to the point of no return.

The doctor put me at the top of his list and by September I was going in for a new procedure that would correct this problem. The surgery itself was not much different from before. Nothing could be done about the damaged flap but the esophagus could be tightened so that the flap would function properly. The real difference is in the procedure. Instead of having to slice me wide open and making me a member of the zipper club he could make three small incisions for a camera and two tools. It had gone from being a major surgery with a long recovery to a day procedure where I could walk out after a few hours. Chris dropped me off at the hospital before work and picked me up at the end of his shift. I couldn't actually walk out on my own since the drugs were still making me woozy but not having to stay overnight in a hospital was worth the wobbly walk to the parking lot.

For the next few weeks my diet consisted of liquids and mush, staring off with gelatine and working my way up to mashed potatoes and scrambled eggs. While recovering from a surgery like this I was expected to lose twenty pounds which was quite alright by me. While not greatly overweight my chiropractor had hinted that shedding ten pounds or so would help my back problems, so I essentially killed two birds with one stone. More importantly though was that after three long years of suffering from a crippling stomach problem I was finally back to my old self. Sort of.

There are a few drawbacks to having my esophagus tightened; I would have to eat slowly and chew my food thoroughly from now on. I realize that having to develop good table manners isn't exactly a drawback, but it took a while for me to get the hang of my new limitations. One other consequence was that I would no longer be able to belch. Now that everything was tightened up it was almost impossible for me to expel air with a satisfying burp, meaning that table manners were the least of my concerns. It doesn't take medical training to know that there is only one other way to release gas from the human body, and it isn't by osmosis.

It was this new side-effect of my operation that led to my new pet name. While everybody has seen the tough, professional woman who never flinches, Chris is the only person who has witnessed and gotten to know my sensitive side. During the difficult times he refers to me as his delicate mountain flower, but now that I can only pass gas from my lower, nether region he also refers to me as his stinky mountain blossom. Thankfully after several years I have developed the eating habits to minimize this problem, but the true test of love during that time was Chris being able to sit through an entire movie with me and acting like nothing was wrong.

Despite this new affliction I was definitely feeling more like my old self. I took it easy through the winter and would always need to be cautious about over-exerting myself, but by late spring I felt like I had a new lease on life. It was our fourth year living in our little house and Chris had come home with some big news about work. After four years of fueling up buses and maintaining the shop he had decided to pursue an apprenticeship in the garage. He could see how frustrated I was with my lack of a teaching career and didn't want me to worry so much about money so he took the next step to increasing his pay. It's true that I was border-line obsessed with our financial situation, and though I applied every year to gain full-time teaching it was becoming clear that I'd never be more than a substitute teacher in this town. Chris had faith that we would always get by but I needed more than that. That's why a couple of months later I told him that I had an interview for a Principal's job… in Alberta.

At first he wasn't sure if I was serious. I was always talking about how much I missed living in that province but he honestly never thought that I'd apply for a job there after we had settled down here. I'd been living out of cardboard boxes for years and this house was supposed to be the end of that. Not only had we thrown away all of the boxes after moving into the house but I had even unpacked many of my tchotchkes, from my antique, Russian tea set to my assortment of collector's plates. The symbolism of me breaking out my knick-knacks was supposed to be the ultimate act of settling down, never to move again. Chris just gave a deep sigh and agreed that we should see how the phone interview goes before jumping to any conclusions. I had put three fleeces before the Lord concerning this job: it would have to pay well; it would have to come with someplace to live; it would have to offer a relocation bonus. During the interview I found out that it came with all three but I still told them that I'd have to think about it.

Chris and I had a long talk after that. It was already the end of June so if I did take the job then I'd have to leave in a matter of weeks while driving across the country on my own to get there. On top of that I would be on my own for an entire year before deciding if the job would be permanent. My Darling hubby has always been very protective of me but not in the jealous, possessive way. Living on the island for eight months had been hard enough and I was coming home on weekends, so he was worried that living on the other side of the country would be too much. He was afraid that if anything happened then he would not be there for me. I called the Superintendent back and told him that I was declining the offer but he just said that he'd give me the weekend to think about it before accepting my decision. That weekend I talked to Mary-Joyce and told her about my dilemma. She understood why I had turned the job down but in her kind, motherly manner she also said that if I didn't give this a try, and remained stuck and unhappy in Sudbury, then I might regret it for the rest of my life.

One of Chris' quirks is that he isn't wrong very often. It's actually quite frustrating at times when I choose not to listen to him only to end up doing exactly what he had told me in the first place. I suppose it's also frustrating for him, but it's a woman's prerogative to change her mind, right? This isn't to say that he thinks he knows everything, he just knows when to speak his mind. Thankfully he also knows how to admit when he's made a mistake, and giving in to fear about this job was one of those times. It didn't take any convincing for him to see that Mary-Joyce's advice was the truth we both needed to hear and he would have to find the faith to let God look after me for the year we were apart. He saw how unhappy I was trying to find work in Sudbury while he knew in his heart that I was capable of so much more than substitute teaching. It was a scary thought to be apart, but this job was something that I needed to do.

We spent the rest of the weekend planning my big trip. You know a town is small when it's only on the most detailed road map. Chris had to use the internet to find this Hamlet in northern Alberta and then mapped out the best route for me to get there. The real concern was finding me a place to stay each night that I would be able to find without a map. We didn't own cell phones even though it was the year 2008 and we didn't have GPS in our vehicles. Instead we made reservations in hotels that were along the main highway which I should have no trouble finding in the dark. On Monday I called my Superintendent back and told him that I would take the job after all. There was no turning back now.

The next few weeks went by in a flash as I sorted through my closet to pick a wardrobe that I'd be able to live with for the next two months. We'd already decided that Chris would come for a visit on the Thanksgiving weekend and bring another suitcase of clothes for me once I got accustomed to my surroundings. We were pretending that this was only a trial year but deep down we both knew that it was the first step to leaving Sudbury. It just so happened that I had to leave on the day after Chris' kids came to visit.

Every summer since we had been in Sudbury they would spend two weeks with their dad. It was the ideal place for southern, city kids to get a change of pace. We'd have bonfires, visit some of the surrounding lakes, climb the mountain out back and pick blueberries, even see the northern lights at night if we were lucky. They did plenty of camping with their mother and her new husband but at our place they could get the feel of the north while sleeping in a bed and being able to watch TV or surf the 'net any time they wanted. Chris' ex would bring them up to us then he would drive them home and get to see his parents as well. It had been a nice arrangement for the past six years but it was looking like this would be their last time to Sudbury. They were teenagers now so there weren't any tears this time when they learned we'd be moving a few provinces over.

I left early the next morning while it was still dark. I'd said my good-byes the night before so we didn't bother waking the kids. I was bringing out my things as Chris packed the car while making sure that I could still use my mirrors properly. Though placing me in God's hands, my hubby still wanted me to be able to make a safe lane change. He was tucking odds and ends in every crevice but I was still bringing out more stuff, and it was then that he realized his mistake. When he had asked me last night if I had everything ready, which I did, he *should* have asked me if I was sure it would all fit in my little Corolla. We had played it cool ever since deciding that we could live apart for a year, but the frustration finally surfaced.

"This isn't a U-Haul, you know!" Chris snapped.

"Well, put some more in the front!" I shot back.

"You need to be able to see," he replied. "I can't help you if you get in an accident."

It was sinking in that I would soon be on my own for the first time since Chris and I had been together. Sure I had gone to the island for a few months, but I wasn't really that far. When not at work we had always been together except for a number of trips that I could probably count on my fingers. We were always together because we *could* be together. It wasn't forced. I remember telling one of my hairdressers about our many road trips and she couldn't believe that we'd been in each other's company for days on end. She said that if she had to spend a whole day with her boyfriend they'd probably kill each other. Chris had also turned down a couple of weekend camping trips with his buddies at work because he couldn't rationalize a weekend away from me. They couldn't wait to get away from their wives for a weekend of drinking, which is normal for northern men, and while Chris did enjoy being around those guys he had no desire to rough it for a few days when he could be home with me. It may sound crazy but that's just the way we are. To put it as simply as possible: we were meant to be together.

I made some last-minute eliminations to avoid any more confrontation and substituted the fold-up inflatable bed with a more compact air mattress. It was either that or I'd have to leave behind some shoes and I was making enough sacrifices as it was. Once he was satisfied that everything was packed properly my Darling gave me a hug and a kiss, then watched me drive off into the dark. We had managed to keep it together for the entire time but once my tail lights disappeared around the bend he went inside, sat on the edge of our bed and cried for the next hour no matter how hard he tried not to. As for me, I bawled my eyes out until I got to the next city, and that was over three-hundred kilometers away.

Putting a Fleece Before the Lord

I look back to my time in Sudbury with memories of contempt. Aside from making a few friends and living in my adorable little house I have a hard time thinking of anything worthwhile that happened in my life. I was constantly worried about money and employment, which for me is not living at all. I could never really tell if God was working in my life so I adopted an old test of faith from the Bible that is referred to as putting out a fleece.

[36] And Gideon said unto God, If thou wilt save Israel by mine hand, as thou hast said,
[37] Behold, I will put a fleece of wool in the floor; and if the dew be on the fleece only, and it be dry upon all the earth beside, then shall I know that thou wilt save Israel by mine hand, as thou hast said.
[38] And it was so: for he rose up early on the morrow, and thrust the fleece together, and wringed the dew out of the fleece, a bowl full of water.
[39] And Gideon said unto God, Let not thine anger be hot against me, and I will speak but this once: let me prove, I pray thee, but this once with the fleece; let it now be dry only upon the fleece, and upon all the ground let there be dew.

[40] And God did so that night: for it was dry upon the fleece only, and there was dew on all the ground. ~ Judges 6:36-40

Chapters 6 and 7 in the book of Judges depict a time when Gideon was chosen by God to deliver the children of Israel from their enemies. This was going to be a miraculous occasion and Gideon was nervous about taking on thousands of enemies with only a few hundred men. Instead of trusting in God right away Gideon asked for a sign that would prove God's intentions. On the first morning he asked for the fleece, or sheep skin, to be covered with dew while the ground around it was left dry, then he asked for the opposite to happen the next day to rule out any chance of coincidence. After these signs were delivered exactly as Gideon had requested he accepts the task and doubts God no more.

If anything, this passage displays how great God's patience is. When you read the full two chapters we find that God first sent an angel to speak with Gideon. Gideon wants to give up an offering to verify that he is indeed being contacted by God so he places the items on a rock which the angel strikes with its staff and instantly burns the offering for God's acceptance. The angel then disappears and Gideon knows that he was visited by a genuine messenger of the Lord, but he still doubts God and asks for more proof with the two fleece tests, *after* an angel had already zapped his offering up to heaven and then disappeared from plain sight *and* God had spoken to Gideon directly! On top of all that, Gideon is personally guided by God every step of the way to defeat the multitude of enemies. He didn't have to figure it out for himself like some of us, and yet he was still rewarded in the end. If our Father could put up with all of Gideon's doubts then I don't feel so bad about my fears.

Accepting a job that was so far away from Chris was a huge decision for me so I also put out fleeces before the Lord. It had to pay well, come with a place to live and offer a moving bonus, and this job had all three. I'd had another job offer that year which didn't fulfill my requests so when this one came through I was a little scared. My salary would be twice as much as what Chris was making at the garage, there was a teacherage to rent for only $250 a month and I would get a $1500 relocation payment. I saw it as a blessing with a price. God had proven himself to me as He had to Gideon, giving me exactly what I had asked for, so to turn it down would have been foolish no matter how scared Chris and I were. I think being afraid to do something this big is normal, and by going ahead in faith and relying on Him to get you through the challenge proves that you believe something better is ahead. I just needed to take that one, huge, scary step towards a better life and become stronger for it in the end.

There are many times that I wonder why I couldn't have gotten this job offer when we were leaving Kenora. God is all powerful, right? He can do anything, so why couldn't he have spared me from six years of misery? Well, it would seem that there is a bible verse for that as well.

47 And that servant, which knew his lord's will, and prepared not himself, neither did according to his will, shall be beaten with many stripes.
48 But he that knew not, and did commit things worthy of stripes, shall be beaten with few stripes. For unto whomsoever much is given, of him shall be much required: and to whom men have committed much, of him they will ask the more. ~ Luke 12:47-48

This verse sounds a little brutal but it can be translated to something like, "Those who are given more will have greater expectations put on them". In the biblical days of servants there were some who were given greater responsibilities than others. It was a great honor to have higher responsibilities, and it came with better privileges, but it also meant that you had much more to answer for if something went wrong because of negligence. In short: I wasn't ready to go to Alberta six years ago. That part of my life held great responsibility which I probably would have messed up somehow. Personally I don't see how, but my "wisdom" hadn't served me very well through most of my adult life so I'm learning to accept what I don't understand.

Something else for me to remember is that my stomach was going to fail me sooner or later but it happened in Sudbury. If this serious problem had happened to me in northern Alberta then I would not have had the time or the opportunity to get it fixed by a leading specialist who lived in a completely different part of Canada. I can only sum up this chapter of my life with the old cliché: God works in mysterious ways.

Chapter Eighteen

The Longest Year of My Life

We had done so well at being brave and not making a big deal out of this separation that I'd completely fooled myself, but once I lost sight of my house in the rear-view mirror it was all over. The reality that this was a permanent move struck me like a clap of thunder and the flood gates opened. There I was, a grown woman driving to a new career while crying like a little kid. I missed my Darling husband already and I'd only been on the road for a few minutes. This new chapter in my life was overwhelming from the start so I gave up trying to fight my emotions and let them fade away at their own pace. Thankfully I was back to my usual self by the time I got to Sault-Saint Marie where I gassed up the car, grabbed a Starbucks coffee and carried on with my adventure as it was meant to be. I ended the day in Thunder Bay after enjoying the elevated scenery that had been our traveling bane almost ten years earlier. I had taken that journey with a man I was just getting to know, and now I was on this road again and pining for him with all my heart.

Unfortunately the rest of my trip was just as emotional as the first day. Driving past Kenora triggered a landslide of memories about Flo and how we had lost her so suddenly. Without warning I was crying again for a dear, old friend to whom I never got the chance to say good-bye. Passing through Saskatchewan re-kindled memories about my son and the horrible ordeal that my first husband had put me through to keep me from my baby boy, resulting in more tears, and then when I finally made it to Alberta and drove through Edmonton I got one more tearful dose from my past. I was re-living the tragedies of my life on this cross-country trek and if I had known then what I know now I never would have left my Florida home over thirty years ago. I dried my eyes for one last time as the highway headed north and I was finally going someplace where I had no history. It was time to leave all of that behind me to build a new life with Chris.

Five hours later I had arrived at my final destination. It was a northern town with a population that is just shy of seven thousand people but there are many conveniences thanks to the influx of rig workers and truck drivers from the surrounding oil and lumber industries. While not a booming town by any means it was much nicer than other northern communities that I have been to. I checked into my hotel and let Chris know that I'd arrived safely. I wasn't actually at my final destination yet but this was the place where all of the local school divisions had their head offices to deal with the many, smaller communities that populated this region.

The next day I signed all of the paperwork to officially accept my one year contract and met my Superintendent in person. He was a friendly man of medium height who seemed very eager to help me get settled in my new position. We didn't discuss the job very much, deciding that it would be best to go over everything when I was in my own office. After a morning of legalities and form signing I set off to deposit my relocation cheque and have a proper look around. The town was divided by a mighty river, and from what I could tell the town had started on the east side of the river and expanded over to the other side when the surrounding foothills got in the way of progress. As far as shopping was concerned it was a combination of the usual bare necessities with a smattering of newer developments added in an attempt to keep people from flocking to the nearest city. It's the kind of place where you can usually find what you need as long as you know where to look.

For the next two days I attended the required orientation for us newbies plus the usual kickoff where the entire division gathered for a Beginning of the Year info session that also doubled as a pep rally of sorts. I made a few new acquaintances amongst the hordes of unfamiliar faces but I suppose it was inevitable that I gravitated to the lone Native in the crowd. He looked to be about my age and seemed to feel just as out of place as I did, and after a short conversation it turned out that we had someplace in common. During my INAC days he had been on one of the reserves that I was in charge of, so with that small bit of common ground we made it through the rest of the day by swapping stories and getting to know one another. Although having a wife and kids in southern Alberta he was a wanderer just like me, unable to find suitable work near his family. I relayed my own experience of leaving Chris behind to pursue my career and by the end of the day we had each made a new friend.

When I checked out of my hotel on the last day it was finally time to head for my final destination: Smallville, Alberta. Smallville isn't the community's proper name, but everything I write about it can be applied to all of the tiny villages and hamlets that I've been to through my life. It's a tidy place with the church, post office and general store all on the same corner of town, but all I was really interested in was the school. I was secretly dreading that it would be a run-down eyesore, but to my relief it had just been re-vamped six years ago and looked brand new. One of the maintenance guys had met me there and we headed into the building to have a look around. All that was missing was the new-school smell and I fell in love with it immediately. There was nothing I could do until tomorrow when my Superintendent would come to fill me in on the details of my job so it was time to check out my new home and unload my car.

The teacherage duplex was located right beside the school and consisted of a two-bedroom unit and a three-bedroom unit with the three-bedroom unit being mine. My neighbour was a single lady who had been living there for the past twenty years and had been a teacher at the school many years ago. Not only was she quiet and friendly but she was only home half of the time which made her the perfect neighbour. The rest of my day was spent moving in and I could hear my poor little Corolla give a sigh of relief as the last of my wardrobe made its way inside.

With that done I went back to the school to use the phone and arrange for the utilities to be put in my name. I wandered the halls for a few more minutes, checked out my classroom and started making mental notes of things that needed to be done. After that I returned home to start the long job of settling in. Organizing the kitchen didn't take long since I'd only brought the bare essentials but my wardrobe was another matter altogether. It's a good thing that each bedroom had a closet because I filled all three with my hanging clothes and then proceeded to fill the top shelves with the folded articles and cover the floors with footwear. By the end of the night I had a place for everything and everything in its place. Now that I had everything spread out it was hard to believe that all of these clothes and shoes were jam-packed into my little car, but the cramped, three-day drive had been worth it. I didn't really know what I was getting into but at least I'd look coordinated while doing it. My final task was to inflate my bed with the electric pump that Chris had insisted I bring and give him a call as I did almost every night for the next ten months.

My Superintendent met me at the school the next morning to give me my network password and fill me in on the details of my job. We got the small talk out of the way as I let him know that I was pretty much settled in at the teacherage, and then I found out some interesting details that had conveniently been left out of the job description. While I had been hired to be the Principal I knew that I was expected to do some teaching as well. That's normal enough in a small school, but when "some" teaching ends up being four days a week it's hard not to feel that the job was misrepresented in the ad. I wasn't being asked to be a Principal who did some teaching; I was hired to be a teacher who also did the Principal's job as well.

On top of that, due to low enrollment and funding cuts this Kindergarten to Grade 9 School was running with multi-grade classrooms which meant that each teacher was expected to teach three grades at once. I also had an experienced teacher on maternity leave and she was being replaced by a new, inexperienced teacher who was new to the multi-grade classroom environment. The charm of my new school was starting to wear off. To hide the panic that was creeping up I decided to try out my new computer password to make sure that I could log in to my account. The Superintendent could see my change in mood and tried to reassure me by promising to give whatever help was available and that my secretary from last year would be a big help to get me on track. That's when I opened up my e-mail and found one that had been forwarded to me from the previous school year. It was a resignation letter from my secretary. It would appear that she had resigned at the end of June without telling anyone except for sending this e-mail that nobody had read yet. Even my boss didn't know what to say now.

To clarify what had just happened, I was expected to teach the three most demanding grades of my school, grades 7 to 9, at almost a full time capacity while also acting as a full time Principal with no secretary. I had been completely misled about the true nature of this job but after driving for three days I had little choice in the matter. Thankfully my boss left me alone at this point while promising to sort out my secretary issue. I sat in the quiet isolation of my office wondering what I had gotten myself into this time. I wasn't sure what was worse; that the school division had no qualms about dumping such a demanding assignment on a single individual or that they would go so far as to deceive somebody to fill the position. God had fulfilled my three fleeces as I had asked, and I came here with the best of intentions, yet it would seem that I would need to struggle through this predicament under completely unrealistic expectations.

In the end I resolved to trust in my Superintendent's promise of doing everything he could to help me through this and in return I would do my absolute best for the school and the community. I was called to this position without being fully qualified to address all of the issues, but there is a well-known quote that says "God doesn't call the qualified, He qualifies the called." Besides, God had fulfilled His end of the deal to get me this job so now it was my turn to do what I could to keep it. To do any less would be letting us both down.

I had about a week to overcome my shell-shocked disposition so I buried myself in my work while staying in constant contact with head office. There were two ladies in particular, my go-to girls, whom I relied on to help me through this avalanche of responsibilities and paperwork. The secretary had also agreed to return for a few months until I could find a replacement. Her reasons for leaving were based on whatever happened last year with the former Principal, so thankfully she was able to put that behind her and help me out for a while. It's probably a good thing that I had come up here on my own since I was spending at least twelve hours a day at the school, including weekends. I only went home to sleep and to maintain the long-distance relationship with my hubby.

My early encounters with community members were a little less welcoming than I had been expecting. Nobody was rude to me but that small town warmth seemed to be missing. I ignored the feeling and figured that it was just me but it didn't take long to find out what was going on. Last year had been a bit of a nightmare, and during our first month of school I learned what this town had endured at the hands of their last Principal. My predecessor had been a small woman with a serious small-person complex. The stories I'd heard described her as a dictator, a bully, and a tyrant. It probably didn't help that her entire staff was taller than she was but I can only assume that she'd been an angry woman who took pride in abusing her power of authority.

After getting to know the community I could see that they were a very tolerant group of people, so the fact that they wanted to run that Principal out of town by Christmas speaks volumes. She managed to stick it out for the entire year but it was a year that everyone would rather forget. It's no wonder the community was looking at me sideways after having such a horrible person ruin their school for a year. Not only would I have to earn their confidence but I'd have to win their trust as soon as possible. I needed to get the message out that this year was not going to be a re-enactment of the last one and the best way to do that in a small town is to attend their church.

I would have attended the Sunday service anyways, but walking into the town church under these circumstances seemed to have an extra-special effect. Of all the Principals that have run the school in Smallville, very few have bothered to live in town and none have ever become part of the church. By doing both

I was giving a strong message about who I was without saying a word. Even more important was that I made many connections within the community that I might not have made if I'd confined myself to the school. Plus, it just so happened that my teacher on mat-leave also attended the church so we got to know each other without having to wait until the next year. It's almost as if it had been planned out for me.

Making up the teaching schedule for the year was an enormous task. Many people don't fully realize how this is done so I will try to break it down in its simplest form. Each student has a dollar value assigned to them, and the total amount dictates how much teacher time and Educational Assistant (EA) time you can buy for the entire year. Because of the school's low enrollment we could only budget for 2.5 full-time teachers. This means exactly what it looks like; we had to teach nine grades for an entire year using only two teachers and a half-time teacher. This made no sense to me so I called my go-to girls for some clarification on how this should work and they told me that I would need to "get creative" with my planning. It turns out that "getting creative" is code for sticking up to six grades with a single teacher for classes such as phys-ed, art and health. You can see now how essential a few EAs become in a small school.

After several hours of juggling classes around and synchronizing teaching times we finally had a schedule that we could work with in which everybody get one preparation period per week, except for me. My secretary was quick to point out that I wasn't obligated to give anybody a prep, especially my EAs, and I'd lighten my schedule by working everybody non-stop like the previous administrator. I thanked her for the input but did it anyways. I wasn't trying to be a martyr but I wouldn't be a slave driver either. I had nothing but time this year so I took my fair share of the teaching hours and stayed late every day to get my Principal duties under control. Besides, true leaders lead by example, not by demand.

When the first day of school came I was as ready as I'd ever be because nothing was going to prepare me for the group of Junior High students that would walk into my room. I would like to say that they were your typically emotional, hormonal and unenthusiastic bunch of teenage students, but I wasn't that lucky. I could only describe them as a mixed bag of worst-case scenarios that seemed to have a constant ugly on for each other. Every day was a crisis situation with this unruly lot and it was all that anyone could do to keep the peace between them let alone complete a single lesson. I probably would have given up completely if it hadn't been for one particular student whom I'll refer to as my Valedictorian, or Val for short.

Val was starting grade seven this year, at the "bottom of the heap" as it were with this group. She was pleasant, polite and very smart, and my little ray of sunshine in an otherwise glum forecast. Val was also highly self-motivated which meant that I could assign her a lesson out of a textbook which would get completed with minimal additional instruction. Some of you reading this book might wonder why I consider that to be special. In fact, many of you will recall your early school years to be just as I described; a short lesson followed by a textbook assignment that was expected to be completed quietly at your desk with the occasional raised hand for getting a bit of help. Those days are far and few between if not completely non-existent. You'll need to bear with me as I indulge in a bit of a rant.

Those of us who went to school up until the 1980s probably remember the regime of spelling tests and math drills. Teachers were simultaneously feared and respected, to a certain degree, and assignments were expected to be completed on time. Most importantly of all; if you didn't apply yourself then you failed the year and had to repeat the grade. That generation of students helped built the world that we live in today. Then in the early 1990s somebody got concerned about students' feelings. I don't know exactly how it happened but suddenly the tried and true act of memorization was replaced with the new concept of expression. Spelling would no longer be taken into consideration for literary assignments as long as the students were adequately expressing themselves with content, and partial marks were given to incorrect mathematics answers as long as the student was on the right track.

This concept meant that children who couldn't spell or learn their multiplication tables could still reach the desired achievement level to be promoted to the next grade, sparing them from the discomfort of watching their friends move on to the next grade without them. There was no longer a penalty for failure and the simplest of tasks were rewarded with praise. Over the next two decades that exact problem has compounded year after year until today when a common confession can be heard over and over again by students; I don't know how I passed because I didn't do anything last year. Though illiterate and mathematically challenged, these students are being shoved along the academic assembly line whether they are ready or not. Even worse is the fact that they know this. I now had a room full of teenagers who hadn't learned anything in years, and they knew that they didn't have to learn anything if they didn't want to because they'd still pass on to the next grade no matter what.

Recent studies are showing that this low-expectation/high-praise method of teaching, and raising children in general, is not giving us the results that were hoped for. Instead of building up self-esteem we have created a generation with low resilience to stress because dealing with difficult situations has been deemed as optional. Combine that with modern technology that puts a calculator and camera in every child's pocket and the recipe for failure is complete. Why learn even the simplest math when every smart-phone can calculate if for you? Taking notes is also viewed as a monumental task. Instead of going through the memory-inducing procedure of writing facts on paper, "clever" students are taking pictures of their lessons, probably never to be looked at again. Being unable to cope with the everyday demands of life has resulted in a lack of discipline, self-direction and responsibility. Now perhaps you'll understand why students like Val are becoming a bit of a rarity.

The month of September was a complete blur as I scrambled to figure out how I was supposed to teach a Junior High class that couldn't read or perform basic multiplication. My shelves of textbooks were all but useless, and despite my extensive teaching background the rules I had lived by up until now no longer seemed to apply. Then there was the teeny-tiny ordeal of running the school. Not only did I have a dilemma in my own classroom but being the Principal meant that everybody else's problems were also my concern. On top of all of that was the non-stop paperwork that couldn't possibly be done by a part-time secretary, adding one more thing to my plate that was already spilling over with responsibilities. The dream of moving here to start a new career, and a new life, was beginning to feel like a mistake instead. I felt like I had been set up to fail.

Of course I kept all of these negative thoughts to myself, especially when talking to Chris every day. As far as he was concerned I was happy to be back in Alberta, which was true, so I simply focused on the inconveniences of small town isolation. Our weekday chats were usually brief since at least one of us was ready for bed by the time we phoned each other, but we would catch up on things during the weekend. I would call Chris every Saturday morning and we'd have coffee together over the phone. We'd talk about the renovations he was doing with the house and I'd find something encouraging to tell him about the school. He would always say how proud he was of me for forging ahead without him and that was the little boost

I needed to keep going. I knew that if I could just make it through this year then everything would fall into place.

The end of September signaled that ever-important event of receiving my first pay cheque. It had been ten long years since I'd had a decent salary, and this single cheque was the final boost that I needed to conquer my doubts. My first order of business was to purchase that essential piece of equipment that has gotten me through so many lonely nights in the past: my beloved satellite television. For the past month I had been watching rented DVDs on a portable DVD player with a ten-inch screen, so it was a long-overdue affair to order my satellite dish and receiver. I would have to wait two weeks for the delivery and installation since my talented hubby wasn't here to do that for me, so to make the wait worthwhile I splurged on my dream TV. I've wanted a SONY flat screen for years but could never justify the cost, but with the constant advances in digital technology that thirty-two inch wide screen (on sale, of course) was now a guilt-free reality. One other important purchase that I made at this time was a plane ticket for Chris. In just a few weeks he would be flying out to see me for an extended Thanksgiving weekend and it couldn't come too soon.

The prospect of limitless TV and a visit from my hubby recharged my spirit like never before. Suddenly everything seemed possible no matter what the obstacle and I started to see things from a different perspective. I couldn't undo past mistakes but I wouldn't hold those mistakes against my students either. I no longer worried about fixing everybody's problems but instead took the approach that I would give everybody and anybody the chance to help themselves while facilitating a proper education to Val and any other students who were inclined to learn.

When Thanksgiving weekend finally arrived I don't think there was a soul in town who didn't know that Chris was coming to visit, although Bobby was probably the first person I'd told. He was an old trapper whom I met at church and he insisted that I was a spitting image for one of his daughters. We made a connection that day and he was one of my biggest supporters right from the beginning. He couldn't resist teasing me when I mentioned my weekend plans of driving to Edmonton.

"Oh, he's real," said Bobby with a mischievous smile. "I thought he was just a story to keep the wolves at bay."

This had actually had been an on-going joke with the people I had gotten to know, whether or not Chris was a figment of my imagination. I told them that if they wanted to find out for themselves then they should be at church on Sunday. I took a personal day from work to make the six-hour drive on Thursday and gave myself some well-deserved me time. I booked a room at the hotel across from the West Edmonton Mall and fit in an evening of shopping, or Retail Therapy as I like to call it. I barely slept that night and was at the airport early on Friday morning to greet my hubby at the arrival gate. We played it cool since Chris knows that I don't like showy displays of affection in public, but once I got my Darling to the car there was some serious kissing going on. The drive back to the hotel seemed way too long, but we finally made it to the privacy of our room for some long, overdue grown-up time.

[Intense, romantic encounter that cannot be printed on the pages of this book.]

A few hours later we were walking hand-in-hand along Bourbon Street in the mall while wondering how we had managed to be apart for two months. The fires of passion were subdued for now so we calmly strolled through the shopping Mecca without looking for anything in particular. We were content just being together and this was going to be the only relaxing day in our schedule. We managed to keep our hands off of each other long enough to catch a movie at the West Ed Megaplex and then grab some dinner before turning in early for the night. For the drive back to Smallville I wanted to show Chris the scenic route which was only supposed to be a bit longer, but the three paving crews that we met along the way dragged that out into an all-day event. The sun was getting low when I finally showed him the town on the river and he did his best to not be under whelmed. We were both tired from the extra-long drive so we finished the final stretch of highway that took us to our prospective new home.

One thing to remember is that nothing was written in stone yet. The goal was to see if this job in Smallville would be a new start for Chris and I and we had to be sure about it before he quit his job and sold our house. The town itself didn't have that many streets, but unfortunately the teacherage was on the one street that looked like a run-down trailer park. Chris didn't comment on the abandoned homes, or the one directly across from the teacherage that looked like a yard sale had exploded, nor did he comment on the plain, empty style of the building that was to be our new home. Moving here and living in the teacherage was a stark contrast to our cozy nest that he had made for me in Sudbury, and I knew that I was asking a lot of him to embrace it wholeheartedly. We didn't discuss anything that night and simply sat together in front of my new SONY 32" flat screen LCD television until it was time to go to bed on my air mattress.

Sunday morning came too soon, and my Darling husband did something for me that he hadn't done since I left home. Making me my morning coffee became a special thing that had evolved slowly over the years we had been together, but Chris had perfected it by the time we bought our little house. It was strong and full of flavour, made with freshly ground coffee in a French press, seasoned with cinnamon and nutmeg and sweetened with honey. What may seem like nothing to most people was one of the little things that he loved doing just for me. Through trial and error I had managed to make my own cup of coffee that was decent enough but it's always better when somebody makes it for you with the added love. After breakfast he got a quick tour of the school before we walked over to the church where everybody got to meet my real-life husband. After the Sunday service there was always a light meal which consisted of coffee and whatever else was brought in by the congregation, but my favourite was Bobby's freshly baked bannock. Chris was invited over to the men's table where he chewed the fat with the husbands and learned a bit more about the town while I sat at my usual spot with the wives and ladies. This little social event usually went on for about an hour but I managed to steal my hubby away after twenty minutes, explaining that he had work to do before I drove him back to Edmonton for his Monday morning flight. Everyone was surprised that he wasn't staying longer but this was all of the time that he could get off of work. Chris could see by the way I interacted with everyone that I saw past the small town limitations and enjoyed being part of something. On our way back to the teacherage he finally brought up the topic of moving here permanently.

"You like it here, don't you?" He asked while looking around. I told him that I did. "Well," he said after a short pause, "I'd better get those renovations done then. We can't sell a half-finished house." In truth we probably could have sold the house as it was but Chris had his standards and liked to do things properly, even if he wasn't finishing the house for me anymore. Back at the teacherage I had a short honey-do list for my hubby. I wasn't fibbing when I told everybody that he had work to do before heading home, but the main job was moving my TV and setting it up properly.

This teacherage must have been built back when electricity was a fad because each room only had one electrical outlet in the most useless location and the bathroom didn't have one at all! On top of that a solitary phone jack had been put in the kitchen as if it were an afterthought making it impossible for me to plug in my satellite receiver to order movies. Even Chris could see that the TV was in the wrong spot but I had warned him ahead of time so he came prepared. He'd brought a heavy-duty power bar with an extra-long cord that was just long enough to move my TV exactly where I wanted it, then he spliced a second phone line off of the kitchen and ran it behind the living room baseboards to complete my satellite experience. Everything was moved and tidy by diner time, allowing us to relax for a few hours before going to bed early and getting up even earlier.

We passed on the scenic route back to Edmonton and reached the West Edmonton Mall just in time for my Darling to catch the shuttle to the airport. We played brave once again as I kissed him good-bye, but I couldn't keep it up for long. He loaded his bags in the back of the van and took his seat, but when he turned to catch one last glimpse of me I was already gone, crying into the mall. The weekend that I had waited so long for was already done and it wasn't at all like I'd imagined it. I wished that we hadn't wasted so much time driving back and forth from Smallville and just stayed in Edmonton so I could've had my Darling all to myself, but I knew that it had to be done. I drove back that day and cried the whole way home, my only comfort being that the decision had been made. We would be making this town our new home.

Shortly after the long weekend I got a visit from one of my go-to girls from head office. I'd requested the meeting because I needed help sorting out some numbers now that my yearly budget was final. I couldn't understand why I was being dinged the maximum salary dollars for each of my two teachers when I knew very well that neither of them was making that salary. The new teacher replacing my lady on maternity leave was nowhere near that level of pay. Her response was that head office used that figure for every teacher in the division as a round number instead of deducting individual salaries. I could see where using the maxed salary per teacher might even out in a large school, but it was a huge discrepancy for our small school that was struggling to operate with the bare necessities. Tens of thousands of dollars were being taken out of my school's budget and we weren't seeing any benefit from it. No wonder the school was struggling. That one small change of only taking out the actual *earned* salaries would leave me with enough money to upgrade all of the school computers, hire more Educational Assistants and even buy more teaching time which would make everybody's life better at the school, staff and students alike. Unfortunately that's how school business is run and I was in no position to argue. I thanked the woman for her time and knew that I'd have to find another way to pay for our necessities.

A few minutes later my secretary brought me a binder that she'd found in the office and assumed that it was mine. As you can imagine I was leaving stuff everywhere in my quest to get this job under control so it's quite possible that it was mine. I took it back to my office and opened it up to see what it was and there was a printout of an e-mail with my name on it. What's more interesting is that this wasn't my binder. My go-to girl had accidentally left it behind and right at the front was an on-going correspondence about me. In the e-mail I was described as being needy and time-consuming, and the message appeared to be an inside joke between my go-to girls whom were supposed to be my support group. How nice is that? What's more concerning is that I had to wonder why she had bothered to print it out. Was she showing other people as well? Was I a joke to everybody? So much for getting professional help. I had every right to grieve this inappropriate behaviour with my Superintendent but I decided to keep it to myself for now. I quietly made a copy of the page for my own records and informed the owner that the binder had been left at my school. At first I was upset, then I got mad, but I soon settled down and decided not to let such petty immaturity, from grown women, get in the way of doing my job. Nothing was ever said about it but at least I knew who I couldn't trust any more.

With that emotional monkey off my back I could focus on a critical aspect of running a small, under-funded northern school, and that would be fund-raising. I'm not sure if the previous Principal had deliberately run the budget into a ten-thousand dollar deficit or if she simply didn't know what she was doing, but either way it was my problem now. Fortunately this particular task allowed me to utilize a skill that came quite naturally to me and has served me well to succeed in the past. If there's anything that I know how to do well, talking to people would be it. It was a bit of a slow start at first since having the title of Principal had the same effect as somebody walking around with the plague, but once the town realized that my efforts towards the school were genuine it was an entirely different story. A few people worked for the local oil company and with their help I soon had a three-thousand dollar donation that I could put towards some badly needed computers. Not only was it a good first step in the right direction but it also got my picture in the local paper.

Publicity is a good way to raise awareness so I gave Mile Zero a call to see if they'd be interested in a story about my school getting a corporate donation. The man on the other end of the phone said he'd be happy to cover the event and that's when I met Jason. He was the editor of the paper, but like every job up here you had to wear many hats so he was also a reporter and photographer. The donation story wasn't only good for the school but it was good for the donator as well. Everybody likes to be in the local paper, and if you can do it while doing something for a school then all the better. Jason's philosophy on news was that the small communities are just as important as the large ones. From then on I made sure to give him a ring whenever we had something happening at the school, and I made sure that there was always something going on at Smallville.

Sometime in October the inevitable happened and the kids asked me about having a dance. It's no shock that the previous Principal didn't do anything like that so I decided to give them a chance. My class may not have been ideal students but that didn't mean that I hated them. We had the understanding that if everything went well then we could have more dances throughout the year, but if there was bad behaviour then that would be it. This brought up the question about whether or not certain trouble-making kids would be allowed to buy tickets.

There were a few families in town that had built themselves a bad reputation and the students were worried that these bad apples would spoil their chances of any future events. I understood where they were coming from but said that it wouldn't be fair to single them out. Everybody was welcome to buy a ticket and enjoy themselves *as long as they behaved.* I emphasized that point to the students to help them realize that it would be up to them as to whether or not we had more dances.

Everybody showed up for the big night, even the trouble-makers, but they were cleaned up and just as well-behaved as any other kid. I'd brought in a local DJ who put on a top-notch show with fancy lights, the smoke machine and really big speakers. The kids were all blown away and the DJ's wife happened to be from Smallville so he gave me a deal. As an added bonus one of the school families unexpectedly picked up the tab for the entertainment. Everybody had a blast and it didn't cost me anything except for my time to supervise.

To top it off I got a visit from the RCMP that night. They knew that there was a dance in town and did a drive-by because they were expecting trouble. I didn't realize that Smallville was on their high priority list because of those troublesome families that the kids had been worried about, but for the past two months the town had been strangely quiet. They had been hearing good things about me and attributed that to their sudden infrequent visits. I had no idea what to say since I didn't think I was doing anything, but the officer just looked at me and said that whatever it was I should keep on doing it. The reason I had the dance was to let the kids enjoy themselves, but the RCMP visit was the icing on the cake.

Things really picked up once it was clear that I had good intentions for the school but a significant moment was when Val's mom, Mrs. L, came to visit me. My staff told me that Mrs. L had always been a huge supporter of the school until last year when nobody wanted anything to do with that Principal. If I could regain her trust then I'd "have it made." I wasn't sure what that meant but I was about to find out.

Mrs. L and her husband had four kids in the school with Val being their eldest. They were going to have kids in this school for several more years to come and they believed that by supporting it they were supporting their children. It's a simply philosophy that was held by a lot of the community, many whom didn't even have kids in the school anymore, but Mrs. L's enthusiasm was the beginning of a dam burst. She came to me with the idea of having a Halloween theme lunch at the end of the month for the entire school. Halloween was her favourite holiday and it showed with the amount of effort that was put into that meal. She and her mother came to the school to prepare the scary-looking food that the kids ate up without hesitation, and I even gave Jason a call to cover the event. Smallville was in the paper again and the town's spirit seemed to be back to normal.

For the rest of the year we had all sorts of news-worthy occasions which included the Christmas concert that had a packed gymnasium with standing room only; a school talent show with some surprising town talent making it to the stage; the town Winter Carnival which involved a day of activities and food on the school grounds; the spring Art Show that our art instructor orchestrated to display the huge amount of artistic skill within the surrounding community; a Volunteer Tea to show my appreciation to everyone who donated their time to make our school so successful, and Jason was there for each event making sure that Smallville wasn't forgotten about. Of all the events that we had, I think the Mother's Day Strawberry Tea and Fashion Show was the most memorable.

Earlier in the year I was looking for a local place to buy some new clothes. Wal-Mart wasn't doing it for me so I asked my staff where they shopped. Some were tall like me so if anybody would know where to get suitable fashions for the above-average girl it would be them. They directed me to a boutique in a nearby town which I think is the best clothing shop in the north, and that's when everything fell into place. The owner reminded me of the actress Shirley Temple (if you are around my age you would know who she is) and we hit it off immediately. I admired her extensive line of merchandise which made me recall fashion shows that I had done for schools in the past. Shirley told me that she used to do fashion shows in this area but nobody had tried that in a long time, so naturally that made me want to have one even more. The end result was a women's-only tea party that hosted a full-length fashion show with me and my staff, plus some volunteers, strutting our stuff down a runway and displaying the wide variety of clothing that the boutique had to offer. It was a lot of work but it was also a huge success. Having Jason there as the only male allowed in the building was a special touch that added a bit more fun to an already spectacular day.

It was the many, positive moments like this that helped me to get through the rough times of the year, but perhaps the most stressful of them all was going home to see Chris for Christmas. Incidentally, this next story should be subtitle "Why I'll never fly with Air Canada again."

Flying to Sudbury was a bit of a hassle since its airport was one of those small ones that could only handle commuter flights from larger cities like Toronto, but my problems started right away in Edmonton. I managed to get a ride to the city with somebody who was going there for a holiday visit and that way I wouldn't have to pay for two weeks of airport parking. I got to the airport without any problems but I did have some trouble getting through security. Chris and I weren't frequent flyers and hadn't been on a plane since the 9/11 disaster in 2001. He had warned me about the tiny plastic bag that all toiletries had to fit in but somehow I forgot about that crucial bit of information when packing my bags. Sure enough, when I went through security with my carry-on bag I was told that I would have to dispose of my toiletries that exceeded the security requirements (all of my stuff). Everything was high-end cosmetics, from my magnum of hair spray to the bottle of my favourite perfume.

"Are you kidding me?" I asked the girl, but she just pointed to the garbage can beside her that was already half full of toiletry products. "I can't believe this!" I complained as I started to discard my items worth a few hundred dollars. "Are you telling me that there's no way for me to keep them?"

The girl just shrugged but another employee informed me that I could rent out a locker for a dollar a day. I thanked her for her honesty while giving the unhelpful guard a cold look as I retrieved my items and hurried off to set up a locker. On my second run through the lineup I had forgotten about the miniature Swiss Army knife on my key chain. The one inch blade and pair of micro-scissors were deemed a national security threat and I would have to leave it behind.

"This was a gift from my husband!" I said, getting a little irate. Again the unhelpful guard just shrugged, waiting for me to toss it into the garbage, but the helpful girl stepped up again. She handed me an envelope and said that if I filled out my mailing information then she would see that it got to a mail box. I thanked her once more and went to a counter to prepare the envelope with my key chain in it. I got into line again as they were making the last boarding call for my flight. The guard at the beginning of the check point gave me a second look.

"You again?" He asked with surprise.

"What can I say?" I said, trying to remain calm. "I haven't flown for over ten years."

He looked at my ticket and saw that I was running behind so he ushered me to the front of the long line where they quickly processed me and sent me on my way. I made it to the plane just in time and sat down with relief. I'd run marathons that were more relaxing than that!

I didn't get to rest for long because there was a change over in Calgary but when I got to my gate there was some sort of delay with the flight to Toronto. Our loading time came and went but there was no announcement. It was almost an hour later when the flight crew hurried through the gate and the boarding finally started. It was getting late so I asked about the connecting flight to Sudbury and was assured that they would wait. I found out later that that's just the standard line Air Canada employees give to all passengers even if it isn't true. Sure enough when we finally landed in Toronto there was a group of us hurrying to the Sudbury departure gate only to be told that the flight was canceled due to delay. Somebody questioned this and the attendant simply stated that crew had to wait for a passenger in Calgary which delayed the flight for too long so we would have to catch the first flight tomorrow morning. There was a lot of grumbling but nobody challenged this blatant lie.

"No, no!" I yelled from the back of the crowd while making my way to the desk. "We were all there for over an hour waiting for *your* flight crew to show up." I'd had enough for one day and I wasn't being kept from my hubby because some Air Canada employees didn't feel like working a little late. "That delay had nothing to do with us. That was *your* fault, so you're going to get us to Sudbury *tonight!*" She could tell that this wasn't going to end easily so she nervously picked up the phone and called somebody, then informed us that the flight would be boarding shortly. I calmed down and took a seat until they let us on the plane, but I made sure to ask if our bags would be on the plane as well.

"Oh yes," she replied, knowing that any other answer would be the wrong one. Forty-five minutes later I was walking across the snow-covered tarmac towards my smiling hubby. I was exhausted and he had no idea what I'd been through today. I gave him a hug and joined the crowd at the baggage claim. They let us stand there for ten minutes before informing us that the baggage hadn't made it onto the plane. What a surprise. It was almost midnight and the end of a long day was made even longer by having to fill out paperwork so that our luggage could be delivered to our homes as soon as it came in. Half an hour later my Darling finally had me back in our cozy little home for a restful, two week break.

As crazy as it sounds, that flight was only a warm-up for the treat that Air Canada had planned for me on the way back to Alberta. My Saturday morning flight from Sudbury to Toronto went fine, and my connector flight to Saskatoon took off without a hitch, but just when I thought that everything should be alright we had to make an unscheduled landing in Winnipeg for a technical issue. Warning bells started going off in my head but there was a two hour grace period between landing and catching my Edmonton flight so I tried to remain calm.

An hour later we were still in Winnipeg and I started to get antsy. It turned out that we had made this emergency landing because one of the toilets wasn't working properly and company policy deemed that it needed to be fixed right away. I had to sit in a plane, listening to crying kids who'd also had enough of waiting, because one of the several toilets on the plane wasn't flushing properly. Unbelievable. It might have been better if the air was circulating but if the plane isn't running then the air stops flowing, so we had to endure ninety stuffy minutes of screaming kids before moving onto the runway again. The plane got into position and then went nowhere for half an hour. The air was blowing now, but we weren't going anywhere because a plane that was trying to take off earlier broke down on the runway! You might think that I'm making this up but it really happened. It took an hour to tow it back to a hanger but we were assured that the connecting flight to Edmonton would not be missed. I think they knew that there would be a lynching if we'd heard otherwise but you can probably guess what we were told at the Air Canada desk in Saskatoon: we had missed the flight to Edmonton.

That in itself was bad enough, but what followed is both inexcusable and unacceptable from a company that is supposed to be our national airline. Everybody who had missed the Saturday night Edmonton flight was nonchalantly told that another plane wouldn't be leaving until Monday. Not Sunday but *Monday*! This woman did not see it as a big deal that everybody would have to spend two nights in Saskatoon to catch a flight that we had already paid for but missed because a toilet had to be fixed that apparently couldn't wait until the plane landed an hour later in Saskatoon. It was the end of the biggest holiday of the year, everybody in the country had spent all of their money and had to be back at work by Monday morning and this clueless individual couldn't understand why nobody was happy to wait until Monday for a flight to Edmonton. I was livid but there was no compromise this time no matter how mad we were. It was only six o'clock in the evening, which I would think was plenty of time to make up for their mistake, but the best Air Canada would do was to put us all on express coaches that would drive us to Edmonton.

Meanwhile, West Jet (who *should* be Canada's official airline) caught wind of this and let everybody know that they had a plane headed for Edmonton but seating was limited. In hind sight I should have joined the mad rush to get one of those tickets but I wasn't going to let Air Canada off that easily. Instead of getting a ticket I boarded the bus and endured the twelve hour drive to Edmonton. It was also a freezing -30 degrees Celsius that night which kept the bus from heating up at all. I really wish I had gotten one of those West Jet tickets.

We pulled into the bus station on Sunday morning but my trip wasn't over yet. Remember the items that I had back in the airport locker? I had no choice but to take a taxi to the airport, get my stuff, then take a taxi back to the place that I had arranged to meet for my ride back to Smallville. I know that if I'd have called my ride and told them about my last twenty four hours that they would have gladly drove me to the airport, but I didn't want to impose. It was my problem and I solved it on my own. It probably wasn't the best way to solve it but I was so tired by that point that I really wasn't thinking too well.

You would think by now that my nightmare would be over, but about half way home we heard on the radio that there had been a big accident on the river bridge and traffic was backed up for miles. I kid you not. My only way home was across that bridge and right now it was sounding bad. I can only thank God that things cleared up just as we got into town so I was able to finally make it back to my stark, lonely, empty shell of a home for six more months of Smallville School goodness.

It wasn't really that bad, but after the weekend I just had there wasn't much of a bright side to anything. I went to bed early, on my air mattress, and I don't think I moved a muscle until the alarm woke me in the morning. Thankfully the friendly faces of my staff and students quickly washed away the past two days of torment, but that didn't stop me from sending a blistering letter to Air Canada about the service I'd gotten over the holidays. I was issued the standard apology letter and a $200.00 voucher to be used on my next Air Canada flight, thus forcing me to use their services at least one more time.

The rest of my year trudged on as I came to grips with the policies of running a school. I managed to hire a new secretary who worked out well but at the end of the year she had to quit. The job prospects for her husband weren't working out up here and they ended up moving back to southern Alberta. I'd also quit calling head office for their so-called support and figured everything out on my own. It took longer to do it that way but I wasn't going to be the subject of any more ignorant e-mails. My go-to girl made a few more visits during the year and I met with her in my best professional manner which she interpreted as standoffish for some reason. Because of that one e-mail I'd made the decision to keep colleagues at a distance and stay on a professional level with everybody from head office. I was a lot friendlier with my staff and the community but I still avoided social calls outside of school business.

Besides attending church and joining the curling club I kept to myself for the rest of the year because I really wasn't sure who I could trust. Some may have viewed this as being antisocial but that one stray e-mail had put my defences up for now. I restricted the majority of my social life to my long distance marriage but my hubby had figured out a way for us to still have a relationship over the phone. Since we both had the same satellite TV provider we would have movie dates on the weekend if there was something that we both wanted to watch. Chris wasn't a big TV person in general and only enjoyed it when we watched shows together. It was the little chit-chat that we'd exchange while watching the show that made TV watching an interest for him, so we'd watch the same movie together while being on the phone. It even got to the point that I would look forward to our dates after a long week at work, and there was only one time when I was so tired that I fell asleep through the movie. Watching movies this way wasn't exactly the same as being right beside each other but it was enough.

Near the end of the year my Superintendent came by to give me my evaluation. I was on the standard one-year probation and this evaluation was the deciding factor as to whether or not I would be granted a permanent position within the school division. Even though I was confident in my abilities I was still nervous about the results, but I shouldn't have been. I had been given an overall performance rating of Superior. In addition to the glowing review my boss offered me a three year contract to continue with the school in Smallville. I would find out later that such a lengthy contract was unusual in this division but I accepted on the spot. Chris was so proud of me when I called to give him the news.

Not only was this a time of good news for me but my hubby had good news of his own. It was now the summer of 2009, and this was the first official housing season after the catastrophic 2008 Mortgage Crisis that crippled the world economy. It was not a good time to sell a house so we had taken Chris' dad's advice and hired a Realtor. I think she had seen her fair share of hopeless causes in the past twelve months as people who had suddenly lost their jobs were desperate to sell their homes in a hurry. She was expecting no less when she went to see our house but instead got completely surprised. Chris' landscaping combined with the natural backdrop of rock and trees gave our house "curb appeal" which was a rare quality in the Sudbury area. Then she walked into the entrance which was the mudroom/laundry room and got a little more impressed. To be fair there was nothing impressive about this part of the house from our point of view, but when a Realtor is impressed with our "nothing" then that tells you what the rest of the houses were like. It's now understandable why she was speechless upon entering the rest of the house and seeing the way Chris had done the open concept. The screened porch at the back of the house was the *pièce de résistance* and she told my Darling that our house had it all. Sure enough it sold in six weeks for more than double what we paid for it with the closing date on August 1st. God's hand seemed to be on everything we were doing.

I ended the school year and returned home as a very happy girl. I completed my job with Superior performance and had a three year contract to show for it. On top of that my hubby's hard work resulted in us being able to pay off all of our debts and hire professional movers to lug our stuff to Alberta. We planned a relaxing, week-long drive across the provinces that didn't involve any stress or worry because everything had finally fallen into place. Unfortunately this chapter was titled "The Longest Year of my Life" for a reason, and it started in the middle of August, 2008. The year wasn't over yet.

We went to the lawyer's office early on the closing date to drop off the keys and to pick up our cheque. The buyers hadn't come in yet but we were told that everything should be in order before noon. We literally had nowhere to go so we hung around downtown until noon waiting for a call. We didn't get one so we called the lawyer ourselves and asked if the cheque was ready. The woman from the lawyer's office told us that the buyer's funding fell through at the last minute and we wouldn't be getting a cheque today. Chris made her repeat that last part because it wasn't registering properly in his brain, and then he called our Realtor. She met us downtown within minutes and was completely beside herself that this had happened.

To make yet another long and painful story short, the buyers were dealing with a mortgage broker, not a bank, and somehow there was a communication error about the down payment. The buyers had shown up at the lawyer's office just after us with the full expectation to get the keys to their new house, but they didn't have a down payment with them. That set off warning bells with the broker and they dropped the entire deal right there instead of giving the buyers some time to get the down payment. We had done everything by the book with this sale by using a Realtor and lawyer to ensure that something like this would not happen, but it did anyways.

The sale of our house was now null and void and there was nothing we could do about it. The lawyer even said that he'd only seen something like this happen about three times in his entire thirty-year career, so of course it had to happen to us. Our options were to give the buyers time to set up a new mortgage or put the house back on sale and start from scratch. The moving truck was already on its way to Alberta so there was no turning back now. We made a very difficult leap of faith and gave the buyers a chance to refinance their mortgage while leaving the Realtor and lawyer to sort this out as we headed for Alberta.

What was supposed to be a well-deserved vacation became the most stressful month of my life. For the entire trip we called the lawyer every day to see if there was any progress but to no avail. Instead of being debt free we were carefully watching our money for the entire time in case we suddenly had an unplanned mortgage payment to make on a house that was supposed to be sold. The utilities and insurance also had to be re-activated in case something happened in our absence. This was not the way I wanted to spend my special week with my special man after we both worked so hard to get through the year. Even worse was that I was starting to get mad with God. I'd been through enough hardship for one year, but the devil was being allowed to take one more stab at my happiness and it was a doozie.

We got to Smallville ahead of the movers and our shipping container was ready and waiting. Before I left for Sudbury I had asked around if anybody knew where I could get a twenty-foot long storage container for my back yard. The teacherage had no basement and I knew that all of our "extras" wouldn't fit in the two spare rooms, so I decided to get serious about some portable storage. One of my regular reliables on the parent committee, who had taken care of the DJ bill from the beginning of the year, told me that she'd arrange everything while I was gone and she came through 100%. I had the container that I wanted but unfortunately I couldn't pay for it yet.

The movers showed up a few days later but our house still wasn't sold. Thankfully I had arranged to put the entire move on our Sears card to get over $400 worth of points, so that got paid off as planned. Weeks went by and the buyers still hadn't secured funding for the house. They said they were working on it but it was going very slowly. Our Realtor was starting to talk about putting the house back on the market, but selling an empty house is always harder. The storage container was allowed to be taken on the good faith that it would get paid for when I got back, but now I had to tell the dealer that I didn't have the money yet. School was starting in one week and I was an emotional wreck because of this latest disaster in my life. Chris and I made a final plea to God to sort this out, but instead of making it an angry demand we appealed to His rational side.

In our prayer we stated that we had lived apart for a year, sold our house and moved here on faith, but we wouldn't be able to do a good job at Smallville if we were constantly worrying about this financial situation. If we were to represent Him properly then He would need to solve this problem before school started by removing the devil's hand from everything we had worked for. On the last day before school started we got the call from our lawyer that the deal had gone through and the money was in my account. We went to town right away and paid off all of the debts that we'd incurred from the move and I gave a final sigh of relief. I could have been mad and resentful that my summer had been ruined but instead I was grateful that our prayer had been heard and answered, ending what was probably the longest year of my entire life.

Leading by Example

"What doesn't kill you makes you stronger" is one of Chris' favourite sayings but I like to think that I'm strong enough already. At the end of chapter thirteen I touched on the concept of spiritual growth through emotional hardship and back at chapter six I mention how a Christian's way of life portrays the type of Christian that they really are. God was now combining those aspects in my life and He seemed to be doing it in a more public way than before. I had thought that being the Smallville School Principal was going to be a job that was contained within the walls of the school, but instead of simply running the school I had become a leader within this community. This brings us to another one of Chris' favourite sayings:

Iron sharpeneth iron; so a man sharpeneth the countenance of his friend. ~ Proverbs 27:17

Just as it takes a strong, metal file to sharpen a metal blade, it also takes a strong Christian to shape and sharpen other Christians. By sticking with this analogy of metal and people we can take the concept of sharpening a bit further. Bad files that are either worn out, damaged or defective will not do a good job of sharpening a blade, but somebody who doesn't know much about tools or metal might not realize the difference. The result will be a blade that may be sharp in some places but it will also be rough and uneven with chips and scratches. Weak Christians have the same effect on people they try to lead.

I use the term "weak" to describe people who are only knowledgeable in small areas of scripture, such as knowing the Ten Commandments inside and out or only practicing the act of forgiveness without addressing the job of raising accountability. New Christians will look to these people as being wise because of what they know, but what they *don't* know can lead to confusion and misgiving. Basing a church on the practice of forgiveness and tolerance won't work unless the difficult task of accountability is also part of the teaching. It takes a good Christian to forgive but it takes a strong Christian to also make people acknowledge their inappropriate behaviour that is damaging to others. It was time to move out of my comfort zone again, beyond being a good Christian, and become a strong Christian and a strong leader.

Giving the appearance of being a strong leader is easy when everything goes according to plan. It's important to set a good example at all times but being able to do so when life gets rough is the true test of leadership. There are many self-proclaimed leaders who know what the right choices are but they lack the courage to make those choices for fear of what others will think of them. They are afraid to stand their ground for what they know to be right and instead choose to go in the direction that will make them the most popular. Some people confuse the two, thinking that if everybody is happy then they must be making the right choices, but there is a bible verse for that too in the second book of Timothy:

[2] *Preach the word; be instant in season, out of season; reprove, rebuke, exhort with all long suffering and doctrine.*
[3] *For the time will come when they will not endure sound doctrine; but after their own lusts shall they heap to themselves teachers, having itching ears;*
[4] *And they shall turn away their ears from the truth, and shall be turned unto fables.* ~ 2 Timothy 4:2-4

Verse 2 refers to preaching the word instantly, without hesitation, whether it be favourable (in season) or difficult (out of season). Tell people when they are making mistakes and don't let them get away with it even if it makes the situation uncomfortable. "Reprove" refers to using a convincing argument to show wrongdoing that might not be obvious, like how to properly observe the Sabbath; "rebuke" refers to unquestionably bad behaviour like blatant lying, stealing, drunkenness, etc., that doesn't even need to be argued; "exhort" refers to teaching with great passion and conviction, not merely reading what's on the page without fully understanding it. Don't just read the word of God but *live* it and set an example to prove that you know what you are talking about.

Verse 3 is telling us why we must "be instant" because a time is coming when people will no longer have patience for sound, biblical teachings. Act now and get through to whomever you can before it is too late because eventually people will want to chase after their own lusts instead of living sensibly. "Itching ears" refers to the people who know what they want to hear (they have an itch) and find a "leader" who will scratch that itch by telling them what they want to hear, not what is biblically correct. Does this sound like the time we're living in?

Verse 4 just emphasizes what is being said in verse 3, that people will no longer want to listen to the truth because it will be too hard for them. They will instead choose to believe in any nonsense or false claims as long as it allows them to continue with their bad behaviour.

To bring this into perspective, there were a few parents in my school who were trying to get things done *their* way instead of being accountable and contributing members of the school. They wanted to excuse their children's bad behaviour as if it weren't their fault or their problem. It was always somebody else's fault that their children couldn't get along with the other kids or follow the rules of the school. They wanted a Principal that would scratch their itch because they couldn't face the truth that the problems stemmed from them and their household, but I needed to do what was right even if it was going to be difficult.

I spent my first year battling many, many struggles that were both personal and within the school. I could have taken the easy path of giving up or giving in because life was getting hard, but instead I prayed for the strength to push ahead in the direction that God wanted me to follow. I did not keep my Christian beliefs a secret from anybody and I even got the chance to fellowship with some community members outside of the church. I spent my first year setting the example and proving myself to the entire community, and the school division, without showing favouritism or special treatment, and I did so with a final evaluation of Superior results. A few people may not have liked the way I was doing things but they had no justifiable reason to say anything against me. My two choices were to either satisfy their selfish needs or to perform my job and my life in the way that God would approve of, so it wasn't really a choice at all.

Chapter Nineteen

Always Do Your Best (but not really)

With our latest calamity under control Chris and I could focus on the job at hand. To distract ourselves from the worry of our house not selling we had spent a lot of time in the school. My Darling was just starting to understand the full scope of my job and all of the expectations that the school division had. There were also going to be a few major changes with the new school year since I would have to break in another secretary and I was also going to have a brand new class of kids with only Val and another boy returning from last year. I can't say that I was disappointed. I'd been keeping an eye on this new batch of grade 7 students when they were in grade 6 last year and I had a good feeling about them. Once my hubby realized the huge workload that was expected of me he suggested putting off his own job search for a few months while helping me get a foothold with my work. We had discussed this option on and off last year but it wasn't until now that he knew it was a necessity instead of possibility.

I introduced him to the ladies at our first staff meeting and told them about the extra help that Chris would provide on a short-term basis. Being a math whiz and a science nut with a graphic arts background made him a perfect fit for everything that me and my staff found challenging. It was decided that Chris would spend most of his time in my room, under my supervision, while also assisting my other two teachers with their science classes. This was great news to my teacher who was back from maternity leave since she found the sciences to be a bit of a struggle due to multi-grade teaching and all of the preparation that was involved. One concern that was brought up was how he should be addressed by the students. Some of my staff thought that having a Mrs. Young and a Mr. Young might be a bit confusing so it was decided the Chris would be referred to as Mr. C which is how I introduced him at our first school assembly.

Being the only male on staff was enough to make Mr. C stand out but he soon became a staff favourite with many of the students. For the younger grades, having Mr. C come into the room usually meant that there was a science experiment soon to follow, but he had the greatest impact on my class where he tutored math and science for both grades. I didn't have a grade 9 student that year so he was able to focus on the new grade 7 class and my two grade 8 students. I would deliver the lessons and then he would spend the rest of the class helping me with the students as if it were second nature. I no longer had to fumble through math and science textbooks to answer the student's questions because the Amazing Mr. C seemed to have remembered every little math and science tidbit from his grade school years. He actually enjoyed those extra, in-class demonstrations like growing crystals or condensing steam onto a beaker filled with ice.

It's almost shameful how much we used Chris during that year of school. What started off as a helping hand during some science classes turned out to be much more as he constantly stepped forward to help my certified staff with anything else that they directed him to. Assisting us with our academics was a great help but he was also the photocopier un-jammer and back-up techie trouble shooter, he took on an equal share of recess duty, he was the publisher of my monthly newsletter and assisted the students in making the school yearbooks, and at the end of the day he was my photocopy mule. Keep in mind that he was a volunteer at the school and never received a penny for everything he did despite putting in just as many hours as a full-time teacher. On top of all that the Amazing Mr. C ran an after-school Rocket Club for the middle and older grades until the weather got cold and then he held the infamous, after-school Game Night for the remainder of the year.

By the time winter set in my Darling was getting a little tired for some strange reason but he wanted to continue with some sort of after-school activity since I was usually there catching up on my Administrative work and lesson planning. If I was going to stay late marking papers and getting ready for tomorrow then he may as well find something to do as well. When Rocket Club was over he wondered if any of my students would be interested in playing some board games. He wanted to show them that you didn't have to be plugged into a computer to have fun. The kids had taken quite a shine to Mr. C despite his stern and sometimes gruff mannerism in the classroom and a group of them jumped at the chance to do some after-school gaming with Mr. C. We didn't realize it at the time but the inception of Game Night would result in a much bigger project for my hubby in the coming years. In addition to the extra stuff that Mr. C brought to the school this year we still held all of the news-worthy events from last year. The Winter Carnival and Fashion Show were the best ones ever and Smallville was a hoppin' and happenin' place for a change.

With all of this extra help I was able to concentrate better on the administration part of my job which was still an uphill battle. There was a power shift at head office and my boss was in the midst of retiring. Unfortunately the new man at the helm would prove to be a severe disappointment to me in the area of leadership. Perhaps my past career life had spoiled me because I'd worked with some of the best educators in the province during my government days. I knew what was expected from a Superintendent but I just couldn't see my new boss keeping up with the demands that came with the title. To make matters worse my go-to girl from last year was his second in command. It was going to be very interesting to see how this school year unfolded.

My new secretary was working out better than expected despite the constant policy changes from head office. Along with the power shift came many "new and wonderful ideas" on how the school division should operate and it was up to the individual schools to keep up with this new Superintendent's vision. That political restructuring would have been enough to contend with for any small school but my biggest challenge of the year was a small but persistent group of troublemakers. They also had their own ideas on how the school should be run which revolved around the notion that their ill-mannered children should be able to act any way they wanted to. They felt that they should be the exception to the rule for no apparent reason, and from what I gathered from my staff these people have been like this ever since they rolled into town. Why the community had tolerated their behaviour up until now was beyond me, but I was starting to feel like I was the only one who *didn't* have any say as to how I should be running the school. Just to be sure I double checked the Principal's pay stub and wouldn't you know it, there was *my* name. I was correct in thinking that my job title wasn't merely a suggestion. With that out of the way I resolved to remind anybody who was in question about it.

I think the most ridiculous part about this battle of futility is that it was over the smallest things. All I was expecting from these kids was for them to come to school with proper footwear, appropriate clothing and to treat everybody with the same respect and courtesy that they were shown. The rest of the students had no problem following these rules, nor did they suffer any ill-effects from complying with what was really just common sense and decency, yet this small group was treating the request as if I were trying to force a New World Order down their throats. This behaviour eventually led to a situation that could not be brushed aside, nor could it be down played as a mere misunderstanding. After a long-overdue meeting involving the parent and my boss it was decided that both of her children would be bused to the next town which was a larger center with a larger school that had more resources to deal with this matter. The parent was visibly unhappy that she could no longer pretend that her child's problems were everybody else's imagination. Hiding from the truth had created a very real and serious situation that needed to be dealt with before it got any worse

Doing what is right for an entire school should not be such a big ordeal but I suppose the town is partially responsible for allowing this behaviour to continue for so long. Many of the community leaders felt bound by the false ethic of turning the other cheek, thinking that it was their Christian duty to tolerate bad behaviour in hopes that the troublemakers would somehow learn to be better people by following the town's example of complacency. Hopefully by now many of you have learned that being a good Christian does not mean that you allow troublesome people to get away with anything they want to. It definitely takes a strong person to confront someone on their wrongdoings, but you'd be surprised how many troublemakers back down at the first sign of resistance. The Bible doesn't teach us to reprimand people in a mean way, only that it definitely needs to be done. Doing nothing about bad behaviour is the same as encouraging it as far as troublemakers are concerned. By not telling them to stop you are giving them permission to continue whether you realize it or not. Sometimes being nice doesn't always get the desired result.

With that business out of the way we finished the school year on a good note and I finally got a restful summer vacation, but by the beginning of August Chris and I were back in the school getting ready for the upcoming year. Now that he'd experienced it for himself my hubby was fully aware of what needed to be done so that we could have a smooth and enjoyable school year. He had been formulating a strategy for the past few months, seeing what did and didn't work for me from an efficiency point of view, and made his own prioritized list of what he hoped to accomplish before the students returned. This included clearing out the forty-year-old textbooks from the classroom shelves to give me more usable space, setting up a proper work station for me in my classroom so I wouldn't need to run to my office as much, and solving our pin board problem in the office.

I am a very organized individual but I'm also what is referred to as "old school". Perhaps it's from my government days but I like everything on paper, so the small pin board in my office, which was really just a 4' x 2' ceiling tile screwed to the wall, was packed to the point of being almost useless. The main office wasn't much better but at least it had a legitimate pin board. The Amazing Mr. C spent an entire day relocating three huge pin boards from their unused locations in the school and placing them where they would do the most good; one went in the main office and the other two in my office. This is probably an insignificant gesture for most people but for me it was yet another indication of how well Chris knew me. For the first time in a long time everybody was looking forward to the school year. Not only was the Amazing Mr. C returning for duty but I had gotten the worst troublemakers out of the school. Chris felt so good about the coming year that he went home to make me a special dinner while I had a last-minute meeting with second-in-command who had dropped by.

For the next hour and a half my hubby cooked me a steak dinner with sautéed mushrooms and onions, baked mini-potatoes, and there was even a bottle of red wine kicking around. By six-thirty the special dinner was getting a little cold so Chris called the school only to get a busy signal. He put the meal in the oven and kept it warm until I got home at seven o'clock. He did his best not to be annoyed and asked why I was so late when I knew that he was making dinner. I looked into his eyes and started to tell him about the meeting I'd had just after he left, but before finishing the sentence I buried my face in his shoulder and broke down into tears, telling him that he couldn't come back to the school!

It took me a minute to compose myself after which I told him what I could about this sudden development. Second-in-command had simply said that it was in the school division's best interest that Chris not be allowed back to the school. I was taken completely by surprise with this news and it was all I could do to ask why. There was no reason or explanation, only that "it would be best" according to their thinking. This wasn't how I planned to start the new school year but it was also clear that this was not open to discussion either. My only recourse was to ask her what I was supposed to tell my husband. How was I supposed to explain this to him, or anyone else for that matter? Nobody gets discharged from a school without committing a serious offense and this is what people would think unless I had a proper reason to explain the school division's decision. It was her turn to feel uncomfortable now, so instead of giving me an answer she just muttered something about the Superintendent giving a directive and the matter was closed. She then hurried out of my school before I could ask any other questions that she wouldn't be able to answer.

I had no idea how I was supposed to go home to my husband, who was making me a special dinner, and tell him that he was no longer allowed to help out at the school. Instead I spent the next two hours on the phone with two of the ladies from church whom I knew I could trust in confidence. They each had an equally hard time understanding what had just happened, especially the part about no reason being given for Chris' dismissal. He had essentially been fired from his voluntary position if that even makes any sense. In fact, this was worse than being fired because proper disciplinary action against anybody in a school had to follow three steps: a verbal warning, then a written warning and then dismissal following only when the first two warnings were not heeded. I was powerless to do anything about the way they were ousting Chris from the school. I had already stirred the pot by getting those troublemakers out of my school so to outright defy this directive would probably be grounds for dismissal.

Strange as it may seem this made a bit of sense to Chris now that he knew what was going on. As he was leaving the school to start dinner he had run into second-in-command and bid her good day on his way out. She remained silent, avoided eye contact and had a slight smile on her face. He didn't give it much thought since there was no reason to think he'd done anything wrong, but it's probably best that he didn't know what she was planning.

We finally ate our celebration dinner although it was no longer the special occasion that was intended, and we skipped that bottle of wine. After a quiet meal Chris wondered out loud how the community was going to feel about this decision, and I knew what he was hinting at. My hubby would have liked to make a very big deal out of this situation, how a volunteer was getting kicked out of a school for no apparent reason, but I told him that it had to be done delicately.

For Chris, delicacy was only meant for eggs and intimate moments, but he knew that I was right in this matter. If I would have let him, my hubby would have gone straight to head office himself and accused my boss of character defamation. To suddenly yank somebody out of a school could only imply that a serious offense had been committed, so he wanted to know what Mr. C was being charged with. He was justifiably mad about this, but being right wasn't going to solve the problem. My only action was to inform my staff that they would have to re-work any scheduling that relied on Mr. C's assistance since he would not be joining us when school started next week. It didn't take long for the entire town to catch wind of the situation.

Now that this was officially public knowledge one of the ladies I'd told had called the school division and spoken directly to the Superintendent. She asked my boss what Mr. C had done to get kicked out of the school and if the community should be concerned. He reassured her that Mr. C hadn't actually done anything wrong, just that there were some complaints made about him that the school division wanted to get sorted out. She then asked who had called in the complaint and was told that it was an anonymous call. This later raised questions from many people as to how a school division could take a complaint to this extreme when it couldn't even be validated. My new boss had thought that this would be a cut and dry situation but he soon found out that he'd opened a big can of worms instead.

Next to my hubby's defense was the formidable Mrs. L. She now had two of her daughters in my class since last year, Val and her younger sister, and Mr. C had made a strong impact on this family with his dedication to helping out at the school. Mrs. L was not so kind with her phone call and pretty much told my boss that removing Mr. C from the school was a mistake. She then wrote a letter to the paper to make her frustrations clear just in case the phone call hadn't done the trick. I can only speculate that my boss was starting to realize that this decision of his was becoming a much bigger situation than he wished it to be.

I was eventually summoned to my boss's office to discuss this matter, though I know that it was a last resort. It turned out that the accusation against Mr. C was that he was doing more than just helping out around the school. Someone from the community reported that Chris had taken over a lot of actual teaching during his first year but nobody had ever mentioned this to me. In truth we had all taken advantage of my hubby's capabilities and used him to his full potential, but at no time was he ever in charge of teaching. He was able to assist after a lesson just as any Education Assistant would, but we teachers had always developed the lessons.

We probably wouldn't have become so dependent on Mr. C if not for the year-long drama that involved the particular troublemakers whom were now going to school in the next town over. There had been a constant need for me to drop whatever I was doing to solve the latest crisis that revolved around those two students, so Chris' options were to sit in the classroom and do nothing for fear of overstepping his bounds or continue with whatever needed to be done. In hindsight it was probably a no-win situation no matter what he decided.

Another complaint was that Mr. C was disciplining the students by giving out lines which my new boss also saw as a concern. Any parent that I'd talked to thought the lines were a great idea, but according to my boss they were a thing of the past; "the way of the dinosaurs" if I remember his comment correctly. I got great results with this form of discipline but I was more or less told not to use it anymore as a means of keeping my class in order, and no effective alternative was suggested either. This man was supposed to be a mentor for all Principals in the division but he had no idea how to help me do a better job.

The final warning sign was when second-in-command had seen Chris helping with the scheduling on that day she came in for the meeting. She had thought this to be inappropriate but it wasn't even a valid concern since subject scheduling was public knowledge. Any parent had access to the same information that Chris used to help us out, but she had deemed this to be the last nail in the coffin. Between the anonymous phone complaints and second-in-command's "concerns" I was starting to wonder who really called the shots at head office. Now the unjustifiable directive to ban my husband from the Smallville school was becoming a publicity hot-spot and my boss was hoping to quietly brush it aside. All of this came about because my husband was being too helpful.

The school year started with a sombre mood and the absence of Mr. C was felt most heavily in my classroom. Chris had set up a mini-office for me in the room which made my life a little easier but the kids were visibly disappointed that he wasn't around. It wasn't our intention for him to become a permanent fixture in the school but it happened all the same. The days dragged on for the month of September and the school seemed a little more boring without Mr. C. He was the one who had time to answer those obscure "how" and "why" questions that kids always come up with at the most inopportune times, and I can recall one such incident during a Language Arts lesson that illustrates this point.

The Grade 8 class was learning about mythology and a question came up about a particular mythical hero. I was stumped by the question but the kids just had to know, so we sat there in silence for a few minutes before one of the girls spoke up. "Mr. C would know," she said, obviously miffed about his absence. "Let's go get him," said one of the boys, lightening the mood a bit as the class laughed at the idea of walking over to the teacherage, which was a stone's throw away, and ushering him back to the school. I made my own stand by being less available, telling everybody that problems would have to wait until the end of the day when I had no classes. Thankfully I didn't have to do this for long because by the end of September the Mr. C ban was lifted. Not once was there an apology given for the way my husband and this entire situation had been treated. We didn't make a big deal about Mr. C's return since it was clear that we would need to be very careful about what he did for us from now on.

Almost as if on cue, one more parent yanked her kid out of my school on the same day that Chris returned. The student was not a problem but the mother was another serious trouble-maker for the school. She showed up near the end of the day with two other women for backup: the mother of the two students I'd already relocated and someone who hadn't had kids in the school for a long time yet was a notorious problem parent in her day. The three of them marched into the school like they were ready for a fight, ordered the student to clean out her locker and marched off again like they were on a deadline. I'm not sure why the mother felt that she needed a support group. She didn't need my permission to remove her child but she was behaving as if she would need to fight tooth and nail to get what she wanted. I was at my computer when this happened and Chris wasn't even in the room, thank God, but that didn't stop the parent from calling my boss to complain that I was playing computer games at my desk while Chris was teaching the class! At least my boss had the sense to call me and get my side of the story, after which nothing ever came of the situation again.

I would like to say that that was the end of my problems with those people, but it wasn't meant to be. For the next two years they sat in the general store drinking coffee and bashing me, my husband and the school. Parents and community members would tell me about what they had heard over at the store, to which I would reply, "And what did *you* say to *them* about it?"

Very few people in the town would stand up to these adult bullies, so the ranting went on despite my discussions with the store owner. She allowed this behaviour in her establishment, not because she agreed with it, but because she wanted everybody to like her. Reprimanding anyone would be bad for business. Even though I no longer had contact with these people in any way they continued to hate me with a vengeance. Badmouthing aside, we still had the best school year ever when Chris came back.

In addition to our usual event-filled agenda I had completed a two-year project of opening our school library into a community library. Mrs. K, my new secretary whom I'd like to think became a friend, had run a library in the next town for many years until the commute became too much. Initially it was a different community member who had approached me about opening the library. We had talked when I first arrived and he said that he'd been trying to get this done for years but none of the previous Principals would give it the time of day. It's no wonder considering the amount of paperwork that was required to get it done, but once I agreed to give it a shot he directed me to Mrs. K and the rest fell into place.

Mrs. K had a true passion for running a community library so the chance to do it in her home town was an offer she couldn't refuse. After two years of filling out forms and attending meetings we were finally recognized as a member of the Alberta public library system. This was a huge accomplishment that we were very proud of and it helped to renew my own interest in public libraries and how important they are to small communities. It was one more feather in my Smallville cap, and that cap was getting mighty full after three very fruitful years.

I'd been told on multiple occasions that being the Principal at Smallville for one year was equivalent to three years of work in a regular school, so I had essentially provided nine years' worth of work for three years of pay. Surely the school division would be appreciative of such devotion, right? I knew for a fact that the community appreciated it because I was told so in person from almost everybody. The only people who weren't happy were the troublemakers and nobody was even listening to them. They could say as many bad things as they liked but anyone who wanted the truth only had to visit me at my school.

Only a few substitute teachers were willing to drive out to Smallville, but they loved being there. We were continually told by visitors that we had the best-behaved students in the entire division. I would have to say that it was my crowning year despite the rough start so at the beginning of my fourth year I was kind of hoping that it would get easier. Ironically enough, and much to our dismay, the troublemakers just couldn't stay away. Those same parents that openly hated me and my school re-enrolled their kids that year which signalled the beginning of the end for me and my hubby.

As if this weren't enough of a challenge I also had to contend with a Judas in my midst. At the beginning of the year I caught one of my staff members trying to throw me under the proverbial bus. She was a prominent community member who was practically revered as a saint by some people, but on more than one occasion she tried to discredit me to my boss. I confronted her on the matter to which she denied everything but it was clear that I'd have to keep her at a professional arm's length for the rest of the year. She was a good teacher but she always had to have her way.

Near the end of the year an all-out investigation was done to see what was going on in Smallville. Fingers had been pointing in every direction since September, from my statements that it was impossible to continue running the school with such a ridiculously small budget to my boss's determination to find fault with me. For three days a small committee scoured through the workings of my school to see where things were going wrong, and at the end of it all their findings were: put more computers in the classrooms, increase the math teaching past the provincial recommendations, and that we needed an extra .5 teaching time. That's it! They couldn't find a single fault with the way I was running my school aside from needing more computers (a funding issue), increasing math classes a bit, and that we needed more teaching time to be more effective. It took a three-person committee three days to tell my boss exactly what we had been saying all along. Unfortunately this was a victory that I couldn't savour and I was never officially given a copy of this report that should have been public knowledge.

This was also the time of year when teaching contracts were renewed but I informed the division that I wasn't interested in the job at Smallville School. I requested a teaching assignment elsewhere in the district. My staff had been worried that this moment would come and now it was official. The only person who remained silent about it was Judas. While at an end-of-year workshop in southern Alberta I mentioned my situation to a gentleman sitting beside me.

"Well," he commented, "with your experience I guess you'll be getting the pick of the crop for your teaching assignment."

Now this is a remark from somebody that works in a *normal* school board with a genuine leader, because this is in fact how it should be. I, on the other hand, was not in a normal school board. People who don't play nice in the sandbox get handed the worst of assignments without any say in the matter, and that is exactly what happened to me. As a final leap of faith I completely resigned from the school division instead of being subjected to that teaching assignment and Chris supported me in every way.

It would be completely understandable for my first year in Smallville to be a horrific mess, but for my next three years to get progressively worse made no sense at all. Despite the constant help from my husband and strong support from most of my staff and community the job of Principal at Smallville School only got tougher every year. Three times I had told myself that next year should be better, but the stress that originated from head office only compounded over time. By supporting the troublemakers and empowering them to disrupt the school they had finally accomplished their goal of running me out of the Smallville school, but not out of the town itself.

It was a difficult decision on many levels. Chris and I had grown close to some of the staff and community members, so to leave the school had an emotional impact. My decision to sever all social connections with the school may have been seen as a snub of some sort but I was really concerned for their well-being. To continue any kind of connection with my former staff might have brought them undue attention from head office. I'm sure that Judas and the troublemakers would have been quick to let my ex-boss know about Mrs. Young hanging around the staff of Smallville, and from what I'd heard through the grapevine their lives at the school were difficult enough. They didn't need the Superintendent putting them under a microscope because he was worried that I was giving out secrets or spreading rumours about him. I hope they understand that this decision wasn't meant to make them feel that they did something wrong. We were a good team and I miss what we had, but it was time to move on.

Then of course there was the financial impact. I went from a six-figure salary to substitute teaching for the local Catholic school board. We had some savings, and our rent was very generous, so by cashing in my teacher's pension we would have enough money to make it through one year. I was a bit terrified to take this step but my Darling had faith that God had a plan. To have taken the only teaching job offer would have surely done me in since my stress levels were already maxed out from that last, brutal year in the Smallville school. We had given the school our very best but the reward for our efforts was having to constantly watch over our shoulder in case Judas or the troublemakers were up to their tricks. That last year helped us realize that I had been fighting a losing battle. It was time for a well-earned rest so we put our faith in God once more and left matters in His hands.

A saving grace that helped us through the hard times was my friendship with a woman who we'll call Mrs. T. She and her husband were our age and their son had attended Smallville School years ago. During that nerve-wracking month when Chris had been kicked out of the school Mrs. T approached us with the opportunity to live in the family farmhouse. They were looking for somebody to occupy it for minimal rent knowing that a house lived in is a house looked after. They had their own house on the next quarter of land but they still wanted to keep the original farmhouse in the family. Mr. T had just put a lot of time into some re-finishing so we drove over to take a look. It was a few kilometers from the school at the end of a quiet, country road, and as we drove up the long lane way I thought it was the perfect replacement for our little gem of a house that we sold in Sudbury. In fact it was even better since it had a usable attic with a dormer that Chris quickly claimed for himself as a studio. Though only a few minutes from the school the house was tucked away in a quiet corner that was surrounded by trees and rarely saw visitors. It even had a wood stove. For a couple of people who were desperate for some peace and quiet it was the ideal place to live, but we also saw it as a Godsend.

It didn't take long for Chris to pack the container, and with the help of Val's parents and her family we were moved down the street by the end of October. Something about the old farmhouse brought peace to my soul while also sparking the creative part of Chris that had lain dormant for a long time. After a winter of soothing wood heating Chris got back to landscaping again. The front of the house had been neglected for years so he completely dug out the overgrown garden and even transplanted a couple of lilac bushes from the back of the property to the front of the house. Among the myriad of farm buildings on the property was a large workshop where Mr. T did his tinkering and parked the tractor during winter. With that at his disposal my hubby was making shelves for the house and screens for some of the windows so we could flood the house with fresh air without letting in the bugs. My Darling knows how much I love having the windows open.

For Chris and I, living in the farmhouse was like living at a country retreat with some of the best neighbours that you could ever ask for. We were no longer constantly exposed to the troublemakers around us, and while that made a world of difference for those last two years of working at the school it made an even bigger difference during the year after.

I realized that I could leave the school because I had done my best despite the odds against me. I'd arrived in Smallville a broken Christian but I had been put through the fires of proving during these four short years and emerged as a strong Christian leader. I was tired, but I no longer had anything to prove. I fulfilled my unusually long contract that God had arranged, so to have kept my job and endured the abuse for the sake of a pay cheque would have been a step in the wrong direction. We felt that we had to make a choice between faith and finances, and for the first time in my life I put my fear of money aside.

God had proven Himself to us over and over again ever since he brought me together with Chris so now it was my turn to prove myself to Him. We would rest this year and give our Father time to work. Chris felt that we had earned a break, so aside from my days of substitute teaching we would hibernate through the winter and see what the new season holds for us. We know He has a plan and we'll be ready to take the next step on the path of the straight and narrow. It was time to live my Testimony of Faith instead of just talking about it.

MOVING ON

One of the hardest things about being a Christian is having non-Christians using the Bible against us. Being told that we have to love everybody no matter what or that God has to forgive them because the Bible says so can be very frustrating if we don't understand scripture ourselves. Even the act of walking away from Smallville School can be misinterpreted as a non-Christian, defeatist attitude until we look to the book of Mark:

And whosoever shall not receive you, nor hear you, when ye depart thence, shake off the dust under your feet for a testimony against them. Verily I say unto you, It shall be more tolerable for Sodom and Gomorrha in the day of judgment, than for that city. ~ Mark 6:11

By reading this scripture we can only conclude that Christians are *encouraged* to move on when it is clear that our efforts are not appreciated. If I had turned tail and run at the first sign of resistance then I wouldn't be able to justify my actions, but after four years of dedicated leadership I think it's safe to say that Chris and I did everything we could. Those who drove us from the school may be proud of their accomplishment but the scripture above indicates that God will deal with them in His own good time.

Speaking negatively of others could also be misconstrued as non-Christian behaviour, but that depends on the situation. If we take a look in the second book of Timothy we find a request from Paul for Timothy to visit him:

14 Alexander the coppersmith did me much evil: the Lord reward him according to his works:
15 Of whom be thou ware also; for he hath greatly withstood our words.
16 At my first answer no man stood with me, but all men forsook me: I pray God that it may not be laid to their charge.
~ 2 Timothy 4:14-16

This passage doesn't tell us what Alexander the coppersmith did to Paul but it was bad enough for him to forewarn Timothy. Paul wasn't spreading idle gossip, he was letting Timothy know that the man was trouble and should be avoided. This is also another example of the phrase "turn the other cheek" not meaning what we think it does otherwise Paul would be happy, if not insistent, to give that coppersmith a second chance. Instead he is leaving judgement in the Lord's hands.

In verse 16 Paul mentions that many other people abandoned him in his ministry, probably for fear of persecution, but he isn't angry with them and prays that God will forgive them. Paul isn't vindictive towards everybody who has let him down but he is wary of those who go out of their way to purposely cause him harm. I've tried to reflect this behaviour in my own lifestyle by always giving people a chance to prove themselves. Anybody mentioned in this book, from my first husband to Judas and the troublemakers, always got my best intentions in the beginning but for some reason they were still compelled to do wrong against me. I don't understand it, Chris can't understand it, but I too will leave it to our Lord to reward them for their works.

These last few chapters may have a negative, almost angry feel to them but this wasn't my intent. While my goal was to be truthful, and somewhat entertaining, I'm not trying to encourage aggressive Christian beliefs with my story. While I would definitely like to debunk the myth that Christians are supposed to be complacent zombies who forgive anything to the point of being abused, we aren't meant to be angry enforcers of God's Law either. We are all different because we are each unique so our paths will be equally diverse, but unfortunately this leads some Christians to believe that they are exempt from behaving properly. By looking to the book of Ezekiel I would like to emphasize one last point that will challenge an older yet traditional Christian view.

10 Therefore, O thou son of man, speak unto the house of
Israel; Thus ye speak, saying, If our transgressions and our sins be upon us, and we pine away in them, how should we then live?
11 Say unto them, As I live, saith the Lord GOD, I have no
pleasure in the death of the wicked; but that the wicked turn from his way and live: turn ye, turn ye from your evil ways; for why will ye die, O house of Israel?
~ Ezekiel 33:10-11

Throughout the Old Testament we see the house of Israel forsake God on several occasions. In verse 10 they become so worried about their terrible track record of broken faith that they wonder how they can go on. God answers them in verse 11, but some scholars believe that the second comma here should actually be a period:

11 Say unto them, As I live. Saith the Lord GOD, I have no
pleasure in the death of the wicked;

When written like this we can see that God wants His people to live as He would live, thus following His commandments. Jesus would later come to fulfill this wish and set the example. Most important is the next phrase where God tells us that he takes no pleasure in the death of the wicked but would rather they turn from their evil ways instead. This one statement removes the justification from any religious group that claims to be killing the wicked in the name of God. From the Medieval crusades to modern terrorism, anyone who tries to use the words of the Bible as an excuse to hate somebody is thwarted by this single piece of scripture. While the Bible mentions many actions and types of behaviour that are deserving of punishment it is no longer our responsibility to deal out these punishments as we see fit. Jesus sat and ate with the sinners while shunning the scribes and Pharisees. Our Lord wasn't condoning their behaviour but he didn't hate them either. He wanted to lead the sinners towards repentance, not force them into submission.

Now a truly troublesome nit-picker will point to the end of Chapter Eight in this book and say "Ah-ha! I see a double standard here. Remember this?"

And the man that committeth adultery with another man's wife, even he that committeth adultery with his neighbour's wife, the adulterer and the adulteress shall surely be put to death. ~ Leviticus 20:10

Bear with me as I skip through a few more verses before coming to a conclusion.

But of the tree of the knowledge of good and evil, thou shalt not eat of it: for in the day that thou eatest thereof thou shalt surely die. ~ Genesis 2:17

[3] *And the scribes and Pharisees brought unto him a woman taken in adultery; and when they had set her in the midst,*
[4] *They say unto him, Master, this woman was taken in adultery, in the very act.*

[5] Now Moses in the law commanded us, that such should be
stoned: but what sayest thou?
[6] This they said, tempting him, that they might have to
accuse him. But Jesus stooped down, and with his finger
wrote on the ground, as though he heard them not.
[7] So when they continued asking him, he lifted up himself,
and said unto them, He that is without sin among you, let
him first cast a stone at her.
[8] And again he stooped down, and wrote on the ground.
[9] And they which heard it, being convicted by their own
conscience, went out one by one, beginning at the eldest,
even unto the last: and Jesus was left alone, and the wom-
an standing in the midst.
[10] When Jesus had lifted up himself, and saw none but the
woman, he said unto her, Woman, where are those thine
accusers? hath no man condemned thee?
[11] She said, No man, Lord. And Jesus said unto her, Neither
do I condemn thee: go, and sin no more. ~ John 8: 3-11

Without going into a huge discussion about this I will simply say that the adulterers were sentenced to the same fate as Adam and Eve when they disobeyed the word of God. Adam and Eve, however, were spared by God's grace. Some will argue that their sentence of death only meant their loss of eternal life, leading to eventual death. Others will insist that Adam and Eve should have suffered instantaneous death but were spared, and Jesus' act of sparing the woman in John 8 would seem to collaborate with this thinking. The morale of the story: just because a sin is *worthy* of death (according to scripture) does not mean that the punishment has to be delivered. In the end it is God's decision, not ours. Christians cannot use the Old Testament as a blueprint to justify hate of any kind because Jesus is our example. His last words to the adulterous woman were to sin no more. It wasn't an order, it was advice. We don't know whether she followed it or not, but when judgement comes she will only have herself to blame if she chose not to heed the words of our Lord.

These are the examples that I tried to follow during my time in Smallville. When I stood my ground against the troublemakers I did not act in anger by simply trying to kick them out. I removed the problem from my school while still providing an alternative for them to continue with their education. I always gave them a chance to look at what they were doing and reassess their actions but unfortunately they couldn't see the opportunity they were given and instead chose to remain angry and spiteful. I did everything I could for them but it is out of my hands now. Perhaps they will be fortunate enough for somebody else to put in the effort to help them but as long as their bad behaviour is excused then I honestly believe that people like them have no hope.

Chris' and my decision to hibernate through the winter turned out to be a good one in my opinion. This year the snow started flying at the beginning of October, and by the middle of October it was here to stay. We burned two years' worth of firewood by the time winter left at the end of April, so working part-time during a six-month winter was exactly the break I needed. It's almost as if it had been planned all along. Chris had started writing when we first moved to the farmhouse, but what started as a new hobby soon became a new career. Game Night had rekindled his love for old-school gaming and after writing a choose-your-own-adventure novel as an experiment he came to realize that he had a knack for putting words together. He has plans to expand his adventure novel into a series but first he needed to complete a different project.

While subbing at one of the Catholic schools I bumped into a teacher whom I knew from Smallville. He'd heard about my sudden career choice and asked how things were going. I told him that we were leaving things in God's hands for the year and living in faith.

"You have no RRSPs or stored teacher's pension?" He asked in disbelief. "No assets at all?"

I told him we were living on my substitute teacher's pay and our hope in God. Upon fully realizing my situation he confessed that he would never be able to live like that and I had to admit that I never thought I'd be able to do it either.

"So what's your husband doing with himself?" He asked.

I told him that Chris had been inspired to write my life's story from the perspective of a spiritual journey, and after our collaboration throughout the six-month winter of 2012-2013 my personal Testimony of Faith was finally done. We had been given a calm before the next storm in my life so we filled it with daily scripture readings, long walks together whenever the weather permitted and lots of job applications. I even managed to reconnect with my son after all these years. Some might think that we did nothing all year but if telling my story helps at least one person through a storm in their life then I think that it was time well spent.

19830434R00178

Made in the USA
Charleston, SC
13 June 2013